PRAISE FOR *VUCA*

'I highly recommend this book to students, scholars, policy makers, entrepreneurs and business persons who strive to succeed and to be as effective and efficient as possible in this "VUCA world"!'

–Dr. Aidin Salamzadeh, Editor-in-Chief,
Journal of Entrepreneurship, Business and Economics

'The caselets chosen are very appropriate and will help understand the concept in a localized context.'

–Arvind Kumar, Delivery Head, Tata Consultancy Services

'The book provides some useful lessons drawn from failures in an increasingly complex world.'

–Dr. Himanshu Rai, Chairperson, MDP,
Indian Institute of Management, Lucknow

'Your work is on a very contemporary issue that post-modern organizations are facing in a global context and will bring insights to leaders in all areas.'

–Pankaj Kumar, Ph. D. Dean (Planning & Development),
Chairman and Professor of Human Resource Management Area|
Indian Institute of Management (IIM), Lucknow

'Building on an incredibly large body of research and professional experience, the authors masterfully inspire our creativity and need for discovery. I compliment the authors on a job very well done.'

–Dr. Shaker A. Zahra, Professor & Department Chair,
Robert E. Buuck Chair of Entrepreneurship, Academic Director,
Entrepreneurship Center, Strategic Management and Organization Dept,
Carlson School of Management.

'This book is a major contribution – a game changer. It is worth every rupee. Buy it and learn.'

–Dr. Gerard McElwee, Professor of Entrepreneurship,
Sheffield Business School, Editor *International Journal of
Entrepreneurship and Innovation*

'The lessons from this book will be of great significance for the development of India's management field and organizations. This is an extremely timely book.'

–Dr. Mike, Michael Gibbs, Faculty Director, Executive MBA Program,
Clinical Professor of Economics,
The University of Chicago Booth School of Business

'The authors remind us that actually there is probably more to learn from failure stories. A great book that should be mandatory for management academics and business managers!'

–Dr. Eric VIARDOT, Director of the Global Innovation Management
Center EADA (GIMCE), EADA Business School

'A must-read for all management individuals in India and abroad.'

–Kishore G. Kulkarni, Ph.D.,
Distinguished Professor of Economics and Editor,
Indian Journal of Economics and Business

'The book offers unique perspectives on dealing with the modern business environment fraught with volatility, uncertainty, complexity, and ambiguity.'

–Dr. L. Murphy Smith, Dill Distinguished Professor of Accounting,
Murray State University (Murray, KY, USA),
Arthur J. Bauernfeind College of Business

'This book is highly readable, innovative, intellectually provocative, current, results-oriented and integrative.'

–Dr. Eric Charles Henri Dorion, Professor at the University of Caxias do
Sul (RS), Brazil, and the University Feevale (RS), Brazil.

'Kudos to the authors for presenting deep insights into the issues in relevant Indian cases.'

–Rajiv Gupta, B.Tech. (IIT), PGDM (IIM)
Management Consultant

'All and all, an excellent volume with the right balance in the correct context.'

–Dr. Sandip Anand, Associate Professor at
Xavier Institute of Management

'An enlightening book!'

–Dr. Jun Li, Senior Lecturer Marketing, Entrepreneurship and Global
Strategy Group, Essex Business School, University of Essex,
Editor *Journal of Entrepreneurship in Emerging Economies*

'This is a fascinating book on a topic long overdue.'

–Dr. Nick Lee: Professor of Sales and Management Science,
Loughborough University

'I am impatient to read volume II of this book, on a general model of the "mind of failure surpassing".'

–Dr. Djamchid Assadi, Professor at ESC Dijon Bourgogne

'I strongly recommend this outstanding book to all scholars, students, and decision makers in practice who want to improve their own decision making capabilities.'

–Dr. Alfred Posch, Professor, University of Graz

'This book reminds us that successful leaders are not only willing to take risks, but must be willing to sacrifice.'

–Dr. Tri Wismiarsi, Regional Editor–*Southeast Asia Journal of Family
Business Management,* Bakrie University, Indonesia

'I hope to have the privilege and pleasure to read this book soon.'

–Paulo Moreira–Consultant at CSW–Competitive Services
in the World Porto Area, Portugal

THE VUCA COMPANY

How Indian companies have faced
Volatility, Uncertainty, Complexity & Ambiguity

SUHAYL ABIDI & MANOJ JOSHI

JAICO PUBLISHING HOUSE

Ahmedabad Bangalore Bhopal Bhubaneswar Chennai
Delhi Hyderabad Kolkata Lucknow Mumbai

Published by Jaico Publishing House
A-2 Jash Chambers, 7-A Sir Phirozshah Mehta Road
Fort, Mumbai - 400 001
jaicopub@jaicobooks.com
www.jaicobooks.com

THE VUCA COMPANY
ISBN 978-81-8495-662-7

First Jaico Impression: 2015

Page design and layout: SÜRYA, New Delhi

Printed by
Rashmi Graphics
#3, Amrutwel CHS Ltd., C.S. #50/74
Ganesh Galli, Lalbaug, Mumbai - 400 012
E-mail: rashmigraphics84@gmail.com

Dedicated to our parents

ACKNOWLEDGEMENT

Words alone cannot express our gratitude to the following persons, whose advice, comments, support and encouragement made this book possible.

Our family members: Dr. Naheed Abidi, Sumaira Abidi, Bhoomija Joshi, Katyayni Joshi, Deepak, Rachna, Arushi, Sidhartha and Paartha.

Our colleagues and mentors: Len D'Costa and Murali Aiyer.

Our friends at Jaico Publishing House: Akash Shah, Sandhya Iyer, Srija Basu and Disha Jayadeep.

And last but not least, our friend and advisor of over 30 years, Sudhir Bansal of Applied Media.

Suhayl Abidi
Manoj Joshi

FOREWORD

This book is a well-documented treatise of some of the well-known corporate debacles in the recent past. In addition to providing interesting details on why these once great institutions or ambitious projects ran into trouble, the authors have tried to logically argue the reasons for each of these failures and have prescribed what could have been remedial measures for turning them around. Another interesting aspect of this book is that the authors have also tried to bring in a global perspective by interspersing their narrative with examples of similar experiences from the global arena.

Although this book is an analysis of why some of India's good companies turned bad, it constantly reminds the reader of the inevitability of VUCA in today's marketplace and the need for leaders to quickly learn what works for their companies and what does not. Institutions and projects fail not because of lack of ambition, inefficient processes or faulty systems but because of their inability to swiftly perceive and adapt to change.

The examples of Indian cases of VUCA failure selected by the authors in this book are topical, and I am sure that readers will easily be able to relate to case studies elaborated in this book and derive greater perspective on why certain institutions or projects fail to succeed. This book is a must read for management practitioners, students, aspiring leaders and all those who believe in continuously sharpening their skills to meet the challenges in a rapidly changing and uncertain environment.

Shikha Sharma

MD and CEO
Axis Bank

So give me a turbulent world as opposed to a quiet world, and I will take the turbulent one.

–Andrew Grove

CONTENTS

Contents

INTRODUCTION

Welcome to the VUCA world! It is a future that is here to stay – entry is neither optional nor avoidable. The VUCA world is characterized by *volatility, uncertainty, complexity* and *ambiguity*. All human beings are affected by the VUCA phenomenon irrespective of whether it is a political, an economic, a business, a natural or a social environment.

In *The World Is Flat*, Thomas Friedman notes that the rate of change today is much different than it was in the past. 'Whenever civilization has gone through one of these disruptive, dislocating technical revolutions – like Gutenberg's introduction of the printing press – the whole world has changed in profound ways,' he writes. 'But there is something different about the flattening of the world that is going to be qualitatively different from other such profound changes: the speed and breadth with which it is taking hold.'[1]

The fate of many leading companies such as Kodak, which failed to navigate the rapid changes brought about in its business environment, and Blackberry, which is on its last leg of existence, is a warning to all organizations that are now facing these inevitable, even unpredictable, changes but lack the leadership, flexibility and imagination to adapt – not because they are not smart or aware, but because the speed of change is simply overwhelming them.[2]

The 'V' in VUCA denotes 'volatility.' It refers to the nature, speed, volume and magnitude of change that does not move in a predictable pattern. 'U' stands for 'uncertainty' – a lack of predictability in issues and events. 'C' denotes 'complexity' – there are often numerous difficult-to-understand causes and mitigating factors (both inside and outside the organization) involved in a problem brought about by an increasingly complex globally intertwined business environment. Finally, 'A' stands for 'ambiguity,' that is, a lack of clarity about events. Each one of these factors comes with many challenges for the leader of an organization, and all four of them combined make it a 'virtual tsunami.'

'VUCA' is a term coined by the US military in the 1990s to deal with a changing battlescape after the Cold War ended, with the emergence of a multilateral, rather than a bilateral, global landscape. This means being ready for situations where adversaries are not visible, the distinction between combatants and innocent civilians are not apparent and the militias continuously change their partners, tactics and so on, such as in Iraq and in Afghanistan and later on in Somalia and in Libya. The US military had to adapt rapidly and improvise to effectively counter weapons and tactics of those opponents, often with an explosion of technology-based but ambiguous field intelligence.

Today, business leaders face a similar, challenging and dynamic landscape, especially after the banking crisis in the 1980s when companies and organizations all over the world suddenly found themselves faced with a comparable turbulence in their business environments and, subsequently, had to rethink their business models.

In 1958, S&P 500 index companies survived on an average of 61 years. By 1980, this figure had dropped to 25 years and by

2011 to only 18 years. Companies fell off the index as they declined in market value, were acquired by others or were threatened by bankruptcy. The decline of once-respected institutions such as Enron, Lehman Brothers and Kodak demonstrate how quickly things can change.[3] Nitin Paranjpe, ex-CEO of Hindustan Unilever Ltd. and presently President of the Home Care Business of Unilever globally, recently said,

> As leaders, we must be absolutely clear that the reasons that helped us succeed in the past will not be why we will succeed in the future. The context has changed. We now need to put on a bifocal lens, where on one hand, we need to look at the 'here and now' and on the other, look to the future.[4]

In a world where business leadership has not yet changed its mindset to the new realities, failures are bound to happen. In this gloomy and hostile situation, leaders should not only just survive, but also thrive. This requires shedding old assumptions and acquiring new mindsets, being more agile and developing the ability to quickly bounce back from adversity. Behavioural changes, rather than just acquiring new competencies and skills, must be emphasized. Resilience and agility cannot be taught but can be learnt. What better way to learn to manage in the VUCA world than to learn from those who failed to do so as failure can teach more than success. Once we know what doesn't work and unlearn it, we are ready to learn new behaviours, models and tools.

Failure! The fear of failure is a worldwide phenomenon, experiencing it is inevitable and running away from it is only human. It is said that if you want to learn about success, talk to a successful person; but if you want to learn about failure, talk to a very successful person.

In the twentieth century, there is no other person who is considered more successful than Mahatma Gandhi. Prior to his death, he had accomplished nearly all that he had set out to do. To associate failure with Mahatma Gandhi is almost a sacrilege, but his first satyagraha in South Africa, to repeal the registration of Indians, was an utter failure; his political career was over before it even began. It was then that Mr. Naidoo, a close friend, encouraged him to reflect on his actions, and Gandhi realized that the reason for failure was his choice of fellow satyagrahis. These were prosperous merchants and traders who had never experienced hunger or deprivation. A day behind bars was enough to weaken their resolve to support the cause. As a result, Gandhi was forced to settle on a compromise with the white administration, which released them, and consequently his reputation suffered. Gandhi reflected on his mistake and for the next satyagraha, he chose Indian coal miners. This was a hardy lot who had seen deprivation and would not weaken in prison. The satyagraha was a resounding success, Gandhi's non-violent protest movement brought him international acclaim and he never looked back. His resilience enabled him to move forward and make the transition from 'Gandhi' to *Mahatma* or 'great soul.'[5]

Leadership involves the readiness to make decisions, the courage to take risks, the willingness to collaborate and to support others to support creativity and the ability to speak one's mind. However, it is not enough to train leaders in these core competencies without attending to the factors that constrain their use.

Resilience is the ability to bounce back from adversity, setbacks and failures. It is a major determinant of success, and it is this that gives highly effective people the stamina for life-long leadership, more so in the VUCA future.

The business environment will always remain volatile and the future uncertain. According to A.T. Kearney's Turbulence Index, our operating environment is probably twice as volatile as it was ten years ago.[6] In the VUCA world, resilience and adaptability are the two attributes that distinguish leaders from mere managers.

In recent years, there has been a deluge of knowledge on 'failure,' especially influenced by the banking crisis and bankruptcy of Lehman Brothers. The business literature nowadays talks a lot about the need for failure in the pursuit of excellence. More than a score of books have appeared. *Harvard Business Review* devoted a full issue (April 2012) to the topic, and there have even been full-page advertisements by successful entrepreneurs (*DNA*, 16 January 2013) extolling the benefits of failure. In the past two decades or so, about 10,000 books have been published about how to succeed as an executive. Added to this are thousands of seminars, training programs and workshops. All this effort and expenditure does not seem to have changed the rate of failure.[7] On the contrary, it seems that those who failed were avid readers of books on how to succeed. Perhaps as a perverse logic, where knowledge on success could not succeed, maybe one can study why failures occur, which could provide some clues on how to avoid, minimize and, most importantly, recover from failure.

No one sets out to fail, but many do at some point in their career. Business failure isn't simply a matter of incompetent leadership. Sometimes the most talented individuals can pursue the wrong path. How do smart people who have been successful for years suddenly begin to make catastrophically bad decisions? Why do they ignore information and insight that is directly in front of them and proceed on a destructive path?

Companies, organizations and empires too fail after a great innings – some spectacularly, like Lehman Brothers, while others sustain on life support for years, like the Mughal Empire for nearly 150 years, General Motors for 40 and Kodak for 25, before calling it a day.

Today, Silicon Valley is the global headquarters of venture capital, but the first venture capital company in Silicon Valley, DG&A, founded in 1959, was not a success. However, those who worked there learned from DG&A's failure and left to form successful venture funds of their own.[8] In India too, Indian Drugs & Pharmaceuticals Ltd. (IDPL) failed, but scientists and executives working there learned from its failure and went on to establish Hyderabad's pharmaceutical industry, notably Dr. Reddy's.

Even immensely successful organizations, like Samsung, produce failures such as its short-lived automobile business. Today, many companies worldwide are on the path of failure, notably some major electronics brands from Japan. Failure is an inevitable part of human journey. When you take time to learn your lessons and use those lessons as stepping stones to greater heights, you transcend failure and are ready to face the VUCA world.

Failure is not a catastrophe, but failure to learn certainly can be. A.G. Lafley, who turned Proctor & Gamble (P&G) into an operations and innovation powerhouse, said,

> My experience is that we learn much more from failure than we do from success. Look at great politicians and successful sports teams. Their biggest lessons come from their toughest losses. The same is true for any kind of leader. And it was certainly true for me. You have to get past the disappointment

and the blame and really understand what happened and why it happened. And then, more important, decide what you have learned and what you are going to do differently next time. What's the single biggest reason that leaders stop developing and growing? They stop becoming adaptable; they stop becoming agile. It's Darwin's theory. When you stop learning, you stop developing and you stop growing. That's the end of a leader.[9]

Sooner or later, all real change involves failure – but not in the sense that many people understand it. If you do only what you know and do it very, very well, chances are that you won't fail. You'll just stagnate, and that's failure by erosion. Ultimately, a successful leader must understand that while mistakes are avoidable, they will still happen because risk is inherent in any activity.

Why write another book on failure? In spite of many failures in the Indian business environment, especially since India started its integration into the global economy, no major work has attempted to bring out the common reasons for all these failures. In addition, most books written on failures primarily focus on character and personality flaws of leaders. This book, besides highlighting behavioral aspects of failure, also details the accompanying reasons for failures, especially mega failures, where systems or structural causes also contributed substantially to it. For example, the US Government Enquiry Report on Lehman Brothers brings out the fact that one of the principal reasons for failure was its obsolete Risk Management System.[10]

It is difficult to persuade an organization to change when managers see themselves as highly competent and successful, already at the top of their game. Aristotle famously said that the gods first send 40 years of prosperity to whoever they intend to destroy. Similarly, R. Gopalkrishnan, Director, Tata Sons, has pointed out that 'it is well proven from the history of men that success (prosperity and happiness) leads to complacency which leads to decline. That is why one must be most alert and watchful at the peak of success. The successful organization sows its own seeds of destruction.'[11]

In this book, failure is not defined only by bankruptcy or liquidation. Substantial gap between expectations and results is also a failure and must be examined. The book is not designed to be critical of any individual or organization but looks at failures in a positive light. It aims to identify key elements of failure, how to face failures, minimize or avoid failures and finally to rebound from failures. All cases have been derived from published articles and reports.

We also need to examine the real reasons for failures rather than simply the superficial ones and apply the 'Five Whys' of Toyota Production System till we reach the unshakable cause. We often read that failure occurred due to financial reasons such as cash flow or because the business environment suddenly went unfavorable, but the real reason may lie elsewhere. To give an example, the official reason for the Fukushima nuclear plant disaster was given as a tsunami. However, later enquiries showed that the extent of disaster was due to a cascade of failures of low standards and investments in safety over a period of time. That itself could be traced back to the pressure of consistently showing good financial results by cutting costs in a regulated industry. Added to this was the false belief in technical infallibility that is inbuilt in the Japanese psyche. 'It was a profoundly man-made disaster – that could and should have been foreseen and prevented. Across the board, the commission found ignorance and arrogance unforgivable for anyone or any organization.'[12]

It is usually success that is written about, and leaders rarely highlight their failures. Even Mr. A.G. Lafley, the formidable CEO of P&G who has written so eloquently about failure, quoted earlier in the chapter, writes about his successful strategies in his book *Playing to Win* while failures are briefly mentioned in appendices although the strategies that brought about the successes also resulted in many failures. Since Mr. Lafley left P&G in 2009, the company has stumbled badly, and he was asked to return in early 2013. What do these sorry tales say about strategy? Rather than explore whether their many strategic successes somehow also sowed the seeds of later problems, Messrs Lafley and co-author Martin coyly note that 'no strategy lasts forever.'[13]

India too is not immune to failures. Big companies, especially where they have substantial influence at the government level, rarely fail and domestic banks, especially state lenders, tend to help companies through tough times by easing loan terms. K.C. Chakrabarty, the ex-Deputy Governor of the Reserve Bank of India, recently said that India's restructuring process is skewed:

> It has substantial bias towards more privileged borrowers vis-a-vis small borrowers. CDR cases are surging in India. In the June quarter, 41 cases worth 205 billion rupees were referred to the CDR cell, from 18 cases worth 46 billion rupees a year earlier. Since the process began in 2001, 57 cases worth 430 billion rupees have exited, of 292 accounts worth 1.5 trillion rupees.[14]

We will attempt to show that all these and many more were avoidable failures.

Who has not faced failure? Amitabh Bachchan, famous for his rich baritone, could not get a job as a radio announcer as his voice was not found suitable. The Beatles were told by Decca Records that 'groups with guitars are on the way out.' Similarly, there are remarkable cases of corporate resilience and turnarounds such as IBM, which was resurrected from near bankruptcy. Our book, too, describes some similar cases from India.

Unless you are an insider at the top level, you have no access to information as events unfold. Insiders can also be biased for many reasons. Therefore, we have largely used media reports, especially news as it happens, so that we could access objective and on-the-spot information.

This book attempts to emphasize the need to encounter failure at an early stage and build a successful journey by learning from them. Complacency kills, and one must, when in a leadership position, steer the enterprise from troubled waters and reach the right harbor at the right time, sometimes sailing with the wind, most of the time sailing against it. Hence, the challenge is to drive a strategy to encounter unknowns.

Mind you, VUCA is not necessarily doom and gloom. While VUCA can provide threats, it can also offer opportunities, especially if you translate VUCA as 'vision, understanding, clarity and agility.'[15]

Our attempt in this book is to present causes that are common to all kinds of failures and their remedies. Each cause is like a pearl that can be put in a necklace, the sum of all causes called dysfunctional learning. This necklace can be worn like a talisman to prevent or minimize failures. Every time you feel on top of the world, immensely successful poster boy and the like, take out this talisman, and it will keep you from slipping. This is the first step in changing behavior and systems that will make your organization stand up to whatever surprises VUCA can throw your way.

NOTES

1. Thomas Friedman, *The World Is Flat* (Farrar, Straus and Giroux, 2005).

2. Lawrence Kirk, *Leadership in a VUCA World* (UNC Kenan-Flagler Business School, 2013).

3. 'Surviving the VUCA World: Modern Challenges, Ancient Solutions,' Human Capital Leadership Institute, September 2013.

4. 'Volatility Is the New Normal,' *Business Standard*, 20 April 2013.

5. *The Making of the Mahatma*, BBC 2 Documentary, Part 1, 2009.

6. A.T. Kearney, *Winning in a Turbulent World* (2012).

7. Lee Thayer, *How Executives Fail* (WME Books, 2007).

8. Leslie Berlin, 'The High-Tech Tortoise,' *Think Magazine*, May 2012.

9. 'I Think of My Failures as a Gift,' an interview with A.G. Lafley, *Harvard Business Review*, April 2001.

10. Financial Crisis Enquiry Report, GPO, US government, January 2011.

11. R. Gopalkrishnan, Speech at IIT Mumbai Foundation Day, 10 March 2003.

12. Dennis Normile, 'Commission Spreads Blame for "Manmade" Disaster,' *Science Magazine*, 13 July 2012.

13. 'Staying on Top,' Review of A.G. Lafley's book *Playing to Win: How Strategy Really Works*, *The Economist*, 12 January 2013.

14. 'Wockhardt: From Debt Debacle to Stock Rocket,' *Reuters*, 19 August 2012.

15. Robert Johansen, 'External Future Forces That Will Disrupt the Practice of Change Management,' Talk at ACMP Conference, April 2013.

VUCA WAS ALWAYS THERE

The VUCA environment is not new. When the Mongols suddenly arrived at the gates of Europe in the thirteenth century, it was VUCA, and the known world changed forever. VUCA brings with it both opportunities and failures. From the dawn of civilization, there have been spectacular failures ranging from the demise of the Persian Empire to the bankruptcy of Lehman Brothers, primarily due to failure to read the impending changes. There have also been sterling cases of phoenix-like rising from failures such as Emperor Babur, who first lost his kingdom and rose again to lay the foundation of the Mughal Empire.

THE PERSIAN EMPIRE

This was the first multination, multicultural and multilingual empire in the world, its extent ranging from Nile to Indus, founded by Cyrus the Great in sixth century BC. Among other innovations, Persian kings revolutionized the economy by placing it on a silver and gold coinage and introducing a regulated and sustainable tax system, promoted agriculture with irrigation projects and instituted an efficient postal system. The empire grew as it accepted and adopted outside influences and an ability to learn from all in a tolerant multicultural society. It influenced the development and structure of future empires. In fact, the Greeks and later on the Romans copied the best features of the Persian method of governing the empire and vicariously adopted them.[1]

The founders of the Persian Empire were hardy nomads who came from mountainous arid country, which made them tough, restless and wandering. Two hundred years later, Darius III ruled from Persepolis, a palace city amidst luxury brought by trade, and rarely ventured out. The rulers assumed 'The Cheese' would always be there. But this success and wealth also brought attention from invaders such as Alexander.

By the time of Alexander's invasion, complacency has crept in, and the systems followed by the earlier Persian rulers, which had led to wealth creation, had been allowed to lapse. This was especially so in the case of the army, which though large had not kept pace with training and development activities, such as cavalry tactics. There was continuous revolt at the boundaries of this far-flung empire, which disturbed wealth creation.

Darius III, relying on his large force for victory, did not see Alexander as a threat. The stage was set for a confrontation with Alexander the Great in 331 BC, who with his small force of about 40,000 twice defeated Darius's larger force of 250,000 with more than 100 chariots, in spite of Darius choosing the battle site, which gave an advantage to his dreaded chariots. However, Alexander's disciplined force, speed and superior cavalry tactics sealed Darius's fate, and the latter fled from the battlefield. Thus, the large Persian Army, which was the most advanced at the dawn of the empire, fell to a smaller Macedonian army with superior cavalry tactics.

BABUR AND THE MUGHAL EMPIRE

We know Babur as the founder of the Mughal Empire. He was the ruler of the small state of Ferghana in present-day Uzbekistan. Many of us are unaware that he had a series of failures starting with his conquest of Samarkand, the rich and powerful Uzbek kingdom on the Silk Route. His victory soon ended with his rout, and as a consequence he also lost Ferghana. He was now homeless and with fewer than forty followers retreated to a remote mountain hideout. Babur writes about his poor diet and harsh life often in subzero temperatures.

> [E]veryone who reads these events will know, what grief and what sorrow and what difficulties I have seen.
>
> —*Baburnama* (1528)

However, his life's learning continued unabated. When his grandmother was returned to him, the first question she asked him was this: 'What did you learn from your failures.' Babur recounted that his obsession with Samarkand was 'like of a boy with a new toy, I could think of nothing else.' He should not have left Ferghana without making adequate provisions for its defense. He made more attempts to take Samarkand and even Ferghana but could not succeed. After every defeat, he would sit down with his close associates and go over the reasons for his failures. Ultimately, he was able to conquer Kabul and somewhat retrieved his fortunes.

Babur had an inquisitive mind and took great notice of the world around him. It was VUCA world and passing caravans brought news of changes taking place beyond borders. He was always aware of the battle tactics being employed around his empire, especially by his enemies. Babur would talk to caravan masters, who were the Google of that age, about conditions in the outside world. From one such interaction, he learned that the Ottomans had given a crushing defeat to the Persians through the use of gunpowder. He immediately sent a general to the Ottoman Sultan for a quantity of field guns, muskets and a Turkish gunner to train his forces. The deployment of this arsenal in several small campaigns in conjunction with his cavalry evolved into development of his strategy and tactics. With every defeat he became a more experienced fighter under adverse conditions, through siege, inside cities, often house-to-house fighting and in mountains with rugged terrain.

Although he started the battle with a prearranged script, he was able to improvise brilliantly when he found that situations demanded changes in tactics. As General Eisenhower once said, 'Plans are useless while planning is essential.'

> All ill, all good in the count is gain if looked right.
>
> *—Baburnama*

After campaigning for almost 30 years, Babur was now ready for his final assault on India. He had a small but well-trained mobile army and had already undertaken several pilot projects to put his cavalry and newly acquired artillery to synergistic use. In addition, he had made four forays into India to understand the defense and tactics of his adversary.

> When one has pretensions to rule and a desire for conquest, one cannot sit back and just watch if events don't go right once or twice.
>
> *—Baburnama*

In October 1525, Babur crossed Indus for the final time and arrived at Panipat in April of next year. He had a force of 12,000, including 4,000 muskets and about 12 field guns.

Life's Lessons Deployed at Panipat

- Babur's Army – 12,000 against Ibrahim Lodi's 100,000 with 1,000 elephants.

- April – hot for Babur's soldiers

- Battlefield – open plains. Babur's experience was largely in mountainous warfare where the size of force does not matter as much as speed and agility. In open plains, Lodi's large army could maul him

- Babur had a long supply line. Lodi was close to his capital

Lodi could wait, and he did wait for one month. However, Babur also had certain advantages:

- His army was well trained while Lodi's army, though large, was not so well trained. It had not seen large-scale battle for a long time

- Babur's advisors were a cohesive team, tested in long years of wilderness, while Lodi had executed 27 advisors in the past few months on suspicion of treachery. He had no pool of trusted advisors when he needed them the most

- Babur had artillery in the form of disruptive technology. Though Lodi had heard of this new invention, he was contemptuous of its application. He said that guns took several minutes to reload while a good cavalry soldier could fire up to ten arrows in one minute on the gallop

Learning from Best Practices

Babur knew that he would be defeated in a traditional face-to-face fighting. Therefore, he laid his battlefield using the knowledge of defensive field laid by the Ottomans against the Persians in the Battle of Chaldiran in 1514. He took Panipat town as the left flank and on the other side he placed 700 carts tied together and covered with hides, with gaps for his cavalry to charge through. Thus, Babur created his defensive battlefield as a funnel so that he could fight in a narrow limited area, his field of expertise. Behind the carts, he placed his guns and muskets.

Now all he needed was Ibrahim Lodi to attack him. One night, to lure Lodi to his battlefield, Babur sent about 5,000 soldiers into the enemy camp to burn tents, create confusion and give the impression that attack had begun. When Lodi's forces retaliated, they quickly retreated back to their camp. The objective of this feigned retreat was to lure the enemy into attack, which he did the next morning.

The next morning, Ibrahim Lodi, sensing an easy victory, used cavalry to engage Babur's forces. His large force could not be maneuvered in a narrow battlefield and Babur used his guns and muskets to full effect. The elephants got scared with the boom of guns and turned around mauling their own forces. Babur's advanced weaponry was the deciding factor in the battle as the Lodi forces, which had only traditional weaponry, were decimated and Ibrahim Lodi was killed.[2]

Babur's innovations were not due to sudden bouts of inspirations but grew out of a lifetime of learning from battles and campaigns, largely defeats, a skill essential for survival in a VUCA world. Lodi was like the CEO of a successful company such as present day Kodak or NOCIL – arrogant, complacent, unable to anticipate disruptive technologies and slow to change, a prisoner of his assumptions and fixed mindsets. Steve Jobs would have immediately identified with Babur as a long-lost twin brother.

However, Babur's later successors, starting with Shah Jahan, could not retain their inheritance and gave way to the British. They built and lived lavishly ruining the state's finances, and the army, though large, had not kept up with the advances in warfare. They lived true to the quote that 'success sows its own seeds of destruction.'

THE EAST INDIA COMPANY

The British East India Company was the first multinational corporation the world had ever seen. It was given a Royal Charter in 1600 and later converted to limited liability joint-stock company for trading in the East. It had a successful run for 275 years and for the first half of its existence, it remained a commercial supplicant, exporting bullion to pay for Asia's luxury goods: first spices, then textiles and tea.

To maintain its monopoly for supply of goods such as tea, cloth and so on, the Company started interfering more and more in internal affairs first through subterfuge and later directly through the use of force. Revenue replaced commerce as the Company's first concern, and the original vision of the company was lost in empire building. To maximize revenue, the company mismanaged the state and was stripped of its operational responsibilities, which passed on to the British government. The East India Company became bankrupt and was dissolved by the same Royal Charter through which it began its journey.[3]

Failures After the Industrial Revolution

Failures after the Industrial Revolution could be called the failures due to disruptive technologies. As we have seen in Babur's case, even in the fifteenth century, disruptive technologies could alter the rules of engagement, as after the Industrial Revolution, technologies replaced existing businesses at an increasingly faster and faster rate. The reasons were not far to see. Complacency brought about by success and management increasingly hard of hearing and contemptuous of emerging threats just as Ibrahim Lodi.

Western Union

Western Union had a monopoly on telegraph business. When Alexander Graham Bell offered to sell telephone patents first to Western Union in 1879,[4] they rejected it saying, 'The idea is idiotic on the face of it. Furthermore, why would any person want to use this ungainly and impractical device when he can send a messenger to the telegraph office and have a clear written message sent to any large city in the United States?'[5] It is interesting to note that Stephen Elop, the CEO of Nokia, made similar comments about touch phones: 'We'd tried touchscreens before, and people didn't like them.'[6] Steve Balmer of Microsoft goes so far as to publicly mock the iPhone, 'Who would use a phone without buttons, after all?'[7] When the iPhone was announced in January 2007, Steve Balmer said the following:

> 500 dollars? Fully subsidized? With a plan? I said that is the most expensive phone in the world. And it doesn't appeal to business customers because it doesn't have a keyboard. Which makes it not a very good email machine ... Let's take phones first. Right now, we're selling millions and millions and millions of phones a year. Apple is selling zero phones a year. In six months, they'll have the most expensive phone by far ever in the marketplace.[8]

Pan Am

Pan Am was a pioneer in air travel and a brand name second only to Coca Cola. Pan Am's founder, Juan Trippe, was the world's first airline tycoon, the imperial sky-god, his company the aviation pioneer that came to be known as America's Imperial Airline. First to fly the Pacific, first across the Atlantic, first around the world, Pan Am was once one of the most glamorous and best-known global corporations. Its worldwide headquarters – the crown jewel – was on Manhattan's Park Avenue, The Pan Am Building, the world's largest corporate office building at the time.

America's heavily regulated airline industry consisted of two parts: the domestic airlines and the international airlines, namely, Pan Am and TWA. The idea was simple: the domestic airlines delivered passengers to international gateways, where the international airlines picked them up and took them overseas. Pan Am, of course, benefited greatly from this arrangement. Until 1978, that is, when the industry was deregulated. It was easier for the domestic carriers to add international service than it was for Pan Am and TWA to build national networks of domestic flights to feed their global service.

It was one of a series of setbacks for the proud pioneer. The expensive 747s arrived just as a recession hit and air travel slowed. Then the Arab oil embargo in 1973 and 1974 increased jet fuel prices, and after that came deregulation. Pan Am was buffeted like a propeller plane in an updraft, handicapped not only by its lack of a domestic route system, but also by an uninspiring succession of chief executives and a top-heavy management. Labor unions also were slow to make concessions. 'Half of Pan Am's problem was caused by circumstances,' a frustrated one-time financial advisor to the company says. 'The other half was caused by the culture, which seemed to make perfectly rational men think they were invulnerable once they walked through Pan Am's doors.'[9]

The Pan Am of legend is long gone.It went bankrupt in 1991, and The Pan Am building was sold and is now called MetLife. It was not defeated by a disruptive technology but by VUCA, changes in the business environment, primarily the deregulation of airlines, that called for agility which monolithic companies did not possess, something our own Air India is very familiar with. If Air India was a private airline, it would also have gone into oblivion a long time ago.

IBM

The transformation of IBM provides a stunning example of phoenix-like rising from near bankruptcy. Twenty-five years ago, IBM was at the pinnacle of success. It had invented General Purpose Computing; its laboratories boasted of Nobel Prize winners, helped put man on the moon and invented the ATM, the hard disk, the floppy drive and many such utilities. By 1984, it was the bluest of blue chips on Wall Street. Soon the downfall started. By the 1980s, there was a pervasive attitude that 'don't tinker with success' with entrenched product and geography silos(somewhat like the Tata Group when Ratan Tata took reins). Executives lose touch in an arrogant and complacent culture. The company missed many technological shifts, and in 1993 posted an $8 billion loss, the biggest in US history. The Wall Street now called it a dinosaur, advocating its breaking up.[10]

Under Louis Gerstner, IBM transformed from a computer hardware company to the world's largest consulting organization, creating an integrated, flexible, service-oriented architecture. It was done through exiting commoditized hardware business; making 9 out of 10 employees focus on customers' solutions;

searching for talent globally; removing layers from fiefdoms (mini-IBMs); making execution more important than strategy; adopting Globally Integrated Support Functions and Clear Performance Measures; and, most importantly, changing corporate culture coupled with re-emphasizing spirit of core values.

The path to success lies in understanding the relevant trends, figuring out how your strengths and resources can capitalize on them and staking out a leadership position.

Iraq War—No Learning from Vietnam

Since World War II, the US Army is trained in fighting large-scale wars. Its assumption was that the enemy is visible and predictable. When the United States got involved in the Vietnam War, a new type of enemy was encountered, one that was invisible, did not give straight fight and believed in hit and run, in short, a guerilla, an adversary that the US Army had not encountered before.

The US military, especially the Army, approached the Vietnam War with a conventional mindset, referred to as the 'Army concept.' The American method of counterinsurgency was 'almost a purely military approach,' which ignored political and social realities on the ground. Instead of focusing on protecting the Vietnamese people and denying the Communists a safe haven, the Army in particular believed that massive firepower was the best means to be 'utilized by the Army to achieve the desired end of the attrition strategy – the body count.' In the end the American defeat was a 'failure of understanding and imagination.'[11]

The Vietnam War was fought from the Pentagon, and local commanders had no say in the matter. Even during the Iraq War the Pentagon used massive amount of data to analyze and direct the war. Defense Secretary Rumsfeld's refusal to listen to men who were specialists in Middle East matters and understood the ground situation was a result of his denial of the reality that the United States was fighting an insurgency and not engaging in conventional warfare. Officers who believed that counter-insurgency strategy was to be employed, including General Petraeus, were transferred to insignificant postings and passed over for promotions. Therefore, officers stopped voicing their opposition to the views of Rumsfeld and his senior Pentagon officials.

Strategic errors are common in war, and this wasn't just about going into Iraq with the wrong strategy. It was a failure; worse, a refusal to adapt. The US Army's fortunes changed when Rumsfeld was removed due to heavy losses and General Petraeus was made commander in Iraq. He brought back, with due promotions, those officers who were punished for airing contrary opinions and decision making was transferred to field commanders who knew the ground realities. An initial refusal to learn from what was going on and later the military's ability to learn and to adapt changed the tide of the war. Change comes from a bottom-up approach. Good leadership is important, but in a complex VUCA environment it would be a mistake to lead through remote control.[12]

Eastman Kodak

As Eastman Kodak begins to adapt to the challenges of bankruptcy, David A. Glocker's company, Isoflux, is expanding, thanks to technology he developed in Kodak's research labs. He didn't steal anything. In fact, before he founded Isoflux with Kodak's blessing in 1993, Glocker approached his managers at the company and suggested they market the coating process he had developed. 'In a nutshell, I went to them and said, "I think this is valuable technology and it's not being commercialized … I'd like to do that if Kodak is not interested,"' he recalls. 'And they said, "Fine, do it."' That was in the year 1998. Today, several patents and innovations later, Isoflux is a growing company. The technology is one of countless innovations that Kodak developed over the years but failed to successfully commercialize, the most famous being the digital camera, invented by Kodak engineer Steven Sasson in 1975. Digital technology has all but done in the iconic filmmaker. Since 2003, Kodak has closed 13 manufacturing plants and 130 processing labs and reduced its workforce by 47,000. It now employs 17,000 worldwide, down from 63,900 less than a decade ago. When new technologies change the world, some companies are caught off-guard. Others see change coming and are able to adapt in time. And then there are companies like Kodak – which saw the future and simply couldn't figure out what to do. Kodak's Chapter 11 bankruptcy filing on 19 January 2012 saw the culmination of the company's 30-year slide from innovation giant to aging behemoth crippled by its own legacy.[13]

Why did Kodak not see the changes that were visible to others such as rival Fuji Films. The reason is not far to see. Twenty-five years back, Kodak had 90 percent of the US market for color films with a 70 percent gross margin. The success had blinded the company into denial that digital photography would replace film roll.

Kodak fits the classic profile of a twentieth-century corporate dinosaur. But the company isn't in trouble because it stood still while the world turned. Rather, Kodak has spent the past decade attempting to adapt to the changing times, often creating innovative new products, but failing to turn them into a sustainable business. Today, Kodak is trying to sell off its cache of digital patents, which may in fact be worth more than the company's market cap. In a way, it's a fitting metaphor for the company's recent history: often great at innovation, but always bad at business.[14]

Iridium

Motorola had been one of the great companies and one of the proudest brands of the United States. The company embodied technology leadership and had a series of inventions to its credit, including the first walkie-talkies for the military and a host of products that laid the foundation of the mobile phone industry. It also pioneered the six-sigma process. Therefore, failure on a truly gigantic scale is not something expected of this immensely successful company led by towering, visionary leaders, a company that was second only to Nokia in sales of mobile handsets.

Motorola launched its Iridium project in 1985, the concept being a constellation of 66 low-earth-orbiting (LEO) satellites that would allow subscribers to make phone calls from any global location. Robert Galvin, Motorola's Chairman at the time, gave approval for go ahead. Iridium was viewed as a potential symbol of Motorola's technological prowess for all the world to see.

In 1991, Motorola established Iridium LLC as a separate company and was the partner with the largest equity share.

Some industry observers felt that Motorola had an additional incentive to ensure that Iridium succeeded, namely, protecting its reputation. Between 1994 and 1997, Motorola had suffered through slowing sales growth, a decline in net income and declining margins. Moreover, the company had experienced several previous business mishaps, including a failure to anticipate the cellular industry's switch to digital cell phones, which played a major role in Motorola's more than 50 percent share price decline in 1998.

On 1 November 1998, the company launched its satellite phone service charging $3,000 for a handset and $3–$8 per minute for calls. The results were devastating. In the end, the company had only 20,000 subscribers instead of the projected 5 million.[15]

On 13 August 1999, two days after defaulting $1.5 billion in loans, Iridium filed for Chapter 11 bankruptcy, making it one of the largest bankruptcies in US history.

Iridium's development took 11 years, during which the mobile phone industry had spread faster and wider reaching places like China and India. Iridium could not be used inside a room, and the customer had to go out in the open to make the connection. A handset the size of a brick, poor data capability and recharging inconveniences made it all the more difficult for business users to adopt this service. Over one thousand articles have been written on the reasons behind the failure of Iridium, but essentially these were few and simple, based on a flawed business model.

1. The long gestation period eroded Iridium's appeal to business travelers. The development of mobile services, both in features and coverage, made Iridium outdated by

the time it was launched. Iridium's prospectus written in 1998 listed 25 full pages of risks. There is little evidence to suggest that Motorola or Iridium made any appreciable progress in addressing any of these risks.

2. The arrogance of technological superiority is deeply ingrained in Motorola's culture and Iridium went forward single mindedly concentrating on satellite design and launch, brushing aside the challenges in marketing and sales.

3. Iridium's board did not provide adequate corporate governance. In 1997, Iridium's board had 28 directors, 27 of who were either Iridium employees or directors designated by Iridium's partners. The composition, not to mention size, of Iridium's board created two major problems. First, the board lacked the insight of outside directors who could have provided a diversity of expertise and objective viewpoints. Second, the fact that most of the board was comprised of partner appointees made it difficult for Iridium to apply pressure on its partners in key situations.

4. The CEO's financial future was tied up in Iridium stocks, and this made it difficult for him to view the project objectively, to cut losses and move on.

Ultimately, the entire business was sold for $25 million.

You have to ask exactly what blinded them to the whole competitive environment. Unfortunately, it points to hubris and the belief in the myth of 'first mover advantage.' Motorola's desire to be the first to chart new territory into civilian aerospace allowed the company to move forward, despite the immaturity of each stage. Motorola was out in front of others on the construction and financing of the satellites. Thus, they probably came to believe that once they established the gold standard, they could monopolize the industry – build it and they will come. Yet, their field of dreams failed to materialize.[16]

This is another case of success sowing its own seeds of failure. Motorola, a successful company, becomes inward looking and complacent leading to downward spiral.

Lehman Brothers

This is the ultimate failure story featuring in countless books, articles TV discussions and its bankruptcy, no doubt, would be dissected and analyzed for years to come.

One can say that the first nail in the Lehman Brothers coffin was driven the day Richard Fuld took over as Chairman and CEO in 1994 and in his first address to the staff laid out his vision and priorities.

The new boss had one simple ambition – to overtake his rivals Merrill Lynch, Morgan Stanley and Goldman Sachs. 'We have inherited and tradition that would let us stand alone and conquer all the people that stand in front of all of us. Basically to crush our enemies like this (teeth clinched).'[17] In his goal to be No.1, he had little time and consideration for his clients and stakeholders. In a recruitment video from 1990, Richard Fuld emphasized the four operating principles of Lehman Brothers. These were:

> First, we are client and customer driven firm; second, attracting, developing, retaining, motivating the very best people that we can find; third, developing outstanding returns. We need outstanding returns to drive shareholder value and allow us to grow and to get resources which encourages

people to buy our stock and our debt and also drive
compensation and fourth work together as a team.[18]

Richard Fuld, in his drive for growth, repudiated three of the
four principles and only went after delivering outstanding returns.
His success on this single-item agenda led to his taking on huge
debts to buy questionable assets, such as sub-prime real-estate,
leading to the bankruptcy. His belligerent philosophy is
remarkably frankly revealed in an internal company video (about
his competitors): 'I am soft, I'm lovable but what I really want
to do is reach in, rip out their heart and eat it before they die.'[19]

One senior Vice President Lawrence McDonald gave an
inside account of the firm in his book *A Colossal Failure of
Common Sense*. '24,992 people striving hard, making money,
and about eight guys losing it. The company was never, never
rotten at the core. That's where all the beauty was. This place
was rotten at the head.' Mr. Fuld surrounded himself with every
type of yes-men and woman he could possibly get. According to
McDonald, by the time 2007 rolled around, he had a real
steamroller. They increased the balance sheet between 2007
and 2008 by over $120 billion. So as the crisis was getting
worse, McDonald says, Lehman was taking on more debt to pay
high-level employees. They were using leverage to increase the
bonus pool and increase the compensation flow to the point
where if you made it to the 31st floor, it was like 'hitting the
New York lottery.'[20]

No doubt, Condé Nast Portfolio ranked Fuld number one
on their Worst American CEOs of All Time list, stating he was
'belligerent and unrepentant,' and he was also named in *Time*
magazine's list of '25 People to Blame for the Financial Crisis.'
The bankruptcy of Lehman Brothers was total failure of corporate

governance. Not only staff, it seems the Board of Directors was also made up of yes-men such as John Akers who was responsible for bringing about the near bankruptcy of IBM. They were reluctant to challenge Richard Fuld.

Each story of failure tells a lesson in surviving the VUCA world. The roots of failure in all cases from Persian Empire to Lehman Brothers should be viewed through the lens of behavioral sciences rather than strategy or operations, the expertise of which is sadly lacking in organizations, leading to many avoidable failures as we shall see next.

NOTES

1. http://en.wikipedia.org/wiki/Achaemenid_Empire#Fall_ of_the_empire.
2. Suhayl Abidi, 'Why Leaders Have to be Learners,' *Indian Management*, October 2004.
3. Nick Robins, 'East India Company: The Original Too-Big-to-Fail Firm,' *Bloomberg*, 12 March 2013.
4. 'Bell Telephone v Western Union (1879),' *The Guardian*, 6 August 2007.
5. Janna Quitney Anderson, *Imagining the Internet: Personalities, Predictions, Perspectives* (Rowman & Littlefield, 2005), pp. 28-29.
6. 'Stephen Elop's Nokia Adventure,' *Bloomberg*, 2 June 2011.
7. 'Nokia's Sorry Story: Mistakes and Misunderstandings – Part 1,' www.articlesnatch.com.
8. Prasad Kaipa, 'Steve Jobs and the Art of Mental Model Innovation,' *Ivy Business Journal*, May/June 2012.
9. Jon Marcus and Gretchen Voss, 'Air Apparent,' *Boston Magazine*, February 2000.

10. Chris Cameu et al., 'IBM's Decade of Transformation – Turnaround to Growth,' IT 509 Woodbury University, 17 February 2009.

11. Andrew F. Krepinevich, *The Army and Vietnam* (The Johns Hopkins University Press, 1986).

12. Tim Harford, *Adapt* (Hachette, 2011).

13. 'What's Wrong With This Picture: Kodak's 30-Year Slide into Bankruptcy,' Knowledge@Australian School of Business, 7 February 2012.

14. 'What Killed Kodak?' *The Atlantic*, 5 January 2012.

15. Sydney Finkelstein and Shade H. Sanford, 'Learning from Corporate Mistakes; The Rise and Fall of Iridium,' *Organizational Dynamics* 29 (2), 2000.

16. 'Iridium's House of Cards: An Analysis,' Knowledge@W.P.Carey, 6 May 2005.

17. 'The Fall of Lehman Brothers,' BBC Documentary, 2008.

18. Lehman Brothers recruitment video from 1999, with an introduction by Richard Fuld.

19. 'No CEOs Paid Price for 2008 Meltdown. Here's Why,' *The Toronto Star*, 14 March 2014.

20. Lawrence G. McDonald, *A Colossal Failure of Common Sense* (Random House, 2009).

INDIAN CASES IN VUCA FAILURE

INDIAN CASES IN YOGA-FAILURE

I

THE DECLINE AND FALL OF SKS MICROFINANCE

A Lesson for Everyone

Swayam Krishi Sangam (SKS) Society, a non-profit, non-government organization (NGO), converted itself into SKS Microfinance, a non-banking financial company-non-deposit taking (NBFC-ND), led by Vikram Akula, an Indian-American with a PhD in political science from the University of Chicago. Modeled after Nobel Laureate Muhammad Yunus's Grameen Bank in Bangladesh, in 2009, it became public limited from a private limited company.

AD 2006 – Vikram Akula, the kurta-wearing CEO of SKS Microfinance, was the uncrowned king of microfinance in India, appearing on the covers of *TIME* and *Forbes* magazines, and Businessweek listing him among India's 50 Most Powerful People in 2009, India's very own Mohammed Yunus. He took SKS to great heights, growing 12 times in five years. In August 2010, the IPO was oversubscribed 20 times.

AD 2010 – Just when Akula was basking in glory, the setbacks started. His firm was mired in controversy over the exit of a CEO whom he had handpicked, farmer suicides and the firm's aggressive debt collection tactics. Finally, in November 2011, he was unceremoniously ousted from SKS Microfinance.

So what went wrong within a short period of only four years? SKS reported a net profit of ₹174.8 crores on total revenues of ₹958.9 crores and an operating revenue of ₹873.50 crores for the year ended 31 March 2010. It had a negative cash flow of ₹541.20 crores for the year ended March 2010.

The IPO of SKS Microfinance made the promoters and other venture capitalists, such as Narayan Murthy's investment vehicle Catamaran and some private equity funds that have stakes in these companies, millionaires. The hapless borrowers continued to live in abject poverty. Earlier, Vikram Akula sold 9.45 lakh shares at ₹639 per share to Tree Line Asia Master Fund (Singapore) Pte for $12.9 million. SKS Microfinance also offered high remuneration to its top management. Its chief executive and managing director Suresh Gurumani was entitled to a consolidated salary of ₹1.5 crores per annum, besides a performance bonus of ₹15 lakh per annum, with annual increments up to a maximum of 100 percent with the board having the liberty to approve any further increase over and above the 100 percent. Another shocking part is that Mr. Gurumani was paid a one-time bonus of ₹1 crore in April 2009, barely five months after joining the company.[1] In short, they did everything that a microfinance company was not supposed to do.

Vikram Akula, founder and Chairman of SKS Microfinance Ltd, blamed Suresh Gurumani's inability to handle the changing dynamics of the microfinance industry in India for the CEO and managing director's ouster after less than two years in saddle. 'Post our IPO (initial public offer), the dynamics of the microfinance sector changed.'[2] In July 2010, Gurumani's remuneration was increased, but by September, his ouster was being discussed by the board. Therefore, his competency was not in question. 'Where I see the problem is that there is a lot of insecurity, where the founders of the company don't want to give control to professionals,' Gurumani was quoted as saying.[3]

Obviously, Gurumani was brought in as a professional face to present to investors prior to IPO. Once the task was over, there was no need for someone who was not an Akula yes-man. For any entrepreneur-led company, scaling operations becomes one of the major problems as the promoters are not ready to relinquish control to professional management and move forward with sturdy systems and processes. It happened here too, as Akula was keen to continue as a hands-on manager. For example, Gurumani wanted to install professional risk-management system, which is crucial for a business where risk is a fundamental concern.

'The latest developments are an unfortunate confluence of circumstances, but perhaps inevitable,' says the head of a leading investment banking firm. 'Reconciling the rhetoric of poverty alleviation through microfinance with the commercial success and a few people getting very rich is going to be a mammoth task.'[4]

Such shenanigans are not unknown in the corporate world. In the United States, the CEO of Duke Energy was fired after one day on the job. His appointment might have been a calculated deception intended to facilitate the merger, and when the merger was over, the board decided he wasn't the right person to run the newly merged company.[5]

The healthy financials started taking a beating. For example, provision for losses rose from 0.9 percent in 2007 to nearly 10 percent in 2011, a rise of 10 times while profits of ₹9.33 crores rising to 28 crores in 2010 turned into a loss of ₹60 crores in 2011.[6] In October 2010, under intense public pressure, the Andhra Pradesh government brought about Microfinance ordinance, primarily alarmed by recovery tactics of microfinance companies, particularly SKS, leading to several suicides, which put many restrictions on the operations of microfinance companies in its largest market.

As Mohammad Yunus said,

> It is not the basic concept of microcredit that has a problem; when it is dedicated to the poor people, to help them, solve their problems. In the business world growth is the key word, if you want to put an IPO and so forth. They say, 'Oh growth rate is so high, fantastic, we'll do it all over India.' You are attracting people to make lot of money with your impressive growth rate. So in order to show growth rate in your performance record you constantly need to push people to do things. The key is that the whole thing (suicides) was triggered by SKS. They were the ones who kind of overdid things in a big way. The aggressiveness that it brought into the picture created all the problems. And then he (Vikram Akula) made personal money out of it. That also irritated the people. That you are saying that you are helping the poor people but I see you are making personal money out of this.[7]

In May 2011, a report by equity analysts at JP Morgan Asia Pacific Equity Research downgraded a stock that was already under pressure and reduced its value to half the listing price ahead of SKS's fourth quarter financial results.[8]

The speed at which the SKS success story unraveled has raised several questions. First, was Akula's revolving door entry and exit as chief executive sensible? Second, does his leadership style – some people we spoke to called it 'arrogant' – cause more harm than good?[9] He always believed that microfinance could be scaled up fast; could be highly profitable. To achieve that scale and heft he needed outside capital.[10]

SKS started by providing small loans exclusively to poor women located in rural areas across India. The loans extended were purely for business and other income-generating activities and not for personal consumption. The key ingredient of a microfinance organization that SKS also followed was to use a village-centered, group-lending model to provide unsecured loans to its members. SKS Microfinance organized prospective clients into groups so that they could address the issue of information asymmetry and lack of collateral by transferring what could be an individual liability to a group liability and holding the group morally responsible for repayment. If one member failed to make the loan payment on time, the company retained the right to refuse loan to that particular group in the future. Thus, the group could make payments on behalf of the individual defaulter.[11] However, to increase its growth rate, SKS made the cardinal mistake of offering loans to individuals. Without the group's moral pressure and with no collateral, there was no way of collecting from defaulters. SKS started running up large defaults that made them use heavy-handed methods to recover loans. The result was suicides, which led to negative media, forcing the government to intervene. Meanwhile, the losses kept on mounting.

Making a rare public appearance for the first time since his November 2011 exit from SKS amid the wave of controversy,

Akula held a packed audience spellbound at the Sankalp Summit 2012, where he admitted he made 'many, many, many mistakes' in his journey as a social entrepreneur. 'I just did not focus on the three Cs: did not focus on culture, code of conduct and control.'[12]

1. Culture is critical. It is important to remain committed to your organization's mission, to define core values and to act with integrity in accordance with those values.

2. It takes rules – defined codes of conduct – to ensure that social enterprises maintain the right kind of culture.

3. It is important for social entrepreneurs to maintain control of their ventures. Not everyone in the social enterprise space is an altruist and is acting with good intentions. Mission drift can be dangerous when organizations lose sight of their social mission and pursue other ends.

This was not all that went wrong. Akula forgot the purpose of business. Peter Drucker said, 'The purpose of business is to create and retain a customer.' SKS's customers were among the poorest in the country, whose well-being was forgotten by the social entrepreneur. The purpose changed, after PE investment took place, to maximization of shareholder value at whatever cost.

It is often seen that with success, the personality of leaders often metamorphoses into a more arrogant and less tolerant one. They start believing what they read about themselves in the media and begin to accept that they have somehow discovered a formula for success. Arrogance leads to overconfidence. Much has been written about this phenomenon. This happened to Richard Fuld who led Lehman Brothers to its bankruptcy as well as to homegrown leaders such as Vijay Mallya. Prior to it, corporations such as General Motors and before that Pan Am have also passed through this phase and paid a heavy price. Not only do leaders become arrogant, but organization culture too starts taking the same hue as dissenters are slowly eased out and debates disappear. Overconfidence isn't a personality trait or a moral failing, but a natural consequence of success that affects almost everyone. As we grow older and more experienced, we overrate the accuracy of our judgments.[13]

Akula later admitted that he should have listened to Dr. Yunus's frequent and forceful warnings that private capital and microfinance were a tenuous and dangerous combination. He admitted to youthful hubris and naïveté and recalled how Muhammad Yunus criticized him and the SKS model, and observed: 'Today, I can look back at what we did and say, "Professor Yunus was right."'[14] It takes courage to eat humble pie and publicly admit that you were wrong.

A humble Vikram Akula is back and this time, he's donning the mantle of sugarcane grower, a sustainable agri-business advocate. He is also focusing on corporate governance in social enterprises as a task force member of the Schwab Foundation for Social Entrepreneurship, and helping budding social entrepreneurs grapple with problems to ensure they don't end up making the same mistakes he did.[15]

In short, the biggest error that Vikram Akula made was to take his eyes off from the purpose of a microfinance organization. The entry of PEs, IPO and so on were all actions that took SKS farther and farther away from its founding objectives. This was a fatal mistake. In a VUCA world, the faster the world changes, the more firmly the organization should be anchored to its vision.

The entry of Gurumani was another mistake. A former banker whose narrowly focused aim is solely to raise the top and bottom lines is not a right choice to head a microfinance organization where empathizing with the customer should be the principal focus. A microfinance organization functions between the space of an NGO and a bank without being either. However, he was right in insisting on introducing processes and systems that a growing organization needs to install.

There is no further need to say that those who live a life of adulation should, very often, reflect and introspect about their motives and actions, and as we are now learning, charisma is often bad for organizational culture.

This is a classic example of greed and aggressiveness, which can destroy an organization in no time. Akula, in increasing his personal wealth and giving indecent remuneration to top functionaries, set an example of what a social entrepreneur should *not* do. Social entrepreneurs by definition take on the mission of bringing innovative solutions to alleviate poverty and in the process launch sustainable organizations. The entrepreneurs can be ambitious and persistent, but always committed to their constituents.

NOTES

1. 'Is SKS Microfinance IPO Being Done at Its Peak Performance?' *Moneylife*, 28 July 2010.
2. 'Gurumani Not Fit to Run SKS Post-IPO, Says Vikram Akula,' *Mint*, 13 October 2010.
3. 'Newsmaker Suresh Gurumani: The Protagonist in a Greek Play,' *Business Standard*, 8 October 2010.
4. 'The Decline and Fall of SKS Microfinance,' *Business Standard*, 22 May 2011.

5. 'Behind Duke's CEO-for-a-Day,' *Wall Street Journal*, 6 July 2012.

6. 'A Conversation with Muhammad Yunus,' *New York Times*, 22 February 2012.

7. Ibid., 4.

8. 'Abrupt Fall from Grace,' *Business Standard*, 20 May 2011.

9. Ibid., 8.

10. 'The Education of Vikram Akula,' *Forbes India Blog*, 17 April 2012.

11. 'Is SKS Microfinance IPO being Done at Its Peak Performance?' *Moneylife*, 28 July 2010.

12. 'The Return of Vikram Akula, This Time as a Sugarcane Messiah,' *First Post*, 12 April 2012.

13. 'The Psychology of Overconfidence,' *The New Yorker*, 27 July 2009.

14. 'The Best of 2012: Making the Most of Missteps,' Harvard Social Enterprise Conference, SKS's Akula Opens Up on Failure, http://www.nextbillion.net, 26 December 2012.

15. Ibid., 12.

II

KINGFISHER AIRLINES

Going Down Celebrity Style

When Kingfisher Airlines was up and flying, it was impossible to travel without noticing its owner, Dr. Vijay Mallya. Before the planes took off, the seat-back televisions showed a video of him, dripping with jewellery, striding through clouds of dry ice amid models of his fleet of aircraft. 'I've instructed my crew to treat you as a guest in my own home,' he announces. 'If you miss anything, contact me personally.'[1]

It was all part of the Vijay Mallya show: the life of a man who was not content with being a successful, astute businessman – but also wanted to be a giant celebrity.

When Dr. Mallya inherited his father's ₹120 crore United Breweries Group in 1984, he displayed his astute side early. His business model was to use debt to acquire other companies till he became the largest manufacturer in his class of products and had 50–75 percent market share in various product categories. The rich cash flow allowed him to retire debts and create surplus to grow and acquire. Vijay Mallya fought many battles with his rivals in the beverage industry for dominance, winning most and as a result regularly hogged limelight in the media. He used his wealth to live a luxurious life and acquire friends in high places. He was known to throw the most sought-after parties, and his lifestyle became an extension of his persona. He became the Group's chief brand ambassador.

When the government of India opened Indian skies to private operators, Vijay Mallya obtained the license to operate Kingfisher Airlines (KFA) in 1993. He promised flyers a class of service not usually seen among the domestic airlines. Jet Airlines was punctual but was for busy executives; Air Deccan was for the 'aam aadmi,' a sort of shuttle service, while the others either didn't matter or were too small. Vijay Mallya didn't disappoint. He brought glamor into the business of running airlines. He handpicked air hostesses, gave away goody bags to each passenger and the welcome at the airport counters had to be seen to be believed. He made you feel special. The corporate sector wanted all top executives to fly Kingfisher, and they came back admiring the service.

One year into operations, KFA shifted focus and moved from an all-economy model to luxury by reconfiguring the planes with a combination of First Class and Economy.

Next, Dr. Mallya made his big strategic mistake. Air Deccan, a pioneering budget airline was desperately looking for a buyer. Vijay Mallya put in his bid, apparently offering more money than a rival suitor. He used the successful business model of the beverages business to acquire, through raising a huge debt. There the similarity ended. Unlike the beverage business which is more recession proof and brings consistent cash flow, the airlines was an entirely different business, capital intensive and small margin with variable cash flow. None of the Indian airlines had made any profit till that time.

It seemed a good deal in the beginning. Mr. Mallya got Air Deccan's huge market share and several aircraft as well, plus an immediate listing as well as the license to fly on international routes as Air Deccan had been in the business for five years – a requirement by the regulator for any airline to fly overseas.

He also acquired the losses incurred by the airline.

He spun off Air Deccan's fleet into a Kingfisher Beverages subsidiary called Kingfisher Red. So, Kingfisher Airlines had an economy as well as business class and flew on trunk routes including the metros, while Red did the rounds of tier-II cities as well as some of the bigger cities.

However, all this came at a cost. Market analysts believe flaws in Vijay Mallya's business plans and style of functioning lie at the root of Kingfisher Airlines' woes.

'Kingfisher made too many changes in their business model and strategies and that led to strategic weakness,' said Kapil Kaul, Chief Executive Officer (South Asia) for Centre for Asia Pacific and Aviation, an airline consultancy firm. This had a major impact on the airline. 'When an airline keeps changing its model and takes to random expansion, there is no time for the airline to stabilise,' said an industry insider, on condition of anonymity.[2]

In a controversial report on the airline, an internationally respected Investment Research firm Veritas points out that Vijay Mallya should never have got into the airline business. 'We believe that the ill-conceived foray into the airline business has already cost Kingfisher Beverages shareholders dearly, and that their ownership of India's premier beverage company sacrificed at the altar of egoistic ambitions.'[3]

Group management felt there was nothing wrong with the airline. The problem, of course, lay in acquisitive excess. In time, the airline became a stepping stone for the pursuit of other adventures. He acquired Whyte & Mackay distillery and announced the acquisition amidst drama and glamor, holding a press conference in London. Among other acquisitions, he added a cricket team quickly followed by a Formula 1 racing team.

The problem with Vijay Mallya was that he was not just into one business but several and each was different from the other. Normally, for such diverse businesses, one would appoint CEOs to run them with a hands-on approach, who would, in turn, report to the Group Chairman.

While the beverage businesses had an experienced team of managers running the show, the others needed the undivided attention of Dr. Mallya himself. More so, for the airline venture. This was where his second mistake came in. The airline had everything going for it: great brand visibility, loyal customers and a wide network. But as a former business partner of Vijay Mallya pointed out recently, he was more like an absentee landlord.[4] The first CEO left in 2005, two months after takeoff of the airline. His successor resigned in May 2006 after a year in the chair. His replacement joined after three and half years in September 2010 when the last professional CEO Sanjay Aggarwal joined (he left in February 2014). Vijay Mallya was seen everywhere and apparently took more than necessary interest in running the airline, but it just wasn't good enough.

The business model was coming apart and losses kept mounting. There was cannibalization from the mother brand. 'If two brands look alike, then obviously, passengers will opt for the cheaper priced,' the former partner, who did not want to be identified, said.[5]

Industry analysts say the third mistake was that the airline should have first consolidated its domestic operations and then introduced international routes. On foreign routes, the competition only gets bigger and with those who have deeper pockets. 'Kingfisher wanted a lot of rights in one go. We also advised them to be gradual but they were hell bent on aggressive expansion,' said a senior civil aviation ministry official on condition of anonymity.[6]

Kingfisher borrowed easy debt to grow fast. Lenders followed 'name lending' rather than project lending, says another investment banker. 'They should have been prudent in lending to the airline, where the first right for its main asset or planes rests with the lessor.' Some lenders, who converted a part of loans into equity shares, have lost two-thirds of the value as investors flee from the stock.[7]

The airline is today saddled with debts and banks alone have a total exposure of about ₹7,000 crores. The airline has cancelled orders for over 120 planes including 10 dreamliners. The downward spiral was accelerating with no cash for day-to-day operations, salaries not being paid, one government or the other freezing the bank accounts for non-payment of dues, outstandings with oil companies, airport authorities and vendors small and big. The end came on when the airline stopped its operations in March 2012. Vijay Mallya, predictably, has blamed everyone under the sun for his failure, except himself. 'Unfortunate that I am being held responsible for Kingfisher Airlines' difficulties, Vijay Mallya.[8]

Regulators say Mallya was overambitious and blaming government policies won't help. 'Kingfisher Airlines tried to be the Emirates of India,' said a senior DGCA official. 'Now they are saying the routes were unprofitable and that's why they cancelled flights ... Blaming the government and the policies won't help aviation industry out of trouble,' he adds. 'It is a free market and if the costs are high, the airlines can raise fares to a reasonable level, be more careful with the route planning and manage their fleet better.' The official said due diligence and feasibility checks need to be done before flying on new routes. 'A mad rush of market share will obviously lead to a situation like this,' he added.[9]

'We should have let KFA grow organically,' conceded Nedungadi, UB Group CFO, who had cautioned Vijay Mallya when buying Air Deccan.[10]

The airline has already undergone a restructuring thanks to very supportive banks that converted debt into equity at two and a half times the then market price in December 2010 and was now looking for a second bailout. The public pressure is very much against bailout, partly a consequence of regular expose of Dr. Mallya's excessive personal life in the fast lane, which runs like a reality TV show. Therefore, the government was playing it safe this time.

The global economic scenario only added to Kingfisher's woes. When the first debt recast happened, the price of crude was about $80 per barrel, which went up to $120 per barrel in 2008 while the rupee went past ₹50 per dollar in 2009, from about ₹32 when the airline was launched.

In a country like the United States Kingfisher would have been declared insolvent under Chapter 11 and put under restructuring. Such a law would have been a saviour for KFA as it would have removed the Chairman and crony directors as a first step in salvaging, bought time from lenders and a professional management would have put forward a more modest but sustainable recovery program. Although Mahindra Satyam is not a parallel case, it was salvaged by the government replacing the management with eminent professionals and restructuring the company before sell off.

The saying goes that the quickest way for a billionaire to become a millionaire is to invest in the airline sector. Over the years, it has seen most bankruptcies, 190, since 1978 in the United States alone, the most recent being American Airlines and Japan and Swiss Airlines before that. Many top names such as Pan Am and TWA have bitten dust. In India too, airlines such as East-West, Damania and so on folded up soon after launch. This sector, predictably in a VUCA world, is one of the first to be affected by any crisis be it financial, war, oil prices or a volcano eruption in a remote part of the world.

There are airlines that are bucking the trend. In the United States, it is Southwest Airlines and in India, IndiGo. IndiGo, which started same time as Kingfisher, is profitable for the past six years under circumstances similar to Kingfisher.[11]

IndiGo started with one airplane and continued its gradual expansion and waited for the mandatory five years to launch its international operations. Still, it wasn't tempted to find loopholes to expand aggressively in what was a rapidly growing market. IndiGo's approach was more measured and professional. Its first CEO was in India 18 months before the launch, and an experienced team at the management/board level has been the key reason of IndiGo's success. The biggest reason for the airline's success is its sharp focus on key deliverables like on-time performance, low fares and consistent onboard and ground service.[12]

A controlled slow growth would have been less taxing on capital requirement, but Kingfisher relied on debt to grow.[13] Author and business adviser Ram Charan underlines the criticality of cash and high management intensity in times of business uncertainty.

> First, if you do not have – or cannot generate – cash in the short term, you are not going to have the long term. Second, figure out how much cash you are generating and then restructure your debt. Third, revamp your business and understand that it needs to be more focused. This might even mean becoming smaller, but it will keep you safe; then you can generate extra cash to fund for productivity.[14]

Some companies and leaders just fail to learn, either from its own past mistakes or from their peers. This is not the first time Dr. Mallya has courted disaster. In 1992 too, he was under heavy debt burden through ill-advised diversification into non-liquor businesses such as engineering, fertilizers and telecom. He was able to extricate himself by selling assets such as Berger Paints, Kissan Products, Best & Crompton as well as growing liquor business and rising realty and so on. Neither have banks learned their lessons and have deliberately chosen to ignore the history of his reckless borrowing and poor record of diversification.[15]

We have not heard the last on KFA and will wait and watch how Dr. Mallya starts flying again and produces a nascent profit. It would be a pleasure to ride his pampered flights again.

To summarize, the principal reasons for KFA grounding are:

- The persona of Dr. Mallya. An aura of apparent invincibility that Dr. Mallya had created and started believing in, which had its origin in a mindset of success built on debt. An individual, iconic centric style of management, more suited to godmen than businessmen. Poor understanding of VUCA world.

- Dr. Mallya trying to do too many things at the same time without spending time to learn any one of these – running an airline, a cricket team and Formula racing, all businesses new to Indian entrepreneurs, plus odd acquisitions now and then.

- Aspiring to be the No. 1 airline in India, asap, which led to a fast expansion program. Starting international operations before consolidating Indian operations, of which the debt-laden acquisition of Air Deccan was a pivotal component.

- Little appreciation and understanding of risk management principles and practices.

NOTES

1. http://www.flykingfisher.com/about-us/chairmans-message.aspx.
2. 'A Tale of Two Airlines – Kingfisher versus Indigo,' *Business Standard*, 21 February 2012.
3. 'Kingfisher Airlines Is a Bankrupt Company: Veritas Invest,' *Money Control*, 29 September 2011.
4. 'The Rise and Fall of a Castle in the Air,' *The Hindu*, 12 November 2012.
5. Ibid., 4.
6. Ibid., 2.
7. 'Air Deccan, Poor Planning Hit Kingfisher's Fortunes: Experts,' *Indian Express*, 17 November 2011.
8. 'Unfortunate That I Am Being Held Responsible for Kingfisher

Airlines' Difficulties: Vijay Mallya,' *Economic Times*, 10 January 2013.

9. Ibid., 7.

10. 'UB CFO Ravi Nedungadi Predicted Kingfisher Airlines Would be a Drain on Company's Finances,' *Economic Times*, 20 February 2012.

11. 'IndiGo Reports Sixth Straight Annual Profit,' *Mint*, 7 October 2014.

12. Ibid., 2.

13. Ibid., 7.

14. 'Cash Is King. Cash Is Blood Supply: Ram Charan,' *Forbes India*, 15 January 2014.

15. Sucheta Dalal, 'Vijay Mallya: Habitually Broke?' *Money Life*, 18 April 2012.

III

NEW CEO OF DHANLAXMI BANK

Check Road Conditions Before Speeding

Dhanlaxmi Bank is a 75-year-old mid-size regional bank, headquartered in Thrissur, Kerala. It aimed to grow to a new age national bank with a pan-India presence. With this in mind, the bank hired Mr. Amitabh Chaturvedi, who cut his teeth with ICICI bank with a history of aggressive growth. He later became CEO of Reliance Capital where in five years the assets grew from ₹1,500 crores to ₹90,000 crores, a testimony to Amitabh Chaturvedi's passion for growth.

Mr. Amitabh Chaturvedi soon after taking over as CEO said that instead of being acquired by a national bank, he would make it strong and look for acquisitions itself.

By the time Amitabh Chaturvedi joined, the bank was under the so-called monthly monitoring of the Reserve Bank of India (RBI) due to financial mismanagement; two representatives of the regulator were on the bank's board as 'observers' and all credit proposals of ₹3 crores and above were to be approved by the board. A subcommittee of the board was involved in every single recruitment, even for a clerk. The bank had about 1,400 employees on its payroll and another 1,500 employees worked on a daily-wage basis.[1]

The bank has a history of CEOs resigning in quick succession. Mr. T.R. Madhavan resigned in July 2005 after being appointed to the post of MD and CEO in February 2004. Mr. P.S. Prasad was appointed to the post in November 2005 and resigned in July 2008 when Mr. Chaturvedi was taken on board.

Amitabh Chaturvedi tried to change the culture, and initially he succeeded in doing so as he bought peace with trade unions by raising the salary level and offering jobs to employees' children. But the honeymoon did not last long as the trade union turned increasingly restless for fear of losing its grip over the bank, and with Amitabh Chaturvedi furious in his pursuit of growth. He opened 66 new branches and converted many extension counters into full-fledged branches to have an all-India footprint. While quite a few of the daily wage-earners got into the payroll, overall the bank's employee strength rose from 1,400 in fiscal 2009 to 4,780 (over 300 percent) by end 2011.[2]

The business also grew at a breakneck speed. For instance, when Amitabh Chaturvedi joined the bank, it had a loan portfolio of ₹2,500 crores and a deposit base of ₹3,400 crores. In the three years, the loan book grew to ₹10,100 crores (229 percent) and deposits to ₹13,800 crores (400 percent). Not too many banks can grow at such a scorching pace, that too at a time when economy has been slowing and the world is yet to come out from the impact of an unprecedented credit crunch in the aftermath of the collapse of Lehman Brothers.

Indeed, Amitabh Chaturvedi could bring down the average age of Dhanlaxmi Bank employee from 57 to 32, manage an all-India presence (out of 275 branches, 128 are outside TN), and increase business manifold, but all this came at a cost. Its wage bill rose from ₹60 crores to ₹220 crores, and the cost to income ratio went up dramatically. He brought his own team of senior executives and apparently, there was some heartburn among some long-serving senior executives that new recruits at the top level were being paid much higher salaries and perks that were out of sync with the volume of business generated. As income did not grow in sync with expenses, the bank resorted to 'accounting innovations' as otherwise it might not have been able to declare profits.[3]

One bank executive described Amitabh Chaturvedi as a 'growth junkie' who spent a lot of money hiring people and expanding the branch network, but failed to show results in income growth. 'Amitabh Chaturvedi saw this (spending money hiring people and branch expansions) as investment, but it was taking time to pay off,' the executive said.[4] An RBI inspection revealed these, but these accounting innovations – which Indian banks do occasionally when they need to show profits – would not have come to light had the trade union been with Amitabh Chaturvedi. The union started 'exposing' him when its membership started dwindling with aged employees retiring and new employees not allowed to join the fold. Amitabh Chaturvedi tried to buy peace by allowing the new hires to join the trade union provided they agree to be governed by the industry wage pact (it amounts to a sharp cut in salary), but it was not easy as a few members of the board had empathy for the union's causes.

One leading business daily said, 'Had the bank been a human being, I would have said she has been suffering from schizophrenia.' Schizophrenia is a mental disorder involving a breakdown in the relation between thought, emotion and behavior, leading to faulty perception, inappropriate actions and feelings, and withdrawal from reality into fantasy and delusion.[5]

A few institutions that kept bulk deposits with the bank at that time declined to rollover deposits and withdrew about 1,000 crores, plunging it into a liquidity crisis and adding a new dimension to the problems that Amitabh Chaturvedi was busy tackling.

Dhanlaxmi had to borrow heavily from the interbank market to plug the liquidity deficit. Amitabh Chaturvedi was ready to sell some of its loan portfolios to other banks to ease pressure on liquidity and was not in favor of stopping giving loans to new customers while the board was against any expansion in business. He also made the cardinal mistake of not raising capital ahead of focusing on loan growth. Had he raised capital in time, the bank would not have been forced to stop lending for the lack of liquidity. That was the flashpoint – the chief executive officer and the board could not reconcile their differences, leading to Amitabh Chaturvedi's exit after being at the helm of affairs for three years.

'Building an institution takes time,' said Murali Natrajan, MD and CEO, Development Credit Bank, and a former banker at Standard Chartered. 'If you are too aggressive, your cost-to-income ratio can go for a toss. If your strategy is not paying off, why would any board support the CEO. If you do not have promoters that are institutionalised, then it is difficult to run a bank.'[6]

During Chaturvedi's tenure, the bank saw most of its efficiency parameters declining. Return on assets fell to 0.23 percent from 1.21 percent between March 2009 and September

2011, while the capital adequacy ratio fell to 10.81 percent from 14.44 percent between March 2009 and March 2011.[7] He tried to do what other have done before in improving the balance sheet through 'creative accounting.'

However, one cannot blame Amitabh Chaturvedi for all the ills of the smaller private sector banks of which Dhanlaxmi Bank is an example, such as corporate governance, trade unions but these issues were there when he joined.

Mr. Chaturvedi's successful background in aggressive institutions like ICICI Bank and Anil Ambani Group created a mindset where speed was everything. He came to an old conservative bank with a preset mind to grow at a scorching pace, like a brand new engine pulling a decades old train

He refused to take time off to understand the culture of a 75-year-old south-Indian conservative institution and moderate the pace to one that is sustainable but tried to adopt the textbook approach of his previous stints. He brought advisers from private sector banks who mirrored his thought process, and there was nobody to play the Devil's Advocate.

His case is similar to Bob Nardelli who was fired as CEO of Home Depot, the largest home improvement/hobby retailer in the United States in 2007 after six years at the helm. He was smart, witty, challenging and an excellent communicator. Home Depot matured as an organization to the point where it needed a more disciplined management approach, and the board believed Nardelli's skills were exactly what were needed. Nardelli came to Home Depot after a successful career at General Electric and became, in the words of GE's CEO at the time, Jack Welch, 'the best operating executive I've ever seen.'

Even then, Jack Welch must have seen the flaws in Nardelli as a potential CEO candidate and he was bypassed in favor of Jeffrey Immelt. Home Depot's freewheeling marketing culture was totally at odds with the systems culture at GE, like chalk and coal. Home Depot was decentralized, entrepreneurial, a haven for independent-minded employees. Nardelli's military-style leadership produced some short-term profits but demoralized the Home Depot workforce. Customer satisfaction surveys took a nosedive. 'He garnered a hard-charging reputation for being tone deaf to concerns of shareholders, employees and customers. He became known for his arrogance, and he alienated the people he needed most. He seemed to eschew feedback so beneficial to any leader. He was "truth starved."'[8]

Home Depot founder Bernie Marcus was known for his 'Bernie Road Shows' where he would travel to divisions across the country and encourage managers to give direct feedback. He would grant immunity during these meetings so 'Managers can ask any type of question no matter how blunt, invasive, or even offensive it might be.'[9]

Regardless of Nardelli's vision for the company, how could he ever achieve his objectives without the alignment, commitment and loyalty of the Home Depot employees?

The stories of Chaturvedi and Nardelli run parallel to each other like long-lost twin brothers till their exit from the respective companies.

The basic mistake Amitabh Chaturvedi made was to assume that there is a formula for success and what works at one organization would also work at another. This is very common in selection of top leaders where past history is taken as a criteria for future performance. In such cases suave, smooth talking extroverts who are able to visualize through polished presentations carry the day at interviews. In a VUCA environment, past success need not transform into future growth. 'Most companies would be glad to hire anybody in the [GE] top 10,' said Jeff Christian, CEO of Christian & Timbers Inc., the firm that presented Hewlett-Packard Co.'s board with eventual CEO Carly Fiorina last year.[10] Ms. Fiorina was fired under ignominious circumstances after five years in the chair. Mr. Chaturvedi should have taken time to understand the culture of an old established institution before making sustainable plans. He should have experimented with opening a few branches in non-traditional areas and shown success there before undertaking large-scale expansion. He comes across as a person who is highly educated and competent with a great deal of charisma, but a non-learner, blinded by his past success, full of assumptions and unshakable mindset, all characteristics of a potential VUCA failure.

In a VUCA world, success comes from the ability to view issues from various perspectives, which requires a consultative leadership style. Days of a steam roller type of leader who could aggressively direct the destiny of the organization are gone, as noted by Jack Welch himself, one of the last such leaders. As a leader, knowing your gaps in self-awareness is one of the most important qualities to possess but also one of the most difficult to acquire. The reason is, in most cases, leaders, like everyone else, view themselves in a more favorable light than other people do. Therefore, a leader's gross overestimations of his behavioral limitations comes in the way of an adaptive leadership style in which the leader values differences, if he is to succeed in a uncertain and volatile environment. It becomes evident that even if the leader comes from a similar industry vertical and also if he brings like-minded people from his old organization, which happens quite often, success is not guaranteed as the ability to view strategic matters from different perspectives gets diminished.

This case also shows that absence of corporate governance at board can be detrimental to a firm's growth in a VUCA environment. It underscores the need for a board where vigorous dialogue can take place in an environment of mutual trust.

NOTES

1. Tamal Bandhopadhyay, 'Dhanlaxmi Bank's Untold Story – Why the CEO Had to Go,' *Mint*, 13 February 2012.

2. Ibid.,1.

3. Ibid.

4. Dinesh Unnikrishnan, 'Dhanlaxmi Bank CEO Amitabh Chaturvedi Quits,' *Mint*, 6 February 2012.

5. Ibid.,1.

6. Anita Bhoir, 'Bankers Like Amitabh Chaturvedi, Murali Natrajan Failed to Change Old Mind Set of Banks Like Dhanlaxmi, Development Credit Bank,' *Economic Times*, 22 February 2012.

7. 'New-Age Heroes Fumble at Old Banks,' *Economic Times*, 22 February 2012.

8. Tim Irwin, *Derailed* (Thomas Nelson, 2009).

9. Sydney Finkelstein, *Why Smart Executives Fail and What You Can Learn from Their Mistakes* (Penguin Group, 2003).

10. 'GE Succession a Leadership Lesson,' *Los Angeles Times*, 3 December 2000.

IV

WOCKHARDT LIMITED

I Have Seen the Future

Wockhardt is one of the top ten drug companies in India with a strong presence in key therapies. It has 14 manufacturing plants in India and abroad and has subsidiaries in the United States, the United Kingdom, Ireland and France. It sells its products in Africa, Russia, Central and Southeast Asia and the United States.

When the Indian economy opened up in the 1990s, many rules relating to overseas investments were eased. This provided a growth opportunity for Indian pharmaceutical companies to expand their presence in the United States, Europe and other industrialized countries.

The generic pharma products (out of patents) market is dominated by multinationals such as Teva and Sandoz and is characterized by low prices and high volumes. It is difficult to build a brand name in generic products.

As with any other ambitious Indian company, Wockhardt Limited Chairman Habil Khorakiwala wanted to grow to be a billion-dollar company by 2009 by tapping opportunities in the generic markets of the United States and Europe. In the beginning, starting in 1998, Wockhardt made small acquisitions in Europe such as Wallis and CP Pharmaceuticals in the United Kingdom. From 2004 onward, the company made one acquisition per year, including two large ones (Table 2.1).

Table 2.1 Acquisitions made by Wockhardt Limited

Company	Year of acquisition	Cost
Esparma (Germany)	2004	$10 mn (divested 2009 for $24.7 mn)
Pinewood Laboratories (Ireland)	2006	$150 mn
Negma Laboratories (France)	2007	$265 mn
Martin Grove (US)	2007	$52 mn

Source: Wockhardt press releases.

As shown in the table, Wockhardt acquired three overseas companies between 2006 and 2007 at a total acquisition cost of $467 million.

Wockhardt quickly grew its revenue from Europe to over $400 million, the largest for any Indian company. It also acquired in the United States to have a sizeable presence in the global generics space.

The strategy was sound and Wockhardt leaders may have charted out a plan to derive cost benefits, move manufacturing to India, cut the flab in operations of these units and increase its gains in steps. But even before the benefits of these operations could concretize, the financial markets across the world started cracking in the second half of 2008.[1]

The timing couldn't have been worse for Wockhardt. The company had borrowed heavily and spent over $450 million for the three buyouts, but its revenues grew by less than $300 million.

To further aggravate the debt crisis, it issued foreign currency convertible bonds (FCCBs), a new instrument worth $108 million, through overseas listings. FCCB is a type of convertible bond issued in a foreign currency. A convertible bond is a mix between a debt and equity instrument. It acts like a bond by making regular coupon and principal payments, but these bonds also give the bondholder the option to convert the bond into stock. The deal looked promising since the Indian rupee was going strong against the dollar in early 2004 and was appreciating gradually to a value of ₹45 per share. The debt-equity ratio went up from 1.32 in 2004 to 2.69 in 2008[2] and 5.5 in 2010,[3] unusual for a pharmaceutical company.

That was done with the anticipation that Wockhardt's share price would reach a level where the bond holders would convert into shares or redemption could give them an exit from their holdings.

At the time, Indian issuers were not considering repayment provisions as their share values were going through the roof.

But that was not to be. Wockhardt, which racked up debt when it spent $467 million on three overseas acquisitions, was pushed over the edge by losses of ₹5.55 billion ($112 mn) on foreign exchange and derivatives during the global financial crisis in 2008.[4] In line with the practice of most Indian-owned companies (Indian MNCs stay away from hedging), it hedged its foreign exchange earnings and suffered heavy losses to the extent of ₹600 crores ($122 mn). Other companies too lost heavily in hedging, but they did not suffer from Wockhardt's compounded problems.

By 2008, the company's net worth had eroded to near-bankruptcy levels as losses mounted with eight quarters of consecutive losses, and loan defaults prompted creditors to threaten it with liquidation. The promoters had to pledge some of their key assets, including the company's corporate headquarters in Mumbai, and had to endure a messy legal battle with bondholders. The company entered India's Corporate Debt Restructuring (CDR) process in June 2009 to restructure about ₹13 billion ($265 mn) in loans, largely from Indian banks, led by ICICI Bank.[5] Its foreign banks settled separately.

To be fair, Wockhardt is not the only Indian company that defaulted on FCCB bondholders. Many companies faced a severe funding crunch, since most FCCBs did not get converted as a result of the conversion price being higher than the market price (with the conversion option out, of course, no lender wanted equity!), and consequently required refinancing at higher prevailing interest rates. Second, the depreciation in the value of the rupee, coupled with the fact that most of the foreign currency exposures were unhedged, exacerbated the issue and ballooned the principal repayment due in rupee terms, consequently complicating the refinancing challenges.

Wockhardt and many other companies such as JCT, Suzlon, were led the garden path by certain investment bankers. According to India Ratings, up to March 2013, FCCB redemption amount of $1.51 billion belonging to 23 companies was due, out of which around 67 percent of the outstanding dues belonging to 17 companies are unlikely to be redeemed on time.[6]

To pay debts, Wockhardt had to resort to selling the proverbial family silver, first its properties in Mumbai, next its hospital business, profitable portfolio of over-the-counter (OTC; sold without prescription) protein products, veterinary business and last its subsidiaries in Germany and Belgium.

Wockhardt is a classic case of dysfunctional learning where speed and scale of ambition override prudent step-by-step approach, an essential requirement in the VUCA environment where future is uncertain and volatile. It also assumes that opportunities are limited (perhaps embedded in the DNA of Indian business, which had to endure decades of socialist economy), and one must take advantage of all opportunities as they appear. When an organization is entering new areas, especially in VUCA, whether new product lines, new markets or new processes, the prudent approach is first to attempt the change on a small scale to learn the new before attempting it on a large scale. This is true of new products where these are taken from lab to markets via test marketing and new processes through piloting. Wockhardt attempted to get into acquisitions on a mass scale (compared to its size), five in a period of seven years without pausing to see the consequences of the first one. The company assumed the future will be stable and therefore it also took on a new financial instrument FCCB to raise funds for these expansions. It also relied too much on the advice of its bankers (and did not do its own due diligence), who probably misguided Wockhardt and did not highlight the pitfalls of new financial instruments. Most of the FCCBs issued in the European markets during the 2006–2008 boom were handled by two Indian investment bankers, both of whom have shut shop.[7] There is a lesson for companies operating in the VUCA environment, that is, not to be swayed by what other companies arc doing but to create their own knowledge base to evaluate information and advice coming from external consultants, especially the assumptions and bias coloring the reports.

Wockhardt has come out of its problems, which led to near bankruptcy, but at a huge cost. It has lost the momentum of its business of the future – healthcare – and from 11 hospitals at its peak, it now has 2 hospitals and is cautiously expanding. It has sold its most profitable French subsidiary, its promising OTC brands and a lot of land in Mumbai. It has also acquired a strong competitor in Sun Pharma as a significant shareholder, which may have designs on Wockhardt.

Habil Khorakiwala has shown boldness in publicly acknowledging his mistakes and thus coming out of denial and purging his company of the ghost of failure. He says that the company's near-death experience has taught him lessons that he hopes will last generations. 'You burn your hands once then it takes time to recover,' he says.[8] Wockhardt Limited was a well-run company and Khorakiwala within a short period has been able to rebound. Due to efficiency programs undertaken during crisis, the company today is leaner and battle hardened. In addition, Wockhardt's focus on the US market, which contributed about 41 percent of revenue in fiscal 2012 from the earlier 28 percent was also a key factor in recovery. Khorakiwala says his organization was reinvented, as people found a way to manage with fewer resources. The market responded by taking its share from ₹250 to ₹1600 in less than a year (it was again back to ₹400 in February 2014 due to new quality-related problems in the US market). It keeps clear of hedging and has sacked some senior managers who handled derivative accounts. Its debt-equity ratio was brought down to below 1 by August 2012. The company has asked bankers, with which it had to enter into a corporate debt restructuring (CDR) agreement in 2009, to advance its exit, one of the few companies to come out successfully from the CDR process. At the moment, credit has been restored, but restoring credibility remains.

New problems surfaced in 2013 (since our writing), and the US Federal Drug Agency has banned products from some plants in India putting a question mark on Wockhardt's early recovery. However, the resurgence of share price during 2014, from ₹416 to ₹1088, shows that investors retain their enthusiasm for the future of the company.

NOTES

1. 'Hard to Believe an Exciting Player Like Wockhardt Is Ailing,' *DNA*, 9 April 2009.

2. http://www.moneycontrol.com/india/stockpricequote/ pharmaceuticals/wockhardt/06/31/   keyfinancialratios/ marketprice/W05.

3. 'Fortune Smiles on Wockhardt Again,' *Mint*, 17 September 2012.

4. 'Hard Work Pays Off for Wockhardt,' *Economic Times*, 30 July 2012.

5. 'Wockhardt: From Debt Debacle to Stock Rocket,' *Reuters*, 19 August 2012.

6. 'No Money, Can't Pay: Mother of All Defaults Looms in FCCBs,' *First Post*, 7 July 2011.

7. 'About 67% of FCCB Due This Fiscal May Default,' *Business Standard*, 11 November 2012.

8. Ibid., 4.

V

JAIN IRRIGATION SYSTEMS
Diversification Sans Knowledge

Jain Irrigation is a pioneering company in the area of drip irrigation. Today it is the world's second largest drip irrigation company with a turnover of ₹3,458 crores growing over 228 percent over five years and a workforce of over 7,000. Although the company is in existence since 1987, the turnaround came when the government introduced a centrally sponsored scheme on micro irrigation in January 2006 to promote efficiency in water use, which had a component of 50 percent subsidy for small and marginal farmers.[1] This policy led to fast growth, but along with growth came pressure on cash flow. Recovering dues from cash-strapped states was proving to be harder each year. Populism has seen some states promise 80–90 percent subsidy but dues are not cleared for months, creating liquidity problems for the Jains who had already supplied the equipment.[2]

Between 1992 and 1994, the company decided to reduce its dependence on drip irrigation and to diversify.

The 1990s offered new-found opportunities, and being a dream merchant, I could not resist the temptation of taking advantage of them to become a large conglomerate. Between 1992 and 1994 we acquired an IT company, took a granite quarry on lease, ventured into merchant banking and even bought an advertising agency. These diversifications happened along with forward/backward integration projects for our existing operations. By March 1997, we were trying to manage 11 different projects involving an investment of ₹400 crores – almost equal to the company's size then. About ₹250 crores was raised by way of debt. All the diversifications were conceived on instinct and in the euphoria that surrounded the economy then.[3]

All these diversifications were disastrous, and the share price dived from ₹365 in February 1994 to ₹8 in October 2000. The working capital was stretched and funds had to be diverted from core business. The lenders took the company to court.

On the 26 November 1997, a half-page advertisement appeared in a major financial daily on behalf of Mr. Bhavarlal Jain, Chairman of Jain Irrigation Systems Limited, apologizing for their recent failures. It began

> I'm sad that for the first time since our inception, we've fared badly. We ventured into 'unknown' areas like finance, IT and granite at the cost of our core business… We have lost money but more importantly, we've lost some of our reputation. I feel it's my duty to account for, to own up, to admit my misjudgements, to apologise.[4]

This was an unusual advertisement, not repeated since then, taking blame for business failures and reassuring the stakeholders.

Diversification into unknown areas not related to the current business is the bane of many companies. For example, Escorts, which was a leader in automotive and related fields, decided to diversify into areas such as telecom via Escotel and white goods. These attempts were not successful and were later on divested. This left their principal business, tractors, vulnerable to competition. 'Our plate is full,' Nikhil Nanda, Joint MD says, adding the group has since eschewed the aggressive diversification of the 1990s.[5]

Jain Irrigation was able to avoid liquidation by selling controlling stake to a Private Equity Fund and using funds to retire debts. The fund exited in 2005 and the core business extension into mango processing and tissue culture paid rich dividends globally. Today, in these fields, the company is the largest in India. It has nearly ₹4,000 crores in topline, and although the share price hovered around ₹80 in early 2013 (₹120 and rising in April 2014), the future is bright. The company, to reduce pressure on working capital, has launched a non-banking financial company that provides loan to farmers for installation of drip irrigation. The farmer receives subsidies directly from the government and can repay the amount. The loan is like a bridge-finance till the farmer is able to pay.

What Mr. Bhavarlal Jain does not say but is evident is that the resurgence of the company is also due to the unpretentious nature of the promoter as well as a culture of humility that pervades the company. For an organization of this size, the headquarters is based not in a metro but in a class B city, Jalgaon, Maharashtra, closer to its customers, who are farmers. The promoters and benefited farmers have given lectures at prestigious institutions such as Harvard Business School and have won prestigious awards such as Financial Times-ArcelorMittal Boldness in Business Award (Environment), 2011. The value-based culture also is ingrained in the operations. Jain's concern for farmers dictates his business. When times are bad for farmers, he does not mind reducing the margins.

The company has since diversified but in areas related to its core business of drip irrigation, where technology can add value to the farmer's efforts such as tissue culture, fruit processing and solar energy. 'Our business model is unique and provides end-to-end solutions to small farmers for making agriculture remunerative by offering contract farming and buyback of farm produce. It adds value to primary commodities and provides sustainable and profitable solutions to farming by providing market access.'[6]

Jain Irrigation's core lessons: 'Early success had blinded us and we thought we could do no wrong. Diversifying into unknown areas without required management bandwidth and eyeing disproportionate growth using debt is not sustainable. That was the lesson of a lifetime for me.'[7]

Businesses are based on ideas, opportunity recognition and orientation. It is imperative that business decisions are carefully stitched and undertaken based on logic, competency available, core competence developed and capability to steer growth. Jains hurriedly and excitedly took decisions without realizing the VUCA element within each business and hence the catastrophe.

The difference between people and companies that slip and recover and those that do not is the ability of reflection and introspection. Bhavarlal Jain did not blame anyone or anything for his company's debacle, compared to Dr. Mallya who has blamed everyone except himself for the downfall of Kingfisher Airlines. It is an exemplary example of true statesmanship to accept failures as a leader 'all failures are mine and all success are yours.' This case also provides a window on how wealth, which can take decades to create, can be destroyed in a short while.

NOTES

1. 'Water Man,' *Indian Express*, 16 December 2011.
2. 'Jain Irrigation Systems: The Good Company,' *Forbes India*, 2 December 2012.
3. 'Diversifying into Unknown Areas without Management Bandwidth Is Not Sustainable: Bhavarlal H. Jain,' *Business Today*, 17 July 2012.
4. Ibid., 3.
5. 'How Nikhil Nanda Is Transforming Escorts to Recapture Its Lost Ground,' *Economic Times*, 23 May 2013.
6. 'Fruits of Innovation,' *Financial Express*, 3 February 2013.
7. Ibid., 2.

VI

SHREE RENUKA SUGARS

Mirroring Columbus

Christopher Columbus said, 'You can never cross the ocean unless you have the courage to lose sight of the shore.'[1] Shree Renuka Sugars (SRS) definitely doesn't lack daring.

India is the second largest producer of sugar in the world after Brazil. It is expected that by 2017 domestic sugar production would be 28.5 million tonnes (MT) compared to 19.8 MT in 2007. Given the past trend in production cyclicality, an additional 3.5 MT of sugar would be needed by 2017.[2] In this industry, which is highly fragmented, SRS, founded by Mr. Narendra Murkumbi in 1998, acquired a sick sugar mill and after turning it around had a vision of emerging as the most efficient sugar processor and the largest marketer of sugar and ethanol in India. The company occupies a pivotal position by being the largest producer in India and fifth largest in the world, operating 11 mills globally with a total crushing capacity of 20.7 MT per annum (MTPA). The company operates 7 sugar mills in India with a total crushing capacity of 7.1 MTPA and 2 port-based sugar refineries with capacity of 1.7 MTPA. It is the second largest exporter of sugar from India with a presence in the Middle East, Southeast Asia and East Africa, among others, and it is a sugar 'supplier of choice' across leading brands in soft drinks, confectionary and so on. SRS's blend of integrated sugar factories and refineries enables it to consume both sugarcane during season and imported raw sugar feed during the off-season, enhancing asset utilization and sustaining balanced cash flows. It has a technical collaboration with Tate & Lyle, one of the world's largest sugar refiners, to meet exacting EU quality parameters. The company has instituted many pioneering practices like directly supplying large institutional buyers, leased manufacturing assets, excellent farmer relationship (timely payment of dues, which is unusual in India), seamless sugar collection networks and so on. It went public is 2005, and the issue was subscribed 15 times.

Sugar production is cyclic in nature, and there are highs and troughs in a five-year cycle. Although sugar production has grown by 2.4 percent per annum from 1991–1992 to 2010–2011, consumption has grown by 3.8 percent per annum in the same period. However, there is wide fluctuation on a year-to-year basis. India will have a gap of 5 MT in demand and supply by the year 2020. The major problems are reduced growth in sugar care acreage, limited irrigation, poor productivity, manual harvesting practices and so on.[3]

Indian sugar companies keep one eye on the monsoons and another on the government, as the unpredictable behavior of both can play havoc. But SRS has been reducing its dependence on both by setting up independent sugar refining capacities.

Investments in a refinery are much lower than for an integrated sugar plant. These plants also run throughout the year, unlike an integrated plant, which operates at peak capacity during sugarcane season. Imports can ensure adequate availability of raw sugar too.

Brazil is the leading producer and exporter of sugarcane, sugar and ethanol. It is also among the most efficient major sugar producers in the world.

With these strategic points in mind, SRS took the step to be the first Indian sugar company to invest in overseas sugar refineries, especially in Brazil.

Its first acquisition was a 100 percent stake in Vale Do Ivai (VDI), a Brazilian sugar and ethanol production company, in November 2009 for ₹1,123 crores. VDI has a combined cane crushing capacity of 3.1 MTPA in its two mills.

On 9 July 2010, SRS acquired 50.34 percent controlling stake in Equipav AA, a sugar and ethanol production company, for ₹1,151 crores. Equipav AA has two mills with a combined cane crushing capacity of 10.5 MTPA and a huge sugarcane plantation facility in Sao Paulo. It also has a bagasse-based power co-generation capacity of 203 MW. Murkumbi also added that the company is interested in further acquisitions.[4]

Both acquisitions combined were twice the size of its Indian operations. SRS recently raised about ₹506 crores through a QIP issue for its expansion plans. It had a post-issue debt-to-equity ratio of nearly 1:1.[5]

SRS's Brazilian acquisition insulates it from India's sugar cycle. Its strategy of building standalone sugar refining plants partially frees it from the ups and downs of sugar cane production crop cycle. In addition, Brazilian cane has higher sugar content and the cane plants have a life three times that of India. A sugar producer in Indian states like Maharashtra and Karnataka (where SRS has its mills) can typically produce around 111.5 kg of sugar from a tonne of cane that costs ₹2,500. In Brazil, one can make 135 kg of sugar from a tonne of cane that costs ₹1,600. In other words, for every rupee spent, SRS can make 90 percent extra sugar in Brazil than in its mills in India.[6] The acquisition's logic appeared sound during the boom period, which it was experiencing at that time.

Two years later, Murkumbi, the poster boy of Indian sugar industry, had all its vital statistics messed up. In 3Q 2012, Renuka do Brasil (RdB), the larger of the two mills, lost ₹116.7 crores. This has proved a drag on the company. Its stock price is ₹15.50 (on 7 January 2015), 7 percent of what it was when Murkumbi made his acquisitions. The debt on the balance sheet has doubled to ₹9,100 crores, and interest expense is one of the biggest destroyers of shareholder value now.

Selling assets is one option. The company has been trying to sell its RdB asset that produces 138 MW from a co-generation power capacity. With power prices low in Brazil, Murkumbi says he's having difficulty finding a buyer. Joe Louis, the legendary boxer, once said: 'Everyone has a plan until they've been hit.' So did Murkumbi. In an interview at his Worli office, in mid-town Mumbai, he admits: 'I myself was not fully aware of the depth of the problem, and it is a new and humbling experience.'[7]

For an Indian company, to acquire two large companies within a short period of six months, in a continent where few Indians have ventured, was very risky. Doing business in Brazil is not that easy. Brazil's somewhat cumbersome fiscal model, infrastructure bottlenecks, high energy costs, high social security charges on labor, high cost of capital and the bureaucracy involved in opening a company are key challenges.[8]

SRS did not anticipate that the business environment will change so quickly soon after acquisition with unfavorable weather condition bringing on the worst drought in a decade, limiting crushing. SRS's experience in India was limited to refining cane, not growing it. In Brazil, it had to manage its own highly mechanized plantations. The previous owners had neglected replanting, and therefore sugar yield was one-fourth of new plants. SRS had to engage in replanting at a huge cost. Due to their poor experience in farming and cash flow problems, the company went slow in replanting. 'We should have managed cane production better in Brazil,' admits Narendra Murkumbi.[9]

The softening of both the Indian and Brazilian currencies against the dollar aggravated the situation, forcing SRS to incur mark-to-market loss. The main concern for SRS is that it is sitting on a pile of debt as high as ₹9,100 crores at last count, which is four times its equity. SRS inherited a little over half of that debt from the Brazilian buyouts. The company also exhausted its war chest of cash to finance the acquisitions. And fund-raising in tight markets to retire debt is proving a difficult proposition in markets plagued with poor investment appetite.[10]

To keep debt payments, SRS needed to sell sugar at 22c per pound while prices in 2012 ranged between 19 and 23c. The cycle was again in a glut phase.

The company's failure was primarily due to two quick acquisitions within a short time. A VUCA environment, with spacing between acquisitions and learning from the first one, would not only have eased its debt and cash flow problems but would also have helped it learn how to run a plant and, more importantly, a plantation in a new business environment. Coming from India, SRS should have anticipated that weather conditions worldwide are changing and the regularity of the monsoon cannot be guaranteed. Added to this is a mindset among Indian businessmen, due to working for decades under the license permit system of the government. They believe that opportunities are few and one should grab whatever one can. Murkumbi was lucky that the opportunity for third acquisition did not materialize or his problems would have been threefold. The truth is, in a VUCA environment, opportunities are many and they will keep on appearing if one has patience. The overconfidence of Murkumbi also emerged from a mindset that the SRS was successful at acquiring sick companies and turning them around and hence, using the same formula, the Brazilian experience should also follow the pattern. 'SRS is another example of an aggressive, first-generation entrepreneur biting off more than he can chew,' says SP Tulsian, a Mumbai-based independent analyst.[11]

One must have a flawless plan A; if not, then plan B and C must be in place. In VUCA, all businesses have the plausibility of failures. Even Christopher Columbus after discovering the new world was jailed and stripped of his title on return to Spain. Ambitious firms diversifying or expanding into newer geographical boundaries must do their homework well in terms of political, social, technical and legal aspects.

The good news is that the two producers are able to take care of their interest payments – RdB had an outgo of ₹89 crores and Vale ₹11 crores in the December quarter 2012. Overall, operating profits of SRS were up, although lower than analysts' predictions. 'Still concerns remain about the huge debt,' says ICICI Direct's Manyal.[12]

The tide may be turning now. The global sugar surplus will be 51 percent smaller in the 2013–2014 season compared with a year earlier.[13] This would raise prices from 2014 onward and SRS should be out of the woods as far as operational losses are concerned, but the huge debt remains, which still requires some creative solutions like bringing in strategic partners or selling non-core assets.[14] In February 2014, SRS sold controlling stake to global food company Wilmar International Limited.[15] Now, if only sugar prices would rise sooner…

NOTES

1. http://www.goodreads.com/quotes/192564-you-can-never-cross-the-ocean-until-you-have-the.

2. 'KPMG: The Indian Sugar Industry Sector Roadmap 2017,' June 2007.

3. 'Narendra Murkumbi. Indian Challenges For The New Decade,' ISMA Conference, November 2011.

4. 'Renuka Sugars Mulls Third Acquisition in Brazil,' PTI, 8 August 2010.

5. 'Brazilian Acquisition Secures Raw Sugar Supplies for Shree Renuka Sugars but Debt Goes Up Too,' *Mint*, 11 November 2009.

6. 'Two Brazilian Acquisitions Have Backfired for Shree Renuka, but Narendra Murkumbi Confident of a Comeback,' *Economic Times*, 23 February 2012.

7. 'What Renuka Sugars Learnt from Brazil,' *Forbes*, 9 November 2012.

8. 'Why Indian MNCs Like Infosys, Wipro, Godrej & Others Find Great Business Opportunities in Latin America,' *Economic Times*, 4 May 2012.

9. Ibid., 6.

10. Ibid., 8.

11. Ibid.

12. Ibid., 6.

13. 'Kingsman Sees Sugar Surplus Dropping 51% as Output Slides,' *Bloomberg*, 1 February 2013.

14. 'Renuka Sugars in Talks with UK, German Firms to Sell Brazil Asset,' *Mint*, 9 September 2013.

15. 'Wilmar to Take Joint Control of Shree Renuka Sugars for $200 Million,' *Mint*, 20 February 2014.

VII

SUBHIKSHA AND VISHAL RETAIL

Too Fast Too Furious

SUBHIKSHA

An IIM-A alumnus, R. Subramanian takes advantage of India's retail revolution and starts a chain of stores for groceries and FMCG named Subhiksha in 1997. He had an excellent track record in business, though not in organized retail (Who had at that time?). He wanted to 'pioneer a new trend' because of what he had found out about the retail industry: that the No. 1 retailer makes the most money, the No. 2 makes some money, while the third (and the others) has to eventually shut shop.'[1] By 2008, his chain had 1,600 stores. His highly educated and experienced Board of Directors included Azim Premji (who also held a 10 percent stake); Renuka Ramnath, a very experienced investment banker; Rajiv Bakshi, former CEO of Pepsi India; Rama Bijapurkar, a Marketing guru, and so on. It had funding from ICICI ventures (IVen), which owned 23 percent stake and was considering an IPO. Then it went into insolvency and closed in March 2009. However, due to the Satyam scam at the same time, this news went relatively unnoticed.

Organized retail is a new format for India and is a highly competitive business, with neighborhood stores and street hawkers at doorsteps. The organized retail market stood at ₹96,500 crores in 2008. The industry has grown at a CAGR of 36 percent between 2004 and 2008.[2] It has low margins and relies upon large turnover for profitability. A large number of items are perishable. The competition intensified with the entry of deep pockets like Birla, Tata, Reliance, Spencer's and so on and entrenched regional retailers like Nilgiri's. Unorganized supply chains, multiple regulations, high rentals and lack of suitable space and manpower are the key bottlenecks for organized retailers. An NSDC study found significant skill/ competency gap at all levels from store managers, logistics and purchase down to front end sales persons.[3] Subhiksha was positioned as a value/discount retail chain, which means high turnover and low margins.

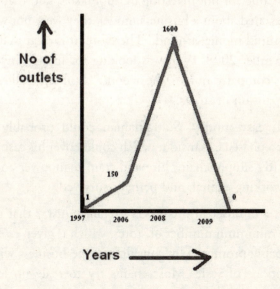

Subhiksha started with a single store in 1997. By year 2000, when first PE investment took place, the number of stores was 50. It rose to 500 in 2006. In a massive expansion from February 2007 to October 2008, the number of stores rose from 500 to 1,650, that is, over 300 percent growth in 18 months. Its revenue grew from ₹330 crores in FY06 to ₹833 crores in FY07 to ₹2,305 crores in FY08, seven times in two years. By October 2008, the company ran out of cash, which led to its collapse.

The company had fixed assets of ₹188.38 crores and inventories of ₹363.92 crores as per the audited balance sheet as of 31 March 2007, but it took loans worth ₹600 crores. 'It is astonishing as to how all these banks sanctioned such huge loans when the company had an equity base of only ₹32 crores.' It speaks volumes about PE investors' due diligence and oversight as well that of banks which provided large loans. Navroz Udwadia of Elton Park International, London, replying to our mail on 4 September 2008 for not investing in Subhiksha, said that while they were excited about a business model, they were not willing to throw 'stupid money around.' Therefore, it is clear that even up to September 2008, IVen was looking for foreign investors to bail the company out of the woods.[5] Still they allowed a massive expansion of stores.

Without easy money, Subramanian could probably have gone in for a phased expansion, which could cover his cash flow, build a sturdy supply chain, hire and train manpower and not strain his working capital, and perhaps survived.

There is a mindset in the grocery retail industry that unless you have a minimum number of stores, which is given as 300, a figure probably promoted by consultants, the business will not have operations of scale. Most chains try to scale up to this magical figure in the shortest possible time. This fast expansion led to the exit of many budding chains such as Spinach of the Dewan Group. However, the inexperienced owners could not get much benefit from their supply chains, which remained retail's Achilles Heel. Subhiksha was no exception, and Subramanian visualized a huge savings through massive expansion. Therefore, the large sums of money raised were spent mainly on store expansion without studying store location and viability and with little investment on strengthening the backend, including supply chain, distribution and replenishment logistics and IT systems, or improving customer experience or even building employee capabilities.

As long as it was operating in a limited geographical market, supply chain issues were not visible, but a fast expansion brought it to a breaking point. It was trying to build a Wal-Mart without the giant's supply chain backbone.

To provide higher margins, the chain started mobile retailing and became the country's largest mobile phone retailer with an annual turnover of Rs 1,000 crores.[6] This was another mistaken assumption. There was little control on inventories and handsets were sold below distributor price. Subhiksha stores were already small and congested and providing space for mobile sales made the space allocation problem even worse. It is known that the mobile market works on low margins and large sale. It would have been prudent to have a test marketing done to evaluate whether customers want to buy mobiles from the same place where they buy their groceries before a pan-India launch.

'We are not mad risk takers. We are not producing movies. We do a lot of research before starting business in an area, and we have back-up plans in place. We work with very good people, and if something goes wrong, we try to take corrective steps,' so said Subramanian.[7]

Subhiksha had to compete with its deep pocket competitors such as Reliance Fresh, Birla's More and Spencer's where it lost out on ambience, size and display. In addition, Subhiksha's staff was poorly trained. It is said that Warren Buffet used to check with his family where they shop and what they buy before investing in retail.

Many attribute the collapse of Subhiksha to the promoter's vaulting ambition.

Overconfidence and aggressiveness were the main reasons for Subhiksha's collapse. Subramanian was a darling of the media at one time, which probably led to this state of mind. In March 2008, the Boston Consulting Group named Subhiksha one of the world's top 50 'local dynamos.' 'We were a darling company that could do no wrong till September 2008 and suddenly we were in trouble,' rues a disheveled Subramanian, as he looked back at Subhiksha's early days – clearly successful – and the recent crisis – without doubt an avoidable tragedy.[8]

Due to generation and access of huge amount of data for front end and supply chain operations, ERP is a critical part of a large-scale retail business. Here too Subhiksha tripped badly. Its system could not cope with the rapid expansion of business. Their payroll system for India-wide employees was a manual system resulting in late disbursement of salaries and other problems. By the time Subramanian decided to upgrade the system, it was too late.

Subhiksha postponed its IPO due to the greed to keep increasing valuation, and by the time they decided to go for IPO, the business environment became unfavorable. Thus, they lost out on badly needed equity infusion. Concedes Subramanian,

> We kept thinking: why dilute equity for shareholders? We
> wanted to keep equity low and raise more debt. This strategy
> will return better money for shareholders as stock market is
> booming. But we should have raised equity in March 2008.
> There was a lot of investor interest in Subhiksha. Not doing
> it then was a mistake.[9]

This started a downward spiral of problem. In the absence of
borrowings, Subhiksha made the cardinal mistake of diverting
working capital to fund expansion. Consequently, vendor
payments were defaulted. They stopped supplies and the shelves
ran empty. Salaries and other statutory dues were not paid.
Security staff deserted their jobs and over 600 stores were
vandalized in November–December 2008.[10]

Time and again history has shown that our addiction for
sales growth blinds us from seeing the draining cash. It also
makes us vulnerable for a black-swan-like recession. It is no
surprise that management guru Professor Ram Charan identifies
cash is the topmost priority in his article 'Basics of
Moneymaking.'[11] He says that the key factors to making money
are the same in any business: *cash, margin, velocity, return* and
growth. These factors should be at the forefront of all analysis
and decision making in every job. No business survives long
without cash. You should know how much cash your business
generates and how much cash it consumes. What are the sources
of it? What drains it? What's the timing of the inflows and
outflows and how is it changing? More revenues (sales) often
mean more cash. But growing a business consumes cash. How
fast can the company expand without straining its cash flow?

Warren Buffett's partner Charlie Munger has this to say after
their loss making entry into retail: 'Retail is a very tough
business. Practically every great chain-store operation that has

been around long enough eventually gets into trouble and is hard to fix.' Like airlines, retail looks like some businesses that make it harder for mediocre to survive.[12]

It seems Subramanian has not learnt his lessons from his debacle. 'We got into trouble during the second half of last year, when we were unable to tie up funds for our ongoing operations. That slowly started choking and has led to paralysis of operations completely now,' he said. 'If the banks and lenders want us to die, then we don't have a choice. We are a golden egg laying duck, we are in trouble. We need their support and upon getting it we will restart operations and repay all debt. It is not easy, but we have to make it happen,' Subramanian said.[13] Six years have passed, and Subramanian is still waiting to restart.

VISHAL RETAIL

There are a lot of similarities in the Subhiksha and Vishal stories. Ram Chandra Agarwal set up his Vishal Garments Store in 1994 – three years before Biyani's Pantaloons and seven years before setting up Vishal Retail. This too was a discount stores model at prices that were much lower than that of other retail outlets and relying on the recent prosperity of middle class for growth.

Vishal raised ₹110 crores from an IPO in June 2007, which wasn't enough to meet its scorching growth pattern. It had 50 stores by then and was aiming for a pan-India expansion to 130 stores in a year's time. As with Subhiksha, it went for short-term debt, which resulted in a big blow to their entire supply chain when the stores didn't happen as intended. Vishal expanded without having the proper capital. They placed orders with suppliers but when the stores didn't work out, the entire supply chain got choked with an inventory of ₹500 crores.

Vishal's distribution center led model failed as it couldn't build an IT network. Buying at warehouses was mostly not aligned to what the customers needed and resulted in dead inventory. Vishal tried to develop private labels in almost every category but had limited scale to support them.

In a newspaper interview, Agarwal was candid enough to list the mistakes that led to his downfall. 'Because of this ambitious attitude I landed in problems but then it also helped me come out of them.' Agarwal admits to some operational lapses. 'I chose the wrong locations and expanded without creating a team. The management information system was faulty, we didn't have any accurate information on supply positions, stock positions or creditor positions,' he says. That ambition often translates into statements that smack of grandiloquence. 'Mark my words – I will be among top five retailers in India in 3–5 years,' says Agarwal. And another: 'Nobody can beat me in finance, sourcing, merchandise and HR.'[14]

To create managerial bandwidth, Ram Chandra Agarwal faltered while recruiting for Vishal Retail. 'Too many bad people came into the organization. I believed in people and employed too many of them without any background check. They did some wrong things in the organization,' he says. He mass hired upward of 200 MBAs from second-rung B-schools without having a strong senior and middle level leadership to guide them in operations. For Jagdeep Kapoor, CMD of Samsika Marketing Consultant, and a close Vishal watcher, 'not having a stake, was a mistake.' In other words, he felt leadership was largely on autopilot with the cult of personality overpowering the rule of many.[15]

It's hard to let go of success when it goes to the head. As an entrepreneur, who started his career as a shopkeeper in Kolkata,

Agarwal was a one-man show, like Vijay Mallya at Kingfisher Airlines. He was seen inaugurating scores of stores and four garment factories in a short while. Vishal floundered beyond the ₹500-crore mark. As is common with on-hand entrepreneurs, Agarwal, who had no corporate training, could not establish structures, systems and processes through which he could direct the fast growing organization. Vishal's Group President Ambeek Khemka says bankers have validated its business model, which is value-retailing and catering to masses in tier-II and tier-III cities. 'The only mistake we made was to grow our business through short-term debt,' says Khemka,[16] which proved costly. The strategy was to grow topline fast through expansion and then approach capital market to obtain funds and retire short-term debts. However, as it happens in a VUCA environment, before it could do so, Lehman Brothers collapsed and it had a snowball effect in reducing fund flow worldwide. Anticipating its expansion, Vishal had placed orders with suppliers (in apparels, Vishal had to place orders six months in advance). When the stores did not happen, deliveries piled up and consumption slowed. 'The supply chain got choked, not just for Vishal but many retailers globally,' says Manmohan Agarwal, a former CEO at Vishal.[17]

Vishal made many other mistakes. When it was ramping up, it spread itself too thin, opening stores across the country. Given that it was selling over 20,000 items in its stores, this made its supply chain complex. 'They needed to expand, stabilise and then expand. But they wanted to be first off-the-block in every town. Your supply chain has to be robust. Even a Wal-Mart is moving step-by-step,' says a supplier with Vishal.[18]

Ultimately, the day of reckoning came in November 2007 when Corporate Debt Restructuring of Vishal debts of ₹730 crores was initiated. Fortunately, it found a buyer in Shriram Capital and PE player TGP and Agarwal got ₹70 crores to start the second innings as V2, although the sale price was a fraction of Vishal Retail's market valuation of ₹2,200 crores in 2008.[19]

His was a clean getaway, unlike Subramanian who got embroiled in several court cases with hints of fraud, which did not go well with any future investors.

Vishal's growth was unprofitable. 'Earlier, credit was cheap and I was expanding recklessly,' says Agarwal, adding that in 2008, he set a ballpark target of Rs 5,000 crores to his employees within 1–2 years. Kapoor, too, vouches for profitable and sustainable growth as the way forward. He quips that it is akin to family planning 'You can't go on producing children, you must nurture them too.'[20]

The biggest change that is seen in Agarwal compared to Subramanian is the way he has reflected and identified reasons for his failures, which has a bearing on his second innings in launching V2 stores. He is more measured in his expansion plans and going for profitable and sustainable growth. Agarwal talks about strengthening the backend in V2, with a firm grip on processes. He claims that now he understands the basics of retail trade such as fill rate, pricing, customer segmentation and marketing strategy much better. Subhiksha and Vishal Retail are symptomatic of the mad rush for expansion when organized retail first burst on the Indian landscape. None had first-hand experience in managing retail, and they did not pause to learn the nitty-gritty such as store location, supply chain, employee training, merchandising, IT backend and so on, while they were being led a garden path by consultants. Availability of so-called easy money made matters worse. Every retailer, whether big or small, expanded stores across India as well as launched numerous formats without any piloting. Learning while doing came at a high cost as the losses mounted and the stores shut down. For example, the apparel chain Koutons, which downsized from 1,400 stores to 1,020.[21] The deep pockets survived while the weaker ones sank.

For the past few years, the imagery of the Indian retail story has been the naked ambition of its biggest players – the building and breaking by Kishore Biyani, the try-again approach of Mukesh Ambani, the tripping of Wal-Mart on its own toes. They have all grown. But they have also bled. Amid these upheavals, stockbroker RK Damani's retail chain, D-Mart, has grown consistently and profitably – and, in trademark Damani style, silently and unobtrusively. D-Mart has not shut a single store since it started in 2000. At last count, it had 73 stores – a fraction of that owned by Ambani and Biyani, but generating per store revenues even they would like. Its revenues have increased from ₹260 crores in 2006–2007 to ₹3,334 crores in 2012–2013, and is projected to hit ₹4,500 crores in 2013–2014, which would make it India's third-largest branded retail chain. It has posted profits at the net level for each of the last seven years.

The early days were about intensive learning, on the job – store layout, billing systems, gaining the confidence of vendors. Damodar Mall (an experienced retailer) and Damani (the other promoter) would pore over books on Sam Walton, who built Wal-Mart into the world's largest retailer. They would travel to the APMC (wholesale agricultural market) market in Navi Mumbai or Crawford Market, in Mumbai, to interact with wholesalers and traders. 'Within six to nine months, we knew we were on to a good thing and had the confidence to apply the model to multiple locations, but testing with our first store in Nerul, Navi Mumbai.' It is not chasing growth, it is well capitalized and debt-light, and its operations generate spare cash. As of March 2013, it had ₹786 crores in shareholder funds and a debt of ₹432 crores. 'With owned properties and no cost of rentals, they are, in fact, building assets on their books,' says Ruchi Sally, director at retail consultancy Elargir Solutions.[22]

The desire to create a business empire through scantily driven strategies in a very dynamic VUCA environment, without hedging the financial exposure and with a poor focus on studying customer behavior, created conditions for downfall. There is little evidence that the promoters learnt anything from successful retailers such as Wal-Mart. Finally, the leader should be wary of believing everything that is written about him in the media.

NOTES

1. 'Retail's Mr. 'No Frills,'' *Business Today*, 18 January 2004.
2. 'Human Skills Requirements in the Organised Retail Sector (2022) – a Report,' National Skills Development Corporation.
3. Ibid., 2.
4. 'R. Sriram: Why Subhiksha Trading Services Collapsed,' *Economic Times*, 25 August 2012.
5. 'Sinking Subhiksha Needs ₹300 cr Infusion,' *Times of India*, 31 January 2009.
6. 'Success Story of Subhiksha, India's Largest Retail Chain,' www.rediff.com, 5 February 2007.
7. Ibid., 5.
8. 'Once Bitten, Twice Not Shy,' *Economic Times*, 26 July 2011.
9. Ibid., 8.
10. Ibid.

11. Ram Charan, *The Basics of Moneymaking*, 2007, http://miltmatters.blogspot.in/2007/06/business-moneymaking-basics.html.

12. Alice Schroeder, *The Snowball: Warren Buffett and the Business of Life* (Bloomsbury, 2008), 288.

13. Ibid., 5.

14. 'Ram Chandra Agarwal on What He Learnt from Vishal Retail's 10 Big Mistakes,' *Economic Times*, 9 March 2012.

15. Ibid., 14.

16. 'Reasons for Vishal Retail's Big Fall,' *Business Standard*, 17 November 2009.

17. Ibid., 16.

18. Ibid.

19. 'TPG, Shriram Group Acquire Vishal Retail for ₹70 Crore,' *Mint*, 14 March 2011.

20. Ibid., 14.

21. 'Debt-Struck Koutons in Talks to Shed 15%,' *Economic Times*, 23 December 2010.

22. 'Radhakishan Damani: Man with the Midas Touch in the Stock Markets,' *Economic Times*, 25 March 2014.

VIII

SUZLON AND GMR

The Curse of Easy Money

Dieticians strongly advise that buffets should be avoided to maintain good health as one tends to overeat. Weight thus gained is difficult to shed. After the unshackling of the economy in the 1990s, a deluge of funds through a buffet of financial instruments, both Indian and foreign, was made available to Indian entrepreneurs and existing companies, some such as foreign currency convertible bonds (FCCBs), for the first time in India.

Coupled with it was crony capitalism of Indian public sector banking and finally magicians in the shape of management consultancy firms that turned these highly leveraged firms and their projects into highly profitable avenues to park money, for which there were no takers in the United States and Europe.

Banks were more than happy to lend money to finance these expansions. And if money couldn't be raised domestically, it could always be raised overseas by issuing FCCBs. The beauty of these bonds was that the rate of interest was almost close to zero. (The lure for investors was that their bonds would get converted into shares at a discount to the market value.) Hence, companies raising money through this route did not see their profits fall because of interest payments. In the prevailing euphoria, these entrepreneurs did not realize that all the money they were raising in the form of debt would eventually have to be returned. Even if they did, they were confident that all these expansions into unrelated territories would soon start making money and would generate enough profits to pay off the debt.[1] Unfortunately, the time has come for the chicken to come home to roost, as it often happens in VUCA.

These scenarios were like Bollywood movies where the story remained the same but the title and characters changed. Real estate companies such as DLF, Unitech and DB realty, to infrastructure companies such as Lanco and GVK, to hoteliers such as Leela, to publishers such as Deccan Chronicle and sunrise industries such as Suzlon, Kingfisher Airlines, Future Group and so on have been able to leverage debts to beyond all prudent levels to fund expansions, diversifications and acquisitions. Real estate companies were buying land and setting up hotels and wind farms, retailers were going into insurance, hoteliers were creating Taj Mahals, publishers were getting into real estate and so on. Now most of them are selling the same assets to repay debts that they incurred to create these assets. As a character in the movie *English Vinglish* (2012) says, '*Entrepreneur, shabd na hua, poori ghazal ho gayi*' ('Entrepreneur' from a mere word has turned into a complete poem).

For example, the debt-equity ratio of some of these companies in 2012 was as follows:

Suzlon Energy: 48.65

GMR Infra: 4.9

GKV Power & Infra: 5.1

HCC: 19.34

Total debt of companies in the BSE 500 index (excluding banking and finance companies) was ₹4.5 lakh crores on 31 March 2007. It rose five fold to ₹20 lakh crores till March 2013. The interest paid rose from ₹22,000 crores to ₹1.2 lakh crores.

As many as 68 out of 400 have a debt-to-equity ratio of more than 2. Many of these debt-ridden companies were once hailed as emerging stars (Suzlon Energy, GMR Infrastructure, GVK Power and Infrastructure, Jaiprakash Associates) on the corporate horizon. However, many are now struggling to service their debt; some are on the verge of insolvency. Many have opted for corporate debt restructuring (CDR), under which banks ease the debt's terms and conditions (reduction of interest rate and increase in tenure).[2]

George Orwell once said, 'Whoever is winning at the moment will always seem to be invincible.'[3] The Indian entrepreneurs went through this phase between 2003 and 2008. They had the Midas touch and the world seemed to be at their feet.

We take two examples here, Suzlon Energy and GMR, as symptomatic of high debt syndrome, and many others fell on the same banana peel.

SUZLON ENERGY

Tulsi Tanti, a first-generation entrepreneur, built Suzlon Energy from scratch to become the fifth largest wind turbine manufacturer in the world. He owned a textile firm with 20 employees and soon realized that the captive wind energy unit he had set up to run his units had better prospects than his existing business. He then set up a green energy company that grew manifold driven by its early-mover advantage in India and the incentive-driven capacity addition in key global markets.

The company's global spread extends across Asia, Australia, Europe, Africa and North and South America with installations of over 20,000 MW and operations across 32 countries. It was truly seen as a shining example of resurgent India.

In 2007, Suzlon made its most ambitious move by acquiring Germany's REpower Systems, after fighting other global suitors. REpower, later renamed Senvion, was seen as the jewel in the crown with its advanced technology, strong market position and robust order book. But in some ways, it has become the albatross around its neck as Suzlon struggles to repay debt raised for the acquisition that cost around ₹8,000 crores. The Indian company is also facing resistance from the German company in its bid to merge and consolidate businesses and benefits from the latter's cash flows and technology – all this at a time the wind energy market faces rough weather globally.[4]

Suzlon and its CEO Tulsi Tanti, the poster boy of yester years, are in trouble. Its FCCB loans amounting to $221 million (₹1,160 crores) matured in October 2012, and the company defaulted on it and its request for extension was rejected by bondholders. The company has a total debt of ₹17,320 crores ($2.7 bn.) as on end September 2014 up from ₹13,360 crores three years back,[5] more than twice its equity base. It has not reported profits for the past three years, and 99.94 percent of the promoter shares are pledged as on Q4FY2014,[6] and, according to Money Control chart, has seen an erosion of 95 percent since purchase of REpower. On top of this, the global demand for wind turbines will shrink by 5 percent in 2014[7] due to lower demand from Europe and the United States. India has also withdrawn tax incentives for setting up wind turbines. However, the long-term future is bright. Tulsi Tanti's wealth has also eroded. From eighth spot in Forbes' 2005 list of 'Richest Indians,' his name disappeared from the list in 2014.

The failure of Suzlon can be attributed to four causes:

1. Acquisition – overpaid for an acquisition that could not be integrated.

2. Consolidation – tardy in implementing quality issues resulting in loss of business such as a large order from Edison.

3. Due diligence – inadequate due diligence due to poor understanding of this vital function resulted in a host of problems at REpower.

4. Risk management – poor assessment of future risks of doing business in global markets.

This is an example not only of relying solely on debt for expansion but also of the lack of due diligence in acquiring REpower and ignoring consolidation, all vital functions in an uncertain and complex VUCA environment. The first is due to blind ambition overriding caution when going abroad for the first time, taking huge loans, assuming that future business environment will remain stable, and the second is due to inadequate managerial bandwidth resulting in inadequate due diligence. Poor due diligence and overpayment has been the cause of failure of many Indian companies acquiring assets overseas, such as Dr. Reddy's acquisition of Germany's Betapharm.[8] Not only has it overpaid for acquisition but it also failed to see that the technology patents of REpower is held by employees and not by the company, and it is the employees who are virtually running the company. Indian companies primarily undertake financial and tax due diligence but are poor at understanding technical, R&D and market and culture-related scrutiny. Suzlon was also eyeing REpower's considerable cash reserves for retiring debts, but German banks had ring fenced it and kept it out of reach of Tanti.[9]

This at a time when Suzlon products were facing a lot of quality-related problems. In 2008, Edison, the US energy giant, cancelled a large order on quality issues. These quality issues made cash flow issue tighter reducing the company's ability to service debts. On court orders, Suzlon has acquired a wind farm owned by Edison against payment due. However, it will take some time before the asset is sold and utilized for debt reduction.[10] In January 2014, Suzlon sold REpower at $1 billion, 40 percent below its purchase price.

GMR GROUP

Telugu business houses were slow to go pan-India as well as global. Organizations such as GMR, GVR, Lanco, IVRCL and so on moved center stage after the liberalization process started in the 1990s with a large state layout for infrastructure development and privatization. GM Rao learnt entrepreneurship at an early age in the family business of jute trading, and his skills were honed at projects such as the turnaround of a sick jute mill. He later turned serial entrepreneur and invested in a host of companies especially Vysya Bank, which brought him handsome returns.[11]

When the government opened infrastructure projects such as airports, roads, power plants and so on for private bidding, Rao discovered his true calling – that of infrastructure development. His successful execution and management of Greenfield Hyderabad airport brought GMR into national limelight.

GMR now has a portfolio of 16 power generation assets, of which 6 are operational and 10 under various stages of implementation, and 10 road assets, of which 8 are operational and 2 are under construction. In the airports sector, besides operating the existing Delhi international airport, the group has also built a brand new integrated terminal, T3, which was commissioned in time for the Commonwealth Games in October 2010. All this was achieved within a short period of 15 years. As a group, Andhra infrastructure companies operate four major airports, a third of all power projects and half of highway projects in India, largely financed through huge debts and private equity.[12]

GMR's troubles stem from its business model. Most projects, whether airports, roads or power plants, are public-private partnership projects in regulated industries, which is a new concept in India with few shining examples as role models. To give an example, the largest infrastructure company in India, L&T, has a mix of projects, those with milestone payments and others on PPP model. This results in a stream of positive cash-flow even under unfavorable economic conditions. For example, the L&T Metro Rail Hyderabad Limited project is based on a revenue model of 50 percent from passenger fares, 45 percent from property development and 5 percent from advertisement and other miscellaneous sources. This reduces possibility of future fare hikes and consequent public and government ire. L&T has divested some businesses like its cement division, which do not come under its core business strengths. On the other hand, GMR feels confident to construct and run power plants, airports and roads and so on, each of which is a complex business in itself.

Few major projects in India reach projected milestones in terms of time and cost, Delhi Metro and Jamnagar Refinery of Reliance Industries being exceptions. Ad-hoc policies that change with political tide, land acquisition problems, inter-ministerial turf battles, turtle paced bureaucracy, which is often paralyzed by corruption issues, all contribute to nightmarish problems for entrepreneurs. *Doing Business 2014*, an annual global index produced by the World Bank, which ranks the ease of doing business in various countries, has placed India at a low 134 out of 189 countries, slipping three ranks since 2013. The reasons are not far to see. When GMR placed all its eggs in PPP basket, it should have visualized these problems, which are not new and have plagued most projects since independence.

The slow pace of execution of projects has adverse consequences for cash flow to service loans and fund future projects, which further restrict access to additional loans and private equity, a sort of cyclone spiral with ever-increasing velocity.

GMR today is faced with myriad problems: feedstock as well as payment from State Electricity Boards in power generation; multiple government bodies playing an obstructing role in Delhi Airport project, which is bleeding; and environmental and forest clearances have resulted in GMR withdrawing from a major road project and Male airport (over which GMR is fighting a messy legal battle) being taken over by the Maldives government.

GMR is learning the hard way that getting projects from the government in India is easier, as it still depends upon high-level relationship management compared to execution of these projects, which have long gestation periods and where the business environment changes rapidly between award and completion of projects.

Instead of consolidating the empire and improving cash flow, GMR continues to take on new projects such as tendering for a new airport in Philippines.

The award of Delhi airport project was won at a huge premium. For example, Airports Authority of India (AAI) is a 26 percent partner but is entitled to 46 percent of earnings. Getting permissions from over 40 government departments was also a challenge. 'When we got into the project, I did not fully know what I was in for,' recalls Rao.[13] Moreover, additional conveniences added to the initial project cost, which increased from ₹9,875 crores to ₹12,700 crores. This resulted in a total debt of ₹30,000 crores, largely for Delhi Airport, more than the net worth of the company.[14]

With the launch of Airport Economic Regulatory Authority (AERA), the new airport regulator, the cosy relationship with the government came to an end. AERA is putting its foot put down on airport fees and questioning the basis of the revenue model. Land banks, which were supposed to be cash cows through hotels, shopping and so on, have not yet materialized.

'Most good airports around the world make more money from their commercial revenues than from their airline revenues,' says Albert Brunner, CEO of BIAL. 'In India, this is a potential that has not been tapped at all.'[15]

As against this, both Cochin and Bangalore airports started showing profits within the stipulated time. It is true that both these airports are smaller, but the principle remains that investors and debtors will not wait indefinitely for returns on their investments. Bangalore airport has been constructed on a modular basis where expansion takes place in line with traffic increase easing pressure on capital expenditure, while Delhi airport takes care of passenger traffic for the next 25 years.

The present failure of GMR essentially originates in the group's desire for a fast-paced growth simultaneously in multiple areas, all with huge capital layouts in regulated projects with long gestation periods, through funds that were primarily derived though debt. The hunger for growth should be tempered with desire for maintaining a positive cash flow.

Indian businesses are poor in risk management and project due diligence, and this fact has come to light in several cases discussed in this book. The Male airport debacle is partially derived from a poor assessment of socio-political situation. It should be assumed that all countries bordering India are more or less hostile to it and look at India as an oppressive big brother. Whenever there are internal political problems, a finger is often lifted at India for interfering in internal affairs and reaction is focused on local Indian businesses. This has happened in Nepal and more recently in Sri Lanka and Bangladesh. In Maldives too, nationalistic feelings have been rising for several years now, and a risk assessment should have taken this into account. The airport project became a casualty of the power struggle. Opposition parties had threatened nationalization during previous regime, perceiving the contract has been won through proximity to previous government at terms unfavorable to Maldives.[16] GMR proposed to build a business center-cum-shopping and entertainment area. This was a double whammy for the locals, say Maldivians. It would wean away shoppers and tourists from Male, while the second runway plan, which would have enabled more tourist traffic and economic growth, was shelved. Tourism revenue is an important issue in a small poor country that depends upon tourism as a major source of revenue.[17]

Most Maldivians who have followed the events over two years say the deal was doomed from Day One. At the ceremony of the inking of the original agreement between GMR and

Maldives government, lawyers and officials from both sides were still reading and trying to understand the papers. 'There was hardly anything ceremonial. People were tense. Many of them simply had not had enough time to go through the document and appreciate the various issues. It was all done in great hurry.' The holes in the agreement were soon exposed, as the provision to levy an Airport Development charge was stuck down by a civil court in January 2012.[18]

GMR also did not take political risk insurance cover. 'Events such as these are the reason why multinational companies buy political risk insurance while embarking on projects in emerging markets. Many investors in Male do buy political risk cover and there is an active market for it,' said an insurance official. However, GMR had not purchased political risk cover for the Male project. The insurance official added that there was not much of a market for it among Indian corporates 'as lenders did not insist on this.'[19] This itself shows how little risk management is understood and practiced by Indian companies. This could be either due to ignorance or simply due to the urge to save a little money.

Its multimillion dollar acquisition of international power company Intergen has also not brought about expected results and now GMR has sold its interest to a Chinese company. In addition, the company is selling other assets in South Africa and Singapore. This should free up much need cash.

Successful entrepreneurs assume that they have found a formula for success, which can be applied in every domain. There is little effort to take pause, consolidate, improve cash flow, learn from your experiences and move forward. Dr. Mallya too went into airlines, F1 racing, cricket franchisee and assumed that these can be run like his successful liquor business.

It is fruitless to blame all problems on the government and on the external business environment. Ad-hoc policy and bureaucratic delays are the norms in government, and these obstacles have only increased, rather than decreased, after the opening of the economy in the 1990s. This VUCA condition should not surprise an astute businessman and precautions should have been taken to reduce risk exposure to PPP projects. The very reason that all domains such as airports, roads and power plants are in trouble also highlight the fact that all these are separate businesses, and experience in one does not replicate itself in gaining insight into another. This problem is not unique to GMR but several infra companies such as Gammon India, Lanco and so on are in a similar situation.

Rating agency ICRA has also downgraded its long-term rating outlook on the company from stable to 'negative.' 'The negative rating outlook reflects the possibility of cash support having to be extended by the group to several operational/under implementation assets which would serve to worsen the already stretched funding position of the group,' ICRA's report says. It has also lowered the rating assigned to GMR infrastructure's short-term loan program because of 'the growing regulatory and political risks' impacting many of the group's assets, including its airports.[20]

It seems GMR has learnt some valuable lessons, which will guide it in its future endeavors. The group has become more measured in its globalization effort. 'We have set clear hurdle rates to evaluate all opportunities and are much more process-oriented on risk. What I did in the past was largely intuitive but the business is much larger and more complex now and gut feel cannot work,' says Rao. The experience has also made GMR avoid some of the other big moves that rivals like GVK and

Adani are making to secure resources. They are the billion-dollar coal mine-development deals in Australia and elsewhere. Rao is also making sure his company is in fighting form. For a family-run company, he has set up a five-member general performance advisory council to evaluate the company every year and rate it on a scale of 1–10. Planning Commission member Arun Maira set up the framework for the council and its scope. Management guru Ram Charan, Rao's mentor, says he has never seen anything like this elsewhere in the world. The other major priority is to maximize cash flow. Rao says he will achieve this by keeping projects at various stages of implementation and operation in his portfolio so that not all are in the same phase.[21]

All high debt companies would do well to remember the banker's motto: 'Topline is vanity, bottom line is sanity, cash flow is reality.'

NOTES

1. 'Biyani, Mallya, Suzlon, DLF: Easy Money Screwed Up India Inc.,' *First Post*, 16 October 2012.
2. 'Out of Debt Trap,' *Business Today*, September 2014.
3. *The Collected Essays, Journalism and Letters of George Orwell: In Front of Your Nose, 1945–1950* (1968 edition).
4. 'Can Tulsi Tanti Salvage Debt Ridden Suzlon Energy?' *Economic Times*, 16 October 2012.
5. 'Suzlon Energy in Talks to Sell German Business for $2.5 billion,' *Economic Times*, 8 January 2014.
6. 'Top Five Companies Which Saw High Levels of Share Pledging in the March Quarter,' *Economic Times*, 30 April 2014.
7. 'Wind Power's Bright Future,' *E–The Environmental Magazine*, 17 February 2014.

8. 'Betapharm: A Pill Dr Reddy's Could Do Without,' *Business Standard*, 30 November 2012.

9. Ibid., 4.

10. 'Suzlon Energy Takes Over US Client Edison Mission Energy's Wind Farm to Recover $208 Million Dues,' *Economic Times*, 3 April 2014.

11. 'The Rise of Rao,' *The Hindu*, 31 December 2012.

12. 'Why the Big Four Andhra Pradesh-Based Infrastructure Companies GMR, GVK, Lanco & IVRCL Are in Trouble?' *Economic Times*, 24 June 2012.

13. 'G.M. Rao: Build, Operate, and Be Damned,' *Forbes India*, 21 June 2011.

14. 'GMR's Delhi Airport Cost Overrun in Focus Gain,' *DNA*, 28 June 2010.

15. 'Are Private Airports in India Ready to Take Off?' Knowledge @& Wharton, 3 April 2008.

16. 'Mauled in Maldives,' *Business Today*, 20 January 2013.

17. 'Why GMR's Project Was Not Good for Maldives,' *Business Standard*, 20 December 2012.

18. Ibid., 17.

19. 'GMR Didn't Buy Political Cover,' *Times of India*, 4 December 2012.

20. GMR Infrastructure Limited, ICRA, November 2012

21. Ibid., 13.

IX

VENKY'S SELF-GOAL
Unfolding Shakespearean Tragedy

In November 2010, India's largest hatchery company, VH Group (owners of the brand Venky's), bought English League Football Club Blackburn Rovers (BRC) through their company Venky's London Limited for ₹163 crores and took over debts of another ₹142 crores. Venky's promised financial support even if the Club was relegated, which it soon did. BRC was knocked out of the English Premier League (EPL) in the 2012 season after losing 1–0 to Wigan Athletic on its home ground in a make or break game. Most fans blamed the owners for the Club's decline, which affected the finances of the Club where revenues largely come from ticket sales, sponsorships and merchandising.[1]

This was the latest bout of ignominy for the once proud 135 years old BRC of Blackburn, Lancashire, in the United Kingdom, a founding member of The Football League, which was relegated from Premier League at the end of 2011–2012 season. The Club occupied top positions till 1932 when its decline started. Till 1992, the Club had a chequered record of wins and relegation to Second and Third Divisions when it was bought by a local steel magnate and lifelong supporter Jack Walkers. Walkers spent millions of pounds in purchasing new stars and brought a new manager, Kenny Daglish. BRC were runners-up in 1993 and lifted the Premier Cup in 1993–1994.[2]

Soon after reaching the pinnacle, the downfall of BRC started, picking speed with the death of owner Jack Walker. It consistently slipped in ranking with an occasional touch of its old form. To improve results, managers were changed in quick succession.

Sadly, this was a chronicle of a death foretold. Anyone with any understanding of events within Ewood Park could see the dynamic was wrong. No leadership. No unity. Owners without a clue. A manager without experience. The fans could see it. It was their club, their concern long after Venky's and Kean had gone. It was their passion. So they protested. It went on all season, this mutiny, this chorus of 'We want our Rovers back.'[3]

Venky's bought BRC hoping to promote their corporate image and flagship Venky's brand through the EPL, which is followed by millions worldwide. Anuradha Patel, VH's Chairperson, said that she didn't know much about football. Her brother, Vineeth Rao, came on board as a Director who didn't know much about football either and used to ask employees about basic things. He relied on Wikipedia to identify various footballers.[4]

The Raos have been accused of being indifferent to the interests of the club. Wayne Wild, the Group Director of WEC Group, a long-standing sponsor and cofounder of the Blackburn Rovers Supporters' Investment Trust (BRSIT), says that Venky's bought the team to build its brand in the United Kingdom and not out of love for the game. 'The moment Venky's came in as owners they replaced all the experienced people, including players, with inexperienced people. They sacked manager Sam Allardyce and replaced him with first with team coach Steve Kean, who had never managed a (top level) team,' says Wild. Kean himself was later sacked. The owners were notorious for not attending matches and for managing the show from India. 'They stayed too far away to know what they needed to do to make the club a success.' The English media and fans were particularly upset by the fact that the Rao family did not even bother to watch the crucial match against Wigan.[5]

Buying an English premier football club made good business sense since there is growing viewership of EPL in India with 147 million viewers,[6] and Venky's could capitalize on it to not only increase its visibility in India but also clear a route to fulfill its growing ambitions abroad.

People were therefore willing to see the sagacity in the move by Venky's to buy a football club steeped in history and prestige equaled only by the Big Three – Manchester United, Arsenal and Chelsea. At Ewood Park, the Rovers' home base, Venky's was received with the same fervor reserved for messiahs. The previous owners, Jack Walker Trust, had been trying for years to find a buyer. Since it won the League, Rovers had fared badly on the field. The rich and ambitious new owners were about to change that.[7] The scene has changed dramatically now and watching Rovers in action doesn't make for happy television experience these days. It's not just the streak of losses that is worrying. Placards and T-shirts declaring 'Venky's Out,' '100% Rovers, 0% Venky's,' and 'Venky's Wake Up and Smell the Chicken,' are a common sight during matches. Fans are upset that Venky's, as they see it, has 'broken all the promises' made at the time of purchase. The company said it would invest in the club. No money has come from Pune yet. Venky's also promised to bring big names such as David Beckham, Ronaldinho, Kaka and Robinho to Rovers. Fans are still waiting, and in fact to raise cash, the Club sold two of its stars. 'Venky's is the worst thing ever to happen to Blackburn Rovers in its long and proud history,' says Kamran Inayat, chief reporter of brfcs.com, a website for supporters. 'They have taken one of the best run clubs in the Premier League and turned it into a circus.' Ouch! How did matters come to such a pass? How did Venky's come to be so disliked?[8]

This is a classic case of mindless action sans understanding. Venky's senior management had no prior experience with football management, not even any kind of sports management. It did not first try to understand the culture and traditions of English football. It failed to understand that to an Englishman the passion for football is like that for cricket in India. This passion converts into the finances and success of the Clubs, irrespective of their wins and losses. Venky's, without any prior understanding of the dynamics of English Football, came with a prepared script that everything is wrong with the Club. In their eagerness to bring about quick changes, they chose to throw out the baby with the bathwater. Its first action was to replace the experienced coach Sam Allardyce with a novice Steve Kean with no Premier League managerial experience. Within the first month of change in ownership, he was 'forced to resign' in September 2012. As Sportingtelligence has documented, Rovers signed a number of players in Kean's tenure that Kean had little or no involvement in signing. Yet, he always publicly insisted the owners were brilliant and supportive, and that all the signings were his own. To fans who knew – or at least suspected – this wasn't the case; Kean appeared to be a complicit puppet who was party to their club's misfortunes. For these reasons, Kean became a target of the fans' ire – not least because the absent owners were not there to take the flak. Kean took it up for them and kept his job by never once being critical of the owners in public.[9]

Next, differences emerged between the board and owners, which took decisions without consulting the former. Soon, the Chairman, Managing Director and Finance Director, the three most experienced persons, left. They were followed in quick succession by manager Michael Appleton who was sacked, then Henning Berg who too was sacked. He lasted 57 days, 10 less than Appleton. Berg has since been awarded ₹16 crores compensation by court for wrongful dismissal.[10] In this merry-go-round, Venky's brought in Shebby Singh, a Malaysian football broadcaster, the most intriguing character in this real-time drama, to clean up the mess. He was designated 'global adviser,' a designation that is unique in the world of club football. Few knew what that title actually meant and what responsibilities Singh actually had to justify his ₹3 crores a year salary, but there was so much confusion surrounding Blackburn at the time that it went relatively unnoticed. It wasn't long before Singh began making a name for himself by putting his foot in his mouth.[11] Soon, he became more hated than the Patels and Raos. According to Wikipedia, he is no longer with the Club.

The continued frustration of fans may have wider ramifications for the company. Simon Kuper, co-author of the widely acclaimed analytical book *Soccernomics*,[12] says fan support is crucial to running a club.

> In this industry, consumer activism is extreme. The consumers gather in one place and shout things in unison, you don't tend to get that in many industries. If at a club, the fans are

chanting against the owners, and want rid of them, it's very uncomfortable for the owners to hang on. Fans have taken out numerous protest marches against Venky's. They have strongly criticised the club's owners.[13]

In November 2011, Anuradha Desai's brothers Balaji Rao and Venkatesh Rao were booed at halftime during a match. They left the stadium soon after.[14]

Club debt rose to £26.3 million in 2011 from £21 million in 2010. Rovers posted an annual pre-tax loss of £18.6 million for the year to end June 2011 compared with £1.9 million a year earlier. Venky's was also asked by bankers Barclays to make a £10 million deposit or risk crossing the overdraft limit.[15] When Venky's took over the Club, they did not visualise the size of funds they are expected to pump in now and at regular intervals. For the time being, they have averted cash crunch by selling promising players the club was banking on.[16]

Simon Kuper, the author or *Soccernomics*, writes that football clubs almost never make profits.

> I don't believe that many owners buy clubs in the hope of profits. It's actually rare for business groups like Venky's to be club owners. Most owners are individual rich men like [Roman] Abramovich [Russian owner of Chelsea] or the Abu Dhabi owners of Manchester City, who buy clubs in the same spirit that they buy paintings or yachts, for the thrill, the vanity, the glamour of it.[17]

This owners club also includes billionaire Lakshmi Mittal, who has an interest in Queen's Park Rangers.

A fan poll of best and worst football club owners conducted by *Sporting Intelligence Magazine* named Venky's as the worst owners in English Football League.[18]

The family is still unable to face the critical situation as the whole-time director of Venky's, Rao, told the *Times of India* that his family was not expecting the relegation. Seriously? If that were true, they were perhaps the only people on the planet to have not read the writing on the wall. Mike Delap, chief editor of Vital Blackburn, a supporters' website, says everyone knew relegation was a certainty based on the past 12 months' performance. Blackburn is not a glamorous town. It has many social and economic problems but the football team was the one source of genuine pride. It had flourished against all odds in the Premier League despite the vastly greater resources of rivals, but the Venky's reign has been the exact opposite. 'They have ruined an established club and smashed all its structures.' In short, Venky's has 'dismantled a once proud club and replaced it with a sheer embarrassment of a club.' Venky's' reaction to the resentment of fans has been a studied silence. The owners also chose to watch the club's descent into one crisis after the other from the relatively cooler confines of Pune. Never mind that it has riled fans further.[19]

The interim CEO Paul Hunt's letter, which was leaked to the press (not by the writer), made some recommendations for saving the Club. A few of these are: Mrs. Desai to allow her executives at Ewood to run the club, a more cohesive PR strategy, more trips by Ewood executives to meet the stay-away owners, owners to visit the club more and asks for the Ewood executives to hire and fire – rather than Mrs. Desai making these decisions, among a list of 10 points. Further, the letter continues,

> The Blackburn Rovers and Venky's brands are both suffering terribly. Whilst there are negative goings on such as protests, complaints, media stories, unhappy fans etc., then both brands are losing brand equity and consequently, losing value. I am

also concerned that the Premier League will intervene soon as they may take the view that their brand is being tarnished by association too. It is all reparable of course but we must start to act now by building bridges with fans and the media as above.[20]

Venky's did take prompt action. They fired the interim CEO.

To conclude, this was another case of dysfunctional learning and failure as a consequence of success. Venky's owners are second-generation businesspersons who received a pioneering and well-run profitable poultry empire as an inheritance. Success came as a result of birth rather than effort. They have not realized that they must learn to dig a well if they want to drink water. A football team was run by incapable, least passionate individuals who would treat Wikipedia as a source of inspiration.

The Board of Directors is made up of family members with two ex-servicemen as Independent Directors. They may be fine soldiers but their prior experience does not show any strategic depth in the industry in which Venky's operate. Therefore, there was no devil's advocate on the board who could question the family's strategic blunder.

The owners, with no prior English Football experience, took actions based on erroneous assumptions and no clear vision. In a VUCA world, anchoring clear vision to strategy is key to success. They assumed that running an English Football Club is somewhat like running a poultry firm. In reality, it is close to religion in English culture. They ran the Club with remote control and were rarely seen on the grounds for a sporting event where passion runs deep. They were deaf to communication with both the management and fans. They did not foresee the financial implications of running an English Football Club.

In short, they tried to run before learning to walk. In a VUCA environment, where the future is fast changing, it is essential to learn the intricacies of a new business (if you can call owning a football club a business) before making large-scale changes, as Wipro did in their Malaysian acquisition, discussed later in this book.

The story is not yet over, and whether Venky's has learnt any lesson or not is something only time will tell as this tragedy of Shakespearean proportions is still unfolding. As the bard rightly said:

> The fault, dear Brutus, is not in our stars,
> But in ourselves, that we are underlings.
>
> —Julius Caesar

The latest news from the Club shows that all is not lost as Gary Bowyer, who was promoted from the coaching ranks last March to become Blackburn's fifth manager in just over two years, is credited with bringing stability with a young team. Over 4,000 fans traveled down to Manchester to see their club play against Manchester City.[21]

NOTES

1. 'Fowl Game,' *Business Today*, 10 June 2012.
2. 'Blackburn Rovers F.C.,' Wikipedia.
3. 'Blackburn Rovers Relegated from Premier League,' *The Telegraph*, London, 10 February 2013.
4. Ibid., 1.
5. Ibid.
6. 'Blackburn Rovers Buyout,' *Economic Times*, 22 January 2012.

7. 'The Best and Worst Owners in English Football,' www.sportingintelligence.com, 31 December 2012.

8. Ibid., 6.

9. 'Fans Celebrate as Steve Kean 'Forced to Resign' as Blackburn Manager,' www.sportsintelligence.com, 28 September 2012.

10. 'Venky's Still Groping in the Dark with Blackburn Rovers It Bought in 2010,' *Economic Times*, 26 May 2013.

11. 'Shebby Singh: The Tyrannical Leader Blackburn Rovers Just Don't Need,' *International Business Times*, 22 April 2013.

12. Simon Kuper, *Soccernomics* (Nation Books, 2009).

13. Ibid., 6.

14. 'The Rovers' Swift Descent From Riches to Rags,' *New York Times*, 27 December 2011.

15. Ibid., 6.

16. 'The Future Looks Black and Burnt for Venky's Blackburn Rovers,' *Economic Times*, 13 May 2012.

17. Ibid., 6.

18. Ibid., 7.

19. 'New Leaked Blackburn Letter Lays Bare Crisis and Torment inside Ewood,' www.sportsintelligence.com, 8 May 2012.

20. Ibid., 19.

21. 'Blackburn Rovers Head to Manchester City with a Little Sanity Restored,' *The Guardian*, 14 January 2014.

X

NANO AND AKASH TABLET I

Jugaad Doesn't Always Work

Clever improvisation locally called 'jugaad' has focused the world's attention on India where you can bring out frill-free innovative products at an affordable price. Research from Indian laboratories has been responsible for cheap ECG machines from GE Healthcare and least expensive cath lab from Philip Healthcare. India is emerging as a hotbed for frugal ideas and low-cost innovations for high-volume value-conscious customers. If innovation is successful here, it can have a worldwide market.

Both Nano car and Akash tablets were designed for such value-conscious customers, who desire the basic in application and can do without many frills that add to the cost.

Both were the result of two visionaries Mr. Ratan Tata, then Chairman of the Tata Group, and Mr. Kapil Sibal, ex-Union Minister of Education as well as Telecom.

NANO CAR

Nano car was the result of the vision of Mr. Ratan Tata, then Chairman of Tata Motors Limited. Competitors scoffed. They said it couldn't be done; it would take a miracle to make it happen. As he explains, he aimed for a safe alternative to a family going out on a scooter. That led us to configure a small car which would be a full-fledged car. We started again in an evolutionary way. Perhaps the bigger, more visible issue is that we needed to benchmark ourselves against something. And we took the Maruti 800 as the benchmark in terms of acceleration – driveability should at least be equal to Maruti and in some areas it should exceed the Maruti.[1]

According to a study conducted by CRISIL, Nano was expected to expand the country's car market by 65 percent.[2] There was an overwhelming response for inaugural bookings. For first 100,000 cars, there were over 200,000 bookings. Delivery began in July 2009.

After the initial launch, the demand tapered off. In November 2010, while overall auto sales in India's booming economy rose more than 22 percent,[3] Tata sold only 509 Nano cars, down from the 9,000 it sold the previous month. In spite of a huge publicity built up prior to the launch, it was not a big hit, and it still struggling to grab the market in spite of its good and convincing features.

Price was a major factor in its initial publicity, and the whole advertising campaign was designed around its price. Its features were a secondary aspect. It was assumed that low price alone would make the huge sales the company was expecting in converting two-wheeler owners into Nano owners. In 2012, the market for two-wheelers was 13.8 million units,[4] 35 percent of which was financed.[5]

Considering the average cost of a two-wheeler is ₹40,000, almost one-third of the owners are unable to purchase a two-wheeler from their own funds. The remaining two-thirds buy using their personal funds. To convert to Nano, a majority of these will have to avail a car loan. To expect them to convert to Nano, at least three times the cost (initial price of ₹1 lakh was unrealistic and price ranged from ₹1.2 to 1.5 lakhs) at high interest rates is very optimistic. In addition, parking a two-wheeler does not require much space, and many are found parked outside even a one-room shanty. To park a Nano car, they will have to look for definite parking space. Ultimately, the market of Nano turned out to be not the motorcycle owners but those looking for a second car.

Large initial demand required the company to build the car at scale from the outset, which proved publicly problematic when the company ran into problems purchasing land for a new factory in West Bengal. Production for the first 100,000 cars was delayed by more than 18 months.

Then it turned out that the car doesn't really sell for the highly publicized ₹1 lakh. In fact, the *New York Times* reports that a fully equipped Nano sells for only about $800 less than the Suzuki Alto, which 'has a bigger engine, more storage space and a longer track record than the Nano.'[6] That last factor is particularly important in the wake of dramatic accounts of some Nano cars bursting into flames, an unfortunate irony for a car touted as a 'safe.'[7]

Nor, it seems, is the car popular with its original target market. Nano customers are not upgrading from motor scooters but people looking for a fun, trendy second car for running errands.

It is not unusual for innovations to run into problems that require further tinkering till product, marketing and price are right. The much delayed launch, the fanfare surrounding

Nano and high expectations did not allow this process to be completed.

It might not have been easy, but had Tata piloted the Nano quietly, on a small scale, perhaps through a limited production run in a small city, like Durgapur in West Bengal or Ranchi in Jharkhand, its engineering, pricing, financing and marketing might have been adjusted far from the limelight to suit the needs of an optimal target customer. Then, like the 'overnight sensations' who seem to have acquired instantaneous talent – but in fact spent years quietly perfecting their craft – the Nano might have made its debut to the wider world with less hype and greater effect. It might not have been a ₹1 lakh car or even an alternative to motor scooters. But when it first appeared in the mainstream, it would have been the right product for the right price in the right market.

It is reported that Tata Motors will be launching a diesel variant at ₹3.5 lakhs. This should be interesting to watch as Tata is known for their diesel technology, and diesel variants of Indica and Indigo models are already in the market.

At last count, 14,800 Nano cars were sold in January–November 2014.[8]

AKASH TABLET I

'I want public services to be delivered through Aakash. I want Aakash to be a platform for 1.2 billion people.' So was launched Mr. Sibal's ambitious project for producing a low-cost tablet device for students, teachers and general public who cannot afford laptops. He further added that 'there are some moments in history (*taking a long pause*) that will be milestones recognized by future generations. This is one such moment.'[9]

For Indian Education Minister Kapil Sibal, Aakash would be proof of India's global stature. In this one device, you can find the high hopes not just of an ambitious politician but of an entire nation.

Sibal said that he was about to give 500 prototypes to students for testing. He announced that the government would distribute 10 million at the subsidized $35 price, while millions more would be available for $60 apiece. The device would have videoconferencing capability, a touch screen, and three hours of battery life – not to mention the ability to turn around India's global reputation.[10] Applying jugaad to the PC looked like a worthy goal.

The idea for the Aakash tablet and troubles that the project brings with it have both been inherited from the One Laptop Per Child (OLPC) project launched in 2005 by Nicholas Negroponte of the Massachusetts Institute of Technology. OLPC's hope was that empowering children in the developing world with computers connected to the Internet will help them learn faster, develop better skills and reach their full potential. About eight years after its launch, the results are in and the OLPC hasn't done so well, both in terms of scores of students and in terms of lowering the price.[11]

Mr. Sibal, like Negroponte, considers Aakash to be the panacea to all problems. It's not just that. Mr. Sibal also wants Aakash to be the cheapest tablet. The product design was given to Indian Institute of Technology (IIT), Jodhpur, a new IIT where the curriculum includes product development along with traditional engineering training. The IIT system has produced world-class engineers and computer scientists, including respected Venture Capitalist Vinod Khosla and Cisco Chief Technology Officer Padmasree Warrior.

After the tender was put out for the production of Aakash, the cheapest bid came from DataWind, a Canadian company run by brothers Suneet and Raja Tuli. DataWind's track record was a single gadget that had flopped. But DataWind's bid was unbeatably low: It would produce 100,000 Aakash for ₹227 million, or $4.3 million and Aakash seemed, finally, to be a reality.

Hundreds of Aakash tablets arrived at IIT Jodhpur for testing. The problems were immediately evident. According to one source close to the university, a third of the devices didn't start at all. Most of those that did either failed the basic drop test, overheated quickly, or saw their screens freeze until the battery with a life of two hours, ran out. A peek inside the box revealed circuitry and imported components held together by electrical tape.[12] Several reviews of the device, including one by respected journal *IEEE Spectrum*, dismissed it as clunky and slow. The result was the start of blame game between IIT Jodhpur and contractor DataWind. To break the stalemate, the government transferred the project to IIT Mumbai. It is not clear on what basis the IITs were chosen for design and DataWind for producing hardware. Neither of them have any experience in producing low-cost mass-produced electronic devices. Today, products are designed and produced using global expertise and supply chain. India does not have any infrastructure for producing mass-market computing devices. A glance at any shop in Delhi's Nehru Place or Mumbai's Lamington Road will tell you that not a single product is 'Made in India.'

The original Aakash tablet, DataWind's Tuli and others readily admit, was a disaster. Underpowered, it had an old-style resistive touch screen that made it almost unusable. (All modern touch-based devices, including the Aakash 2, have capacitive touch screens.) As a consequence of learning from failure, the commercial version of the Aakash 2 tablet, known as the Ubislate, and its price are a marvel of functionality. It's a 7-inch tablet with a processor about as fast as the one contained in the original iPad. Sure, it's occasionally slow when compared to tablets costing ten times as much, but it's perfectly suited to be the sole computing device of a student in a developing country like India. And, as other reviewers have noted, it's more than good enough to find a place in the homes of consumers in rich countries, as well.[13]

The first Akash failed because:

• The vision was not backed by a sturdy execution strategy.

• The developer and manufacturer were not on same wavelength. The specifications kept on changing.

• The product was hastily launched without rigorous testing, same as the Nano car. IIT Jodhpur is a new institution, which did not have the infrastructure for techno-commercial study and testing.

The Government is not in the job of product design and manufacturing, which it tried to do. Tablet design is a nimble activity as technology and market are fast changing, especially in a VUCA world, where companies like Blackberry and previously Iridium have learnt at a heavy cost. When Akash I was launched in October 2011, only 10 percent tablets in the markets were priced below ₹10,000, while it was 70 percent in July 2013. The cheapest tablet in the Indian market as of July 2013 was Wishtel Ira Thing 2 retailing at ₹2,990. This device has less RAM than Akash 4, but in all other respects it appears to be the same.[14]

Image and perception are as important as the product. Both suffered in Akash as in the Nano, reducing their marketability in the future.

The history of innovation is filled with false starts and innumerable obstacles. There is no innovation that succeeds in all its elements from lab to market in first attempt. However, success comes to those who learn from their errors and build that learning in future projects.

It is also seen, in our hierarchical corporate culture, that when visionary people such as Mr. Tata or Mr. Sibal voice their desires, perhaps to create something for posterity to remember them, no real dialogue on the feasibility takes place internally. Every person in the organization, which holds the leader in awe, races to ensure that the desire is converted to reality. Mr. Tata, perhaps in hindsight, would be more remembered for instituting a prize for the best failed idea. 'Failure is a Gold Mine!' proclaims the now retired Chairman, hoping to leave the sprawling company with enough of an innovative spark to keep it relevant on the global stage.[15] That failure should increasingly be seen as a central part of any business strategy that would perhaps be viewed as the most enduring legacy of a leader who will long be remembered for putting India on the global corporate map.

However, at this stage, neither of these two products can be seen as total losses as revisions continue to be launched at regular intervals with new features and marketing plans, in the hope that something may click.

NOTES

1. 'Interview With Ratan Tata: Making of Nano,' *Economic Times*, 11 January 2008.

2. 'Small Nano Attracts Really Big Numbers,' *Hindustan Times*, 13 January 2008.

3. 'India's 2010–11 Vehicle Sales Seen Up 12–13%,' *Mint*, 8 January 2010.

4. '2-Wheeler Industry to See 4–5% Volume Growth in FY13: ICRA,' *Business Standard*, 9 July 2013.

5. 'Urban India Doesn't Like to Finance Two-Wheelers,' *Mint*, 10 January 2013.

6. 'Tata's Nano, the Car That Few Want to Buy,' *New York Times*, 9 December 2010.

7. Matt Eyring, 'Matt: Learning from Tata's Nano Mistakes,' *Harvard Business Review*, January 2011.

8. http://autoportal.com/newcars/tata/nano/sales-statistics/.

9. 'Aakash Is No Silver Bullet,' *The Hindu*, 29 March 2013.

10. 'How the Failed Aakash Tablet Is an Object Lesson In India's Long Road Ahead to Tech Innovation,' *Fast Company*, 18 June 2012.

11. Ibid., 10.

12. Ibid., 9.

13. 'Is India's Ultra-cheap Akash Tablet Doomed?' *New York Times*, 1 January 2013.

14. 'Will Akash 4 Deliver the Goods?' *Mint*, 7 July 2013.

15. Rita Mcgrath, 'Failure Is a Gold Mine for India's Tata,' *HBR Blogs*, 11 April 2011.

XI

RANBAXY LABORATORIES LIMITED
Conspiracy of Silence

There are two ways to be fooled. One is to believe what isn't true; the other is to refuse to believe what is true.

–Søren Kierkegaard, author

There was a time in the 1990s when Ranbaxy Laboratories Ltd was talked of as one of the handful of Indian companies that had the potential and the business vision to be a future multinational coming out of emerging markets such as India and China. Today, that promise lies wasted, destroyed by a culture of systematic and sustained falsification of records, so crucial in the pharmaceutical business. This episode has shaken the foundation of the Indian pharmaceutical industry, which exports products valued at $15 billion annually. Ranbir Singh and Gurbax Singh, the men who started the company in 1951 (and lent their names to it) could scarcely have thought that their endeavor would soon be among India's leading pharma companies. That success began under Bhai Mohan Singh, who acquired the company in 1952 and laid the seeds for its rapid rise.[1]

His son, late Parvinder Singh, recognized the opportunity to reverse-engineer and produce off-patent drugs and sell them cheap in markets like the United States and Europe, where the high prices of the original drugs had rendered them out of the reach of the poor. The strategy paid rich dividends and by 2005, the company was posting over a billion dollars in global sales. His untimely death in July 1999 may well have loosened all controls at the company, and in the quest for growth, which was scorching through the decade and the early 2000s, the men who ran the company after him, including his sons who headed the company then, clearly sacrificed quality.[2]

One wonders why companies and their leaders do not possess the ability to learn from others, as exemplified by Glaxo Smith Kline's (GSK) quality problems at their Puerto Rico Plant, which resulted in a record fine of US$750 million by FDA, the US Federal Drug Agency. This quality problem, which was totally avoidable and which grew in severity and complexity over a period of time, was replicated by Ranbaxy, which followed in the path shown by Glaxo. The matter is even more perplexing considering that the Glaxo case was widely and threadbare analyzed in the media, both print and television.

A former quality control (QC) manager at GSK, a whistleblower, exposed a series of contamination problems at their drugs factory in Puerto Rico, and subsequent cover-up by company bosses. The company repeatedly ignored serious failings, including mold and fungus in tablets and capsules, mixed drug types and doses in the same bottle, wrong labeling, different strengths in same bottle, presence of micro-organisms and so on. The QC manager first warned her senior management of the numerous violations after being sent by GSK to investigate problems in July 2002, following a warning letter to the company from FDA.

Over the next 10 months, she repeatedly alerted a string of GSK executives to a catalogue of breaches, only to be blocked and eventually sacked in 2003. Legal papers show that GSK plant employees lied to FDA inspectors and that the company's executives refused to acknowledge the gravity of the violations and act. This deception was undertaken because the FDA would not consider approvals for two new treatments until the issues mentioned in the warning letter had been resolved. The two products were subsequently approved by the regulator.[3]

Court documents show how the QC manager was gradually sidelined, despite increasing complaints to a growing number of senior bosses as she recommended that GSK stop shipping all product from this plant, stop manufacturing product for two weeks in order to investigate and resolve the issues raised and the impact on released batches, and notify the FDA about the product mix-ups.[4] After being ignored by the CEO, she then reported the company to the FDA in August 2003. In October, after another conversation with GSK's compliance department, the whistleblower told the regulator that the company had no intention of acting on her report; three weeks later the FDA began its own investigation. In a statement, the drugs group said: 'We regret that we operated the Cidra facility in a manner that was inconsistent with current good manufacturing practice (cGMP). GSK worked hard to resolve fully the manufacturing issues at the Cidra facility prior to its closure in 2009.'[5]

GSK was fined a record US$750 million by the FDA, and the whistleblower got US$96 million as a reward.

The first warning signals for Ranbaxy came in September 2008 when the FDA issued two warning letters to Ranbaxy and an import alert for generic drugs produced by two manufacturing plants in India. The FDA release cited serious manufacturing deficiencies affecting over 30 different generic drugs. Within six months, the FDA halted reviews of all drug applications, including data developed at Ranbaxy's Paonta Sahib plant in India, because of a practice of 'falsified data and test results in approved and pending drug applications.'[6]

But with Japanese pharma major Daiichi Sankyo Co. Ltd buying a controlling stake in Ranbaxy for up to $4.6 billion that year, the warnings were swept under the carpet as personal fortunes swelled. Clearly, while the operational abilities of the Singh brothers, Malvinder and Shivinder, might have left something to be desired, their timing was impeccable as they made nearly $2 billion from the deal with Daiichi Sankyo. The same cannot be said about the due-diligence process followed by the Japanese company before acquiring the tainted Indian company.[7]

Circa 2003. Dinesh Thakur returned to India from the United States in 2003, where he worked for ten years with a leading US pharmaceutical company, to take up a senior quality management position with India's largest drug company – Ranbaxy Laboratories. He came across evidence of systematic fraud. The company was manipulating research data as well as producing substandard drugs.

In an expose carried out by *Fortune* magazine in August 2004, suspecting serious deviations from GMP as defined by international regulatory agencies, Thakur's boss Dr. Raj Kumar, R&D Head, who too had joined Ranbaxy around that time, directed Thakur to put aside his other responsibilities and go through the company's portfolio – ultimately, every drug, every market, every production line – and uncover the truth about its testing practices and where the company's liabilities lay. The first action he took was to stop Ranbaxy's antibiotic for his three-year-old son's ear infection, which was not getting better in spite of three days' intensive therapy.[8]

Thakur gave each of his project managers a part of the world and asked them to compare Ranbaxy's manufacturing data against the claims made to regulators. His own efforts began with a visit to a company regulatory official. It was a depressing conversation. The official explained that the company culture was for management to dictate the results it wanted and for those beneath to bend the process to achieve it. He described how Ranbaxy took its greatest liberties in markets where regulation was weakest and the risk of discovery was lowest, such as Africa. He acknowledged there were no data supporting some of Ranbaxy's drug applications in those regions and that the management were aware of this.[9]

The heart of good manufacturing is documentation. Without it, there is no way to verify quality, investigate problems or know whether your drug will improve health or lead to its deterioration. Since the minutest changes can make the difference between a robust product and one that degrades and becomes toxic, each step must be recorded and validated. Any misrepresentation, mixing of data streams or deviation from procedure invalidates – and potentially adulterates – the drugs.[10]

Ranbaxy was used to operating under India's lax drug regulatory mechanism and systematically manipulated the FDA's honor system where the US drug agency relies on data provided by the companies themselves. 'We depend on that information to be truthful,' a senior FDA official said. The rough outlines of the fraud at Ranbaxy first emerged in a 2008 court filing by the US Justice Department. However, its extent and depth and the involvement of top company executives had not been previously revealed. *Fortune* magazine has also uncovered evidence that the company's misconduct continued well into 2009, even after the FDA restricted the company's activities.

The *Fortune* magazine's account is based on more than 1,000 confidential Ranbaxy documents, including internal reports, memos, e-mails, hundreds of pages of FDA documents obtained through Freedom of Information Act requests and court records.[11]

As Thakur's project managers gathered data and interviewed company scientists and executives, they stumbled onto Ranbaxy's open secret: The company manipulated almost every aspect of its manufacturing process to quickly produce impressive-looking data that would bolster its bottom line. 'This was not something that was concealed,' Thakur says. It was 'common knowledge among senior managers of the company, heads of research and development, people responsible for formulation to the clinical people.'[12]

Lying to regulators and backdating and forgery were commonplace, he says. The company even forged its own standard operating procedures, which the FDA inspectors rely on to assess whether a company is following its own policies. Company scientists told Thakur's staff that they were directed to substitute cheaper, lower-quality ingredients in place of better ingredients, to manipulate test parameters to accommodate higher impurities and even to substitute branded drugs in lieu of their own generics in bioequivalence tests to produce better results.

Six other pharma veterans who worked for Ranbaxy in the United States as recently as 2010 told *Fortune* they found themselves in a corporate culture like nothing they'd ever experienced before. Executives approached the regulatory system as an obstacle to be gamed. They bragged about who had most artfully deceived regulators. Until 2005 the company didn't even have a functioning patient-safety department, and patient complaints piled up in boxes, ignored, uncategorized and unreported to the FDA as required.

After just ten days of intensive research, the R&D Head, who compiled the findings into a four-page report for then-CEO Brian Tempest.

The confidential report laid bare systemic fraud in Ranbaxy's worldwide regulatory filings. The company not only invented data but also fraudulently mixed and matched data, taking the best results from manufacturing in one market and presenting it to regulators elsewhere as data unique to the drugs in their markets.

For its HIV drugs, the report found that Ranbaxy had used ingredients that failed purity tests and blended them with good ingredients until the resulting mix met requirements. Such a combination could degrade or become toxic far more quickly than drugs made from the high-quality materials.

In a 'private and confidential' e-mail sent to CEO Tempest along with his report, Kumar noted that 'it appears that some of these issues were apparent over a year ago and I cannot find any documents which sought to address these concerns or resolve the issues …' Kumar emphasized that he could 'not allow any information to be used for any dossier unless fully supported by data.' He made it clear that he planned to follow the law.[13]

CEO Tempest had assured Kumar that the company would do the right thing. So on an evening in late 2004, several months after assigning Thakur to dig up the truth, Kumar found himself before five members of the scientific committee of the board of directors, including Tempest and the Chairman of the board.

Kumar made clear that Ranbaxy had lied to regulators and falsified data in every country examined in the report. 'More than 200 products in more than 40 countries' have "elements of data that were fabricated to support business needs." Business needs,' the report showed, was a euphemism for ways in which Ranbaxy could minimize cost, maximize profit and dupe regulators into approving substandard drugs.[14] No market or type of drug was exempt, including anti-retrovirals purchased by the United States and WHO as part of a program to fight HIV in Africa. In Europe, for example, the company used ingredients from unapproved sources, invented shelf-life data, tested different formulations of the drug than the ones it sold and made undocumented changes to the manufacturing process.

In entire markets – including Asia, Latin America, Africa, United States and Europe – the company had simply not tested the drugs and had invented all the data. Noting Ranbaxy's agreement to manufacture brand-name drugs, 'We have also put our partners (Bayer & Merck) at risk by using suspect data.'[15]

Kumar proposed a drastic course: pull all compromised drugs off the market; repeat all suspect tests; inform regulators of every case of switched data; and create a process for linking the right data to the right drugs. 'A short-term loss of revenue is better than a long-term losing proposition for the entire business.'[16]

Kumar completed the presentation to a silent boardroom. Only one director, a scientist, showed any surprise about the findings. The others appeared more astonished by Kumar's declaration that if he was not given full authority to fix the problems, he would resign.

The silence told Kumar everything he needed to know.

Within two days of the board meeting, he submitted his resignation: 'Given the serious nature of the issues we discussed,' he wrote, his only choice was to withdraw 'gracefully but immediately.' He had been at Ranbaxy less than four months.

As in the case of Glaxo, the company forced Thakur to resign. The reason – he was accused of watching porn sites after the management had asked the IT department to plant porn IP sites on his computer. He then complained to the FDA and as in case of Glaxo became a whistleblower. The FDA banned products from three plants. Ranbaxy had to withdraw several products and even lost the opportunity to exclusively launch off-patent atorvastatin, the biggest drug in the US market. Ranbaxy eventually settled the case in May 2012 by pleading guilty and paying a fine of $500 million (around ₹2,800 crores). The total loss is still being ascertained. The loss of business in the US market alone is estimated to be $1 billion, the cost of loss of reputation, incalculable.[17]

The company has since acknowledged that in 2003 and 2005 it was informed of cGMP violations by consultants it hired to conduct audits at its Paonta Sahib and Dewas facilities.[18]

Ranbaxy's is no ordinary misdemeanor. The US Department of Justice said the company had 'pleaded guilty today to felony charges relating to the manufacture of certain adulterated drugs.' Felony is a serious criminal charge. By accepting to pay a criminal fine and forfeiture and agreeing to settle civil claims, Ranbaxy may have succeeded in effecting damage control. That does not, however, mitigate the seriousness of its actions.[19] The damage done to India's substantial drugs export business is incalculable.

Both Daiichi and Shivendra Singh, ex-Chairman of Ranbaxy, are blaming each other in a Singapore Court. In 2014, Daiichi sold the troubled company to Sun Pharma.

WILFUL BLINDNESS

What led to this huge failure at Ranbaxy for which the company is still paying the price? One obvious reason could be 'wilful blindness,' that is, why we ignore the obvious at our peril as analyzed in the book *Wilful Blindness* by Margaret Heffernan. It comes into play when people deny truths that are too painful, too frightening to confront. The problem arises when we use the same mechanism to deny uncomfortable truths that cry out for acknowledgment, debate, action, and change. The sheer complexities of many businesses mean they are impossible to fully manage – no one can know everything that is happening in an organization. Organizations naturally 'self-select' people who fit in with map of reality (people with a different point of view get weeded out), leading to a consensual (and closed) view – they see what they want to see and do not see what they do not want to see and when presented with 'facts' we will often choose to ignore them rather than sway from our point of view.[20]

Ranbaxy and many other companies are in the habit of hoodwinking the Indian regulatory authorities, which do not have the will or manpower to take on such powerful companies. Ranbaxy started taking these shortcuts in African and Latin American countries and as their appetite increased, they developed the mindset that they can mislead American authorities too. We have an innate drive to be in groups. Physiologically we are programmed to belong. When rejected, the same chemicals associated with pain are released in our bodies. And when accepted into groups, opiates ('pleasure') are released. When we are in a team, it helps validate our self-image and our views (which we will go to great lengths to protect).[21]

So it is no surprise that we try to stay inside groups and not be rejected. This leads to high levels of compliance (sometimes even when it crosses our own moral boundaries). The more people who witness an improper situation, the less likely anything will be done about it. Our compliance (and hence willingness to turn a blind eye to things) is partly driven by our learned response to obey authority figures. At Ranbaxy, as more and more managers got involved in this complicity, which led to increased business in global markets, the inverse value system got further ingrained in the organization culture.

The book further points out that it takes courage, perseverance and an outsider's perspective to dare to challenge. In Ranbaxy's case, it was two recent appointees who unraveled this gigantic fraud.

As we have seen in a majority of cases, speed is a major cause of failure. Ranbaxy Laboratories' desire to quickly launch products in the US market led to most of the data fudging and other malpractices in the company, as claimed by two former executives of the company to *Economic Times*. 'Most of the tampering happened at the time of filing the Abbreviated New Drug Applications (ANDAs) to FDA in the hope of getting a first to file (FTF) in the US market,' said a senior executive of the company who did not want to be identified. The United States has a provision under Hatch Waxman Act where generic drug makers can make a killing during a six-month window of marketing exclusivity if they file the first valid ANDAs with FDA. This is an incentive given by the FDA to encourage launch of cheaper generics.[22]

The same article further reports that the strategy of Ranbaxy, it is alleged, was to falsify data in its filing, but then get the quality of the product right between the periods of filing the application and launching the drug in the market. 'These are not issues which one could easily spot during inspections of facilities,' said a former executive. That probably explains why multiple auditors and regulators who descended in hordes after Ranbaxy's FDA problems became public couldn't find much fault with the facilities. That could also explain why Ranbaxy's sample of drugs randomly picked from the markets across global markets and tested by several regulators didn't fail the quality tests

The company's latest MD, Arun Sawhney, said in May 2013 that Ranbaxy was a different company now. 'The steps we have taken over the recent years reflect the wide-ranging efforts of the current board and management to address certain conduct of the past and ensure that Ranbaxy moves forward with integrity and professionalism in everything we do,' he said.[23]

However, the ground realities tell a different story. Even five years after Daiichi Sankyo bought Ranbaxy, and replacement of two CEOs, the new management was not been totally able to eradicate the compliance problems at their plants. As late as September 2013, Ranbaxy's Mohali plant (the third one) was put on import ban by the FDA due to quality problems.[24] Further, the company's Tonasa plant, which manufacturers bulk drugs called Active Pharmaceutical Ingredients (APIs), was banned from supplying to the United States in November 2013. This is a much more serious problem as the current import ban has been slapped on the company's only remaining facility in India that was supplying active ingredients to Ohm Laboratories, New Jersey – Ranbaxy's only remaining FDA-approved facility. It was getting over 70 percent of the APIs it needed from Tonasa. The latest development has killed market expectations of a quick turnaround in Ranbaxy's operations.[25]

LACK OF EFFECTIVE CORPORATE GOVERNANCE

The second reason could be the inadequate mechanism of corporate governance in India and Ranbaxy in particular. Among the independent directors at Ranbaxy in 2004 were Tejendra Khanna, retired IAS Secretary, Government of India, and later Lt. Governor of Delhi; Vivek Bharat Ram, an eminent industrialist; Gurcharan Das, former CEO of Proctor & Gamble; and other experienced business personalities. Ranbaxy's shareholding data as on 31 March 2004 shows that promoters' shareholding was 32.04 percent, while foreign shareholding and Indian institutions' shareholding were 32.98 percent (including FII's shareholding of 22.68 percent) and 15.16 percent, respectively. One would expect corporate governance of the highest order with the illustrious board and significant foreign and institutional shareholding, however, the reality was different.

The corporate governance failures manifested in the board's failure to check fraud, the absence of adequate risk management systems and the perpetuating unethical culture. It may be appropriate to conclude that independent directors did not act diligently. It has been reported in the media that Tejendra

Khanna and other board members were present in the science committee meeting held on 21 December 2004, in which detailed presentation was made on widespread lapses and fudging of data. If it is true, they cannot claim innocence.[26]

Corporate integrity is about culture and sadly ours is a culture where unethical behavior is condoned and rewarded. [27] In case after case quoted in this book, the boards have allowed the company in their charge to slide into avoidable failures by not discharging their fiduciary duties to stakeholders. Lax external supervision, either by government or chartered accountants, only emboldened the boards to allow the wink-and-nod culture to embed. As more and more Indian firms seek to do business abroad, this culture of wilful cheating would be hard to shake off. Enron and Arthur Anderson are examples of the extreme penalties that companies pay when their corporate behavior strays from their vision.

It is not only Ranbaxy that failed to learn from others, but more recently, the FDA has come down heavily on Wockhardt Limited, another large Indian drug company, where products from its two plants were banned from entering the United States. It seems mindsets are hard to change.

This whole exercise also shows how difficult it is for an organization culture to change. It is slow and costly. Ranbaxy's problem seems to be one of a culture so steeped in deceit that it may well need enterprise-wide cleansing and reorientation. To avoid such gigantic failures, it is more appropriate to do things right in the first place. Don't soften the brutal facts. Solutions don't begin until problems are named, described, owned and confronted. When you don't dig into your own issues, someone else will dig your grave.

NOTES

1. 'How Ranbaxy Lost Sight of a Vision in Pursuit of Short-Term Profit,' *Economic Times*, 24 January 2014.

2. Ibid., 1.

3. 'GlaxoSmithKline Whistleblower Wins Record £61m Payout,' *Guardian*, 27 October 2010.

4. Ibid., 3.

5. Ibid.

6. 'Ranbaxy Forged Data, Test Results, Says US Drug Regulator,' *Business Standard*, 26 February 2009.

7. Ibid., 1.

8. 'Dirty Medicine,' *Fortune*, 15 May 2013.

9. Ibid., 8.

10. Ibid.

11. Ibid.

12. Ibid.

13. Ibid.

14. Ibid.

15. Ibid.

16. Ibid.

17. Ibid.

18. 'Ranbaxy Holds Up an Ugly Mirror to Corporate India,' *Mint*, 26 May 2013.

19. Ibid., 18.

20. Margaret Heffernan, *Wilful Blindness* (Doubleday, 2011).

21. Ibid., 20.

22. 'Rush to Quickly Launch Products & Get US Nod Led Ranbaxy to Fudging,' *Economic Times*, 24 May 2013.

23. Ibid., 22.

24. 'Indian Drugmaker Ranbaxy Faces New US Regulation Woes,' *Fox News*, 16 September 2013.

25. 'Ranbaxy Stocks May Take More Time to Improve, Long-Term Investors Proceed Cautiously,' *Economic Times*, 25 January 2014.

26. 'Corporate Governance Failure at Ranbaxy?' *Business Standard*, 9 June 2013.

XII

ARVIND MILLS

Phoenix-Like Resurrection

Success can be achieved in two ways. One is like climbing a ladder. It is fast, but a ladder can be unstable and you can fall to where you started from. The other is like climbing a mountain, where you experience ascent, descent as well as plateau on your way to the peak. As we have seen, many companies use highly leveraged debt as ladder to finance growth. However, if the market does not behave as projected in strategic planning, the interest and capital payments can cripple the company. Once they fall, the next rise is through mountain climbing, that is, learning through experience.

Arvind Mills, the flagship company of the Lalbhai Group, founded in 1931, is one of India's leading composite manufacturers of textiles. It produces a range of cotton shirting, denim, knits and khaki fabrics. It is India's largest denim manufacturer apart from being the world's fourth-largest producer and exporter of denim. In the early 1980s, the company brought denim into the domestic market; thus started the jeans revolution in India.

In the 1990s, the Lalbhai Group decided to put all its eggs in denim market and took on huge debts to finance capacity expansion. Its total long-term Indian and international debt was estimated at ₹2,700 crores.

At the time Arvind Mills started this expansion, the composite textile industry was already in decline in its major centers – Mumbai and Ahmedabad. A high wage structure, low productivity and surplus labor in the textile mills rendered its businesses unviable in most of the product categories in which it competed. The emergence of power looms in the 1970s further exasperated the problems faced by Arvind Mills. The government's indirect tax system at that time also reduced the profitability of its product lines. In the mid-1980s, Arvind Mills switched to high-quality fabrics requiring technical superiority that the power looms could not hope to match.

That period saw Arvind at its highest level of profitability. There could be no better time, concluded the management, for a rethink on strategy. The Arvind management coined a new word for it new strategy – 'Reno vision.' It simply meant a new way of looking at issues, of seeing more than the obvious, and that became the corporate philosophy. The national focus paved the way for international focus and Arvind's markets shifted from domestic to global, a market that expected and accepted only quality goods. An in-depth analysis of the world textile market proved an eye opener. People the world over were shifting from synthetic to natural fabrics. Cottons were the largest growing segment. But where conventional wisdom pointed to popular priced segments, 'Reno vision' pointed to high-quality premium niches. Thus in 1987–1988, Arvind entered the export market for two sections: denim for leisure and fashion wear, and high-quality fabric for cotton shirting and trousers. By 1991, Arvind touched the 1,600 million meters of denim per year mark, and it was the third largest producer of denim in the world.[1]

The demand for denim took a nosedive, and in 2001 and the company came close to bankruptcy by defaulting on interest payments on loans. It was losing ₹1 crore per day. This bankruptcy was averted through deft negotiations with 85 Indian and international lenders to restructure the loans.[2] It was at this time that Sanjay Lalbhai drafted a proposal for restructuring its entire debt. In a way, this proposal was a unique one, because it had never been tried before in India, and it made the task of convincing the lenders to agree to this plan a more complex one. As a result of the restructuring plan, the interest burden came down substantially and got Arvind Mills the distinction of becoming the first Indian corporate to restructure its entire debt in a single go.[3] Also, post restructuring, Arvind reported a profit of ₹10 crores for the first quarter of the financial year 2002, after a gap of three years.[4] The boom in demand rebounded to such an extent that in spite of its huge capacity, Arvind is buying denim from the market to meet its order book. The average denim price realizations have jumped 20 percent due to buoyancy in the denim industry, shift in market mix, product mix and rupee depreciation. Constant thrust toward product innovation has helped Arvind meet the fashion needs of Levi, Gap, Old Navy, Zara, Nautica and so on. Looking at the return of denim only recently with a new wide base, industry observers expect denim buoyancy to continue for the next few years.[5]

The sheer instinct of Sanjay Lalbhai to survive in the business coupled with some bold and frank decisions had enabled Arvind Mills to come out of its problems and stand on its feet once again. In Sanjay Lalbhai's words, 'The key learning from this experience was to not leverage the balance sheet. If things no one can plan for happen suddenly, there will be financial problems.'[6] What went wrong with Arvind's denim strategy?

The company decided to enter the international market in a big way in the 1990s. Till then, it was largely a domestic player with little exposure to foreign markets. The denim expansion plans took place, probably on the advice of a major international strategy consultant, in spite of early indications that alternative cotton fabrics were slowly replacing it. Dressy, feminine styles were reintroduced over the course of the decade, as women's fashion moved away from the more unisex styles of the 1990s.[7] The company should have first dipped its fingers in the water, tested its temperature and then immersed its entire body. In other words, the first steps, especially in a market that is not only new but also more complex than the domestic one, should be small. Learn from it and gradually accelerate as advised by Peter Senge in *The Fifth Discipline*.[8]

Taking a discontinuous, 'bet-the-company' leap could send the company barreling down a deep and dangerous crevice, ending in the thud of extinction. With revenue increases of 25 percent a year, the world's best growth companies do it a few steps at a time, each bringing options and new capabilities as suggested by a McKinsey study.[9] No formulas, just astute bundling of competences, skills, assets and relationships. Each step makes money in its own right; each is a step up in that it adds new institutional skills that better prepare the company to open up and take advantage of opportunities; and each is a step roughly in the direction of a broader vision of where the company wishes to be. The staircase approach of continuously compounding skills and options is consistent with the competitive reality of most industries. The competitive landscape is changing so rapidly that it is impossible to predict paths several years ahead. Building a staircase explicitly recognizes that the appropriate strategy for any company depends on where it is today and on the state of the world down the road. As Peter Senge says, 'Go slow to move fast,'[10] a paradox that will keep companies from extinction in a VUCA world.

Arvind Mills should also have developed peripheral vision to see the changes taking place in the economy, especially in the United States, which affects purchasing power, as well as paid close attention to changing fashion trends. This would have moderated the company's ambitions.

NOTES

1. http://www.arvind-amd.com/history.html.

2. 'Arvind Mills: From Near Bankruptcy to Reinvention,' *Economic Times*, 14 December 2012.

3. 'Arvind Mills Ltd.: Restructuring Paying Off,' *The Analyst Magazine* (IUP), July 2002.

4. Bernadette D'Silva and Annie Beena Joseph, 'A Study on the Implications of Corporate Restructuring,' *Sanchayan* 2 (1), 2013.

5. 'No Longer the Blues,' *Economic Times*, 28 January 2002.

6. 'Arvind Mills: Wearing the Right Fit,' *Business Today*, 5 August 2012.

7. '2000–09 in Fashion,' Wikipedia.

8. Peter Senge, *The Fifth Discipline* (Crown Publishing, 1990).

9. Mehrdad Baghai et al., 'Staircases to Growth,' *McKinsey Quarterly*, November 1996.

10. Ibid., 8.

WHY FIRMS FAIL

Behavioral and Systemic Factors

In our journey to uncover common causes for failures in a VUCA world, we went through the history of failures as well as review some contemporary cases from India. There are certain common causes that link all failures, whether historical or contemporary, empires or corporates, in this book and out of it.

These causes for failure can be classified into two groups: (1) human or behavioral and (2) systemic or organizational. However, for celebrities such as movie or sports stars, the cause is primarily behavioral. It can even be said that organizational or systemic causes are also a result of behavioral ones.

BEHAVIORAL CAUSES

Arrogance or Hubris

> The person who is the star of previous era is often the last one to adapt to change, the last one to yield to logic of a strategic inflection point and tends to fall harder than most.
>
> –Andrew S. Grove, *Only the Paranoid Survive*

One word that repeats itself in most cases is 'arrogance' and also related to it is 'hubris.' There are countless books, articles, movies, videos and so on that universally call 'arrogance' *the king of failures*. 'Hubris' is the cause for the downfall of celebrities in entertainment, sports or business. This is also the conclusion of a majority of case studies in this book. Jim Collins in his book *How the Mighty Fall* provides an insightful analysis and his chilling message is: 'Whether you prevail or fall, endure or die, depends more on what you do to yourself than on what the world does to you.'[1] Most failures are self-inflicted wounds that are allowed to fester and ultimately poison the leader and his organization.

Mike Tyson was one of the greatest boxers of all time. By 1988, he was the undisputed heavyweight champion of the world and held the record as the youngest boxer to win the WBC, WBA and IBF heavyweight titles in 20 years. By 1990, Tyson seemed to have lost direction, and his personal life was in disarray. He was arrested for rape and theft and spent time in jail. After his parole in 1993, he easily won his comeback matches and made a huge fortune. On 9 July 1997, Tyson's boxing license was rescinded for biting an opponent's ear. It was followed by Tyson's conviction for assaulting two motorists. In August 2003, after years of financial struggle, Tyson filed for bankruptcy. He was also convicted of possessing drugs.

Later, Mike Tyson went public to reflect on his life and career:

> I wanted to see myself as a tough guy. Nothing in the world is more humbling than getting your ass kicked.[2]
>
> The first stage of my life was just a whole bunch of selfishness. Just a whole bunch of gifts to myself and people who didn't necessarily deserve it. Greatest man on the planet? I wasn't half the man I thought I was. If I allow myself to think that I'm a super, great megalomania fighter, my ego, my self-absorbed would take me to a very dark place and I am not willing to go there any more.[3]

It's just a simple question of humility. If you're not humble, life will visit humbleness upon you. I was too into that character, that 'Iron Mike' guy. And that guy was pretty toxic for me at that particular time. So I had to get away from that. This is just a part of me that I just don't like and don't understand. Tyson has changed for the better. He's always been regarded as the worst guy on the planet but behind that tough image? he shows there is a soft, gentle one that melts like butter. Tyson is now a changed man and for the better.[4]

Do we all have to go through this trauma to understand ourselves?

Nothing brings to light the power of arrogance in bringing about failures than the career contrast between Sachin Tendulkar and Vinod Kambli. Both started their careers in February 1988 with an unbeaten partnership of 664 runs. It seems incredible now, but at the time many observers believed that Kambli was the more talented of the two. And it is the reckless combination of talent and serial indiscipline that makes Kambli a 'reverse sweep.' Kambli followed his fellow world-beater into the Indian side in 1993 at the age of 21 and proceeded to start his test career like a new Don Bradman. In his first seven tests, he hit two double hundreds and two other hundreds and had an average of 113. It was all downhill from here. He was to feature in only another ten test matches, playing his last at the age of 23, and by then his average had slipped to a still creditable but now mortal 54.20. Kambli also featured in the one-day side, from which he was dropped and recalled nine times before playing his last ODI in 2000.[5] Later, he tried his hand at acting and many other ventures, all flops. Very recently, Sreesanth has also fallen in the same trap.

In contrast, Tendulkar was a model of discipline and decorum. He did not speak much and let his bat do the talking. He also suffered failures and off-form but did not allow these to take hold of him. He says, 'My family was always there to keep an eye and keep me grounded at all times.'[6] He did not blame anybody for his occasional poor showings while Kambli has blamed everyone under the sun for his debacles, *except* himself. Vinod Kambli had all the promise of a cricketing great, a person who got several chances to prove himself but chose to bowl himself out repeatedly. With each inning Tendulkar became a more polished diamond while Kambli remained a rough-cut.

Unlike Kambli, comedian Johnny Lever did not start his career with a bang.

> My first show was in Patkar Hall next to Bombay Hospital. It was a total flop. I was so nervous standing in front of all those people that I completely froze. I forgot all my lines and the audience booed me off the stage. I realised that day that you have to earn the audience's appreciation. They aren't fools.

To his credit, Lever didn't slink off, tail between legs. He practiced long and hard, got back on the same stage, and won the audience over. 'I had this determination to make it, on that very stage. It was like a fire within me. And I did.'[7]

Success and the adoration that breeds can bring unimaginable riches in India. But you can play the game two ways. Be aloof but businesslike and watch the money roll in, as Tendulkar did, or get sucked into the fame game, something Kambli, with his sudden passion for bling and booze, did rather too enthusiastically for those running Indian cricket. When it came, his fall was sudden and permanent.[8]

Throughout history, hubris has been cited as a common reason for leadership failure. One of the more famous examples of hubris at work was Napoleon's Russian campaign of 1812 in which he lost his army and his empire. In June of 1812, Napoleon Bonaparte was ruler of the Empire of France, King of Italy and master of the European continent. At the head of the Grand Army, numbering over 500,000 men, the largest force ever assembled at that point in history, he set out to conquer the one nation in Europe he had not yet subjugated – Imperial Russia. In December of the same year, less than 20,000 of those men would make it home alive, and all that General Napoleon had accomplished in his meteoric career would soon be lost by Emperor Napoleon. Napoleon was a republican general who rose to power after the French Revolution. First, he took the title of dictator and later crowned himself emperor repudiating the principles on which the Republic was founded.

Many explanations have been offered for the rout, poor planning, bad weather, insightful Russian leadership, but the real reason, which brought about all these other reasons, was Napoleon's arrogance and hubris. Hubris has been defined as exaggerated pride, self-confidence or arrogance born largely out of narcissism. Napoleon possessed all its symptoms: unbounded confidence given his past successes and the accompanying narcissism, the adulation that fed that narcissism. As a result, he was able to convince himself that, despite all of the obvious obstacles, he could, through force of will, succeed in bringing Russia and especially Emperor Alexander I, the sole power on the Continent that refused to pay him homage, to their knees. His campaign was less about the need to thwart the hostile intentions of a rival power, and more about the need to satisfy a hubris-infected personality with an arrogant confidence about what great feats could be accomplished.

Napoleon clearly excelled in the skills of warfare, as he planned and implemented winning campaigns. Before the

Russian invasion, he had amassed a record of 35 wins versus only 3 losses. Well before the invasion of Russia, Napoleon's top lieutenants argued that the chances of failure and the cost in lives and materiel were high. Napoleon rejected their warnings, pointing out that his plans called for a quick, decisive and therefore low-cost campaign. He had conducted such campaigns before and saw no difference this time. He mistakenly believed that the Russian campaign too will be over quickly within three months, by autumn, and his army would return home triumphant before winter set in; consequently, he did not prepare for an extended winter campaign.

Napoleon's Russian campaign clearly reflected a reliance on what had worked well in the past, to the point that former innovations became standard operating procedure. This predictability served the Russians, who consistently refused to play by Napoleon's established rules of warfare. Napoleon's strategy was designed for quick victory while Russian strategy was to lure Napoleon more and more into Russian territory, thereby prolonging engagement. Russians embarked on a scorched-earth policy and burned or destroyed anything that could benefit Napoleon. All cities and villages were burned and food, livestock and bridges were destroyed. Napoleon could not engage the Russian Army, which simply was not there. It had retreated to its vast Eastern territories. When winter set in, Napoleon's army had neither warm clothing nor food or shelter, and the soldiers died in their thousands. When Napoleon decided to retreat, his remaining soldiers died at the hands of Russians irregulars who were acclimatized for winter life.[9]

Among the present-day leadership behaviors that may reflect hubris are making unsound and over-priced corporate acquisitions, pursuing growth for its own sake and knowingly violating the standards of acceptable conduct. All present, more or less, in case studies examined in this book. Research has shown that over 70 percent of M&A do not add value.[10] These actions sometimes suggest that such a firm's management believes the world, and the major forces in it, including financial markets, government regulators and competitors, are wrong, and that they are right, and are not governed by the same forces.

In recent times, the debacle at British Petroleum (BP) shows in clear terms the consequences of hubris where the CEO took a route similar to that of Napoleon. When Tony Hayward took over BP in 2007 – after the oil giant had experienced a series of calamitous accidents – he vowed that safety would be his top priority. So how did he come to preside over one of the worst industrial disasters in history? A *Fortune* investigation reveals a saga of hubris, ambition and a safety philosophy that focused too much on spilled coffee and not enough on drilling disasters. It's not easy to blow up an offshore oil rig. It requires an astonishing collection of failures big and small, human and mechanical, by individuals and by organizations.[11]

Tony Hayward was in a hurry to take his company to the top of the list of global petroleum companies and to secure his place among the immortals. He tried to achieve this by first drilling in riskier and dangerous places such as offshore leases, becoming the biggest player there. Over time, the deepwater gulf emerged as the engine of new US oil production. The second was cutting costs. BP was hampered by a starched, rigidly hierarchical management culture dominated by company lifers. Bureaucracy ruled and operating costs were sky-high. As a result BP's profit per employee was half that of Exxon. Hayward was determined to reduce it. However, in spite of public posturing to the contrary, he reduced costs in such a way as to seriously hamper safety standards. With this twin strategy the company reach

No. 2 position in Platt's ranking of global energy companies from No. 7 in five years, and then in April 2010, the Deepwater Horizon blast occurred. During the various press conferences and other public platforms, Hayward came out as an insular person, with little sympathy for hundreds of fishermen who lost their livelihood due to spillage and the damage done to the environment. He blamed everyone except himself.[12]

As in the case of Ranbaxy, the cost to the company in terms of money and reputation has been incalculable. To start with, BP established a $20 billion escrow fund to pay damage claims. Its market valuation has lost 50 percent value, about $50 billion. The company is fighting hundreds of cases, and it will be several years or decades before final cost to the company, which is estimated to be in the region of $90 billion, is known. Typically amongst the world's top five energy players, BP dived to 118th in 2011 from 2nd in 2010, reflecting the huge losses it suffered as a result of the Deepwater Horizon disaster in the Gulf of Mexico, the world's biggest offshore oil spill.[13]

Hubris, the sin of overweening pride or arrogance, is invariably the basic condition that undermines societies and individuals in classical literature. But we seem to have forgotten that hubris has its influence in the real world as well. It is often seen that companies that construct magnificent edifices such as headquarter building, stadiums and so on often decline[14] soon after, just as the Mughal Empire's decline started with the completion of the Taj Mahal. It is no coincidence that our own Sahara Parivar's problems started soon after Mr. Subrata Roy named a stadium after himself.

According to Tim Irwin, in his book *Derailed*,[15] where he charted the highs and lows of six CEOs, there are four qualities that are tied to failure:

Authenticity: Alignment between the inner and outer person. What you say and what you do regarding beliefs, values and behavior. Creating real value – enduring, meaningful, authentic value – isn't about theater.

R. Thyagarajan is founder and Chairman of the Shriram Group, which finances 20–25 percent of India's trucks. Thyagarajan is so low profile that many may not be aware that he founded the group in 1978 with ten friends who put in ₹10,000 each. Today, it has nearly ₹45,000 crores under management and employs one lakh people.

When asked whether he had a vision when he started out in such a small way that one day he would be guiding a ₹50,000 crore group, he laughs, 'Certainly not.' Is he being modest? Thyagarajan says he does not believe in false humility or false modesty. But he is truly a man of minimal needs. He drives a Maruti Alto, didn't own a house till 12 years ago and holds less than 3 percent in his listed companies. He doesn't have a cell phone either. Shriram emerged unscathed during the end of the 1990s when NBFCs were falling like nine pins. It never defaulted on a payment and did not lose its deposit base either. Thyagarajan insists that a business should look at what value it is adding to the community. 'We don't want to make money through smart deals.' It is no wonder that his companies are favorites with private equity funds.[16]

> I cannot distrust people. I don't start with suspicions. This goes for private equity investors or partners. In 1990, when Ashok Leyland and Tata Motors took 15 percent stakes in the company some people said, 'Oh, they are big players and they will swallow us.' I did not think so. When we made people branch managers, we gave them total freedom to

decide on the quantum of money to lend and the risk mitigation steps. I shared my opinion on what I thought, but the decision was theirs. When someone who runs a particular business disagrees with me I ask them to run it. I don't interfere. For instance, when we do a fixed deposit mobilisation, the branch manager will not just fix a target for others; he will first take a target for himself. So, we never ask our colleagues to do things that we ourselves could not do. When we started our business, it was customary to repossess [take back the vehicle if the loan wasn't repaid] through an outside agency. We did it ourselves. We would explain to the customer that he wasn't managing his property well, and that if we took back the vehicle we could minimise his loss. The result – Shriram Transport Finance has delivered large returns for not one but multiple investors; ChrysCapital made 10 times its investment a few years ago, and TPG made 7 times its investment a few weeks ago when it sold its stake in the company.[17]

Listening come easy to him. His idea for entering the field of insurance came from one of his branch managers. His role as angel investor has gone unnoticed. He has been quietly helping people who come to him with good ideas, including employees seeking to set up business. Whenever he has spotted a technocrat with a vision, he has backed him unconditionally. He does not see the need to publicize such ventures. He just says that one should not fear failure.[18] The behavior of Thyagarajan contrasts with that of one of the top business leaders of India at one time, Phaneesh Murthy, who headed Infosys Marketing and was later made iGate CEO. His organizational achievements were undermined by his private life, which led to his being fired from top positions not once but twice. Some people never learn.

Leadership is often a struggle. Yet societal taboos often prevent leaders from talking openly and honestly about their struggles for fear of being perceived as ineffective and inadequate. Social mores reinforce the myth that leaders are supposed to be perfect and that struggle is a sign of weakness and a source of shame. It is hard to keep these societal views in perspective, especially when facing significant challenges. The best leaders learn to sidestep these unrealistic expectations by accepting themselves for who they are today while continually striving to be better tomorrow. These individuals come to understand that struggle is a natural part of leadership and that it is often the struggle itself that unlocks the potential for the greatest growth. Instead of denying the struggle or feeling diminished by it, they learn to embrace it as an art to be mastered. Consequently, they develop skills, capabilities and practices that help them cope with – and even thrive in the midst of – challenge and adversity.[19]

Self-Management: Insight, sensitivity, impulse control, optimism and persistence.

Sushil Patil, a civil engineer, is a dalit businessman from Nagpur, Maharashtra. From an early age, he had witnessed financial strain and caste prejudice. Like the day his father had to request the engineering college to waive his final year fees. He could never forget his father bowing before the Dean. His father went for 15 years without a promotion while his higher caste colleagues got regular pay hikes and other benefits. This humiliation made Patil resolve to have his own business, never an easy objective for a dalit man. Between 1996 and 2003, he started several ventures such as software, poultry farming, facility maintenance, stock broking and so on and all failed. In the end, he decided to return back to civil engineering and took a job in a civil engineering firm for six months to learn project management skills. In 2003, he started his own company in the field of engineering, procurement and construction. Initially, getting work from big power companies was a big task, and Patil spent hours outside their offices. 'I mostly failed, but I never quit,' he says, adding that many people did not take him seriously because he was a dalit entrepreneur. 'They thought this was not my cup of tea and that I would shut my business after some time.' People from upper castes were reluctant to work with him as employees. In order to break into this system, he started offering concessions to clients. Several projects, large and small, started coming his way as clients started liking his commitment and professionalism, ability to complete jobs within time and cost. Now, he runs a company with over ₹350 crores in revenue and staff of 480, of whom 150 are dalits, many of whom he has trained. Patil did not rave and rant about high caste prejudices but took it as one more obstacle he has to cross on his way to success.[20]

Humility: Channeling one's ambition into excellence in performance rather than self-promotion.

One journalist reported that Carly Fiorina, the ousted CEO of HP, used the word 'I' 129 times in a 30-minute talk. She took over most of the decision-making roles at HP rendering the position of COO superfluous. No doubt, she was fired unceremoniously at Chicago Airport.

A. Velumani doesn't own a car. He makes do with a small living quarters above his large lab in Navi Mumbai, but still ends up sleeping in the lab most nights. Nothing in his lifestyle will give away the fact that the valuation of Thyrocare Technologies, the chain of diagnostic laboratories he founded

in 1996, has doubled to ₹1,320 crores in three years. It has a
network of 700 franchises that conduct more than 20,000
investigations daily. Thyrocare shares up to 60 percent of its
revenues with its franchises, the highest in the industry.
Velumani, the son of a landless farmer from Tamil Nadu, hopes
his company will notch up revenues of ₹150–160 crores this
financial year (2013–2014) on the back of aggressive expansion
funded by large doses of PE money. Thyrocare has the lowest
rates for diagnostics services in the country: a strategy that
Velumani claims is by design. 'I may have the lowest revenues
in the business and my costs are the lowest too, but our profit is
the highest in the industry,' Velumani told *Economic Times*.
Thyrocare's EBITDA margins, he claims, are about 60 percent.
Velumani believes in his celluloid hero Rajnikant's words: 'All
your limitations will become your strengths one day.' Velumani's
story puts to rest a mindset that success comes only to aggressive,
fast-paced leaders.[21]

Courage: Choosing to do the right thing under difficult
circumstances.

When Jain Irrigation suffered huge setbacks due to their
diversification into unrelated areas, its founder and Chairman
Bhawar Lal Jain issued an advertisement in *Economic Times*
apologizing to his stakeholders for his misjudgments. 'Not
many in the management team agreed with my decision to
apologise but nevertheless I went ahead to cleanse my
conscience.'[22]

The absence of any of these characteristics can lead to failure
and the chances increase as the number of these characteristics
increase in an individual.

Irwin explains that derailment doesn't happen overnight. It is a long process. He argues that 'derailed leaders progress through five stages as they head toward their demise.'[23]

Stage One: A Failure of Self-/Other-Awareness

There is a Chinese saying: 'One disease, long life; no disease, short life.' Those who know what's wrong with them and take care of themselves accordingly will tend to live a lot longer than those who consider themselves perfectly happy and neglect their weakness.

Many leaders have blind spots that lead to failure, but they are under the impression that their brilliance at work would override all personality weaknesses. The case of Phaneesh Murthy, former Global Marketing Head of Infosys and iGate who was fired from both these jobs within a period of 11 years for identical reasons, clearly underlines the need for keeping a look out for blind spots.

Stage Two: Hubris: Pride before the Fall

Great enterprises can become insulated by their performance and start regarding success as an entitlement. When this happens, one company after another starts to 'market by assumption' assuming that they know more about what customers want than the customers themselves.

As we have seen, Napoleon was a very successful campaigner in Western Europe with his lightning strikes, and he demolished Austro-Hungarian and Italian empires. Similarly, Dr Mallya successfully divested his portfolio of companies that were his core and concentrated on building his liquor business, which he ultimately made No. 2 in the world with Kingfisher as an outstanding brand with huge recall value. His model was acquiring companies through debt, which would be serviced through strong cash flow and also contribute to further growth.

In this phase, internal warning signs begin to mount, yet external results still remain strong. These early derailing trends are explained by the company as temporary, 'not that bad' cyclic, 'our fundamentals are strong etc.' In their denial, the management brushes aside unfavorable information and magnifies favorable ones.

John Collins in his book *How the Mighty Fall*[24] writes that this early derailing trend is also visible when management makes undisciplined leaps into areas where they cannot be great or grow faster than they can manage effectively. He argues that these new diversifications stray into areas that are new to what led the company to greatness in the first place or are without the right managerial pipeline in place to achieve excellence. This starts the downfall spiral process.

Napoleon, took his successful warfare strategy to the Russian campaign. He received many warnings from his generals and also when the Russians refused to take a stand and fight, he should have made a strategic retreat or been satisfied with a part of the Russian territory that he had captured before winter set in.

Like Napoleon, Dr. Mallya extended his debt-led acquisition model to acquire unrelated businesses such as an airline, a Formula One racing team and an IPL cricket club. At one time, he had ordered over 100 aeroplanes, including five dreamliners for Kingfisher Airlines. His jettisoning of top personnel in quick succession shows that his talent pipeline was inadequate.

He was given several warnings not only by his close associates but also by experts in external agencies such as DGCA.

It is important to monitor for hubris because it can lead to devastating consequences such as Lehman Brothers. Boards must learn to distinguish between the confidence of an executive who, in the face of opposition, pursues an entrepreneurial vision and the blind disregard of an executive suffering from hubris. Confidence and arrogance may be intertwined, as in the case of Napoleon, who was both a military genius and a slave to his own narcissism. However, the lesson of history is clear: All too often, successful leaders with many positive qualities become their own worst enemies by succumbing to their narcissistic inclinations and allowing hubris to cloud their vision. When an organization and its leader have achieved their ambitions, they must not allow hubris to erode their hard-earned accomplishments. One should remember what the fool in Shakespeare's play told King Lear: 'Have more than thou showest, speak less than thou knowest.'

An essay, 'The Dark Side of Charisma,' written in 1990 by three psychologists argued: (1) there is a systematic relationship between personality and managerial competence, and (2) certain kinds of people with identifiable personality characteristics tend to rise to the tops of organizations, and these people are potentially very costly to those organizations. Flawed managers fall into three types. One is the High Likability Floater, who rises effortlessly in an organization because he never takes any difficult decisions or makes any enemies. Another is the *Homme du Ressentiment*, who seethes below the surface and plots against his enemies. The most interesting of the three is the Narcissist, whose energy and self-confidence and charm lead him inexorably up the corporate ladder.

Narcissists are terrible managers. They resist accepting suggestions, thinking it will make them appear weak, and they don't believe that others have anything useful to tell them.

> Narcissists are biased to take more credit for success than is legitimate. They are biased to avoid acknowledging responsibility for their failures and shortcomings for the same reasons that they claim more success than is their due. Moreover: Narcissists typically make judgments with greater confidence than other people ... and, because their judgments are rendered with such conviction, other people tend to believe them and the narcissists become disproportionately more influential in group situations.[25]

When you read the business press, it's easy to get the impression that all you need to do to make your company great is add a charismatic CEO. Find the next Steve Jobs, Jack Welch or Phil Knight and you're halfway home. And maybe you would be – if you happened to sign that one-in-a-million leader. The problem is that, among charismatic executives, for every Steve Jobs, there is at least one Dick Fuld – maybe more. Persuasive and strong-minded, Fuld presided over the downfall of Lehman Brothers. Nor is Fuld alone: 6 out of 18 of Germany's most recent winners of the title 'Manager of the Year' were responsible for dramatic missteps, including Daimler's disastrous acquisition of Chrysler Corp. under CEO Jürgen Schrempp.[26]

Stage Three: Missed Early Warning Signals

Here denial sets in and unattended small problems grow into larger problems, as Warren Buffet says. 'There is never just one cockroach in the kitchen.' Problems are usually a sign of other problems. Situations can be retrieved till this stage with corrective action and reorganization.

Napoleon brushed aside his Generals' advice for the Russian campaign. Similarly, Dr Mallya was advised by his internal colleagues as well as regulatory authority DGCA to go slow and especially not to go international till he had consolidated his domestic operations. He continued to micromanage Kingfisher, including technical matters such as scheduling, and in spite of having a CEO, many senior managers continued to report to him creating dual power centers, which undermined the CEO. He staked almost his entire liquor business to save a sinking airline.

The risks gone bad in Stage 3 eventually assert themselves and typically result in a sharp decline in sales and a staggering loss.

Stage Four: Rationalizing

Napoleon kept on hoping that he would be able to engage the Russian army at the next turn or next town so that he could annihilate it. In spite of advancing winter, he kept on taking his army deeper into Russia.

Dr. Mallya for two years kept on repeating that he had a 'savior' in the form of a strategic investor, which would be revealed soon, but it turned out to be largely illusionary. In a letter to employees who had not been paid for months and which led to severe hardship and even one suicide, Dr. Mallya wrote:

> Why should I spend every day to keep our airline afloat if the actions of our own colleagues lead to loss of guest confidence and lower income by cancellation of flights or low load factors that result from uncertainty? What is the confidence that I can give to investors who I am in dialogue with? ... If

some colleagues feel that I will be pressurized by flight cancellations, they are wrong. Instead, I will stop my own support as a few are effectively holding the entire company to ransom.

For the first time, Mallya admitted he had trouble running the airline in his letter. 'I appeal to all of you to try and understand the *extreme hardship that I am going through* ... The promise to pay salaries is now made only when there is a threat of a strike and mostly it turns out to be a false one,' said a pilot. It is sad and surprising to note Vijay Mallya expecting his employees, including pilots, to work for free and not demand a salary. Mallya had told *TOI* that he would recapitalize the airline 'FDI or no FDI.'[27] The extreme hardship that Dr. Mallya referred to was carried out at London's five star Dorchester Hotel.

Stage Five: Derailment

In Stage Five, accumulated setbacks and costly false starts erode financial strength and the individual spirits of management to such an extent that the leaders abandon all hope of rebuilding a new future. Irwin concludes that eventually the organization atrophies into utter insignificance; and in the most extreme cases simply disappears as a result of running out of cash as happened at Subhiksha.

Once Napoleon's army was decimated in Russia, he did not have the resources to fight back his other enemies which decided to rise when he was down. In the battle of Waterloo on 18 June 1815, his long sworn enemy Britain jointly with Dutch and Prussian allies called the Seventh Alliance defeated Napoleon and took his surrender, and the emperor ended his days as a prisoner at the Isle of St. Helena.

At Kingfisher, with employees no longer willing to work without payment, lessors taking back their planes, the DGCA not allowing the airline to restart operations without a viable plan in place, non-payment of provident fund, service tax, income tax, airport operators, and finally banks taking the airline to courts for payments due, there is little likelihood of the airline taking off in the near future. Why has the airline not yet been declared bankrupt? It is more to do with laws and crony capitalism than the merits of the business to sustain. Air Asia has shown that it is cheaper and easier to launch a new airline rather than taking over Kingfisher. Therefore, the chance of Kingfisher ever flying even under a new owner is very remote.

Tim Irwin in his book *Derailed* asks a question, 'How can people with long successful careers stumble and fail?' In *How the Mighty Fall*, author Jim Collins asks a similar question regarding companies that fail after decades of stability and growth. In the book *A Mind of Its Own*,[28] psychologist author Cordelia Fine throws some light on this question. The wonder organ that is the human brain allows us to solve complex problems, learn languages and decode the wonders of the universe system. The same brain hides a dark side. Your brain manipulates, distorts and censors evidence to fashion a more palatable version of reality for itself. It is swayed by emotions that cloud judgment. Prone to wild irrationalities, stubbornly close-minded, it finds evidence for its pre-established beliefs where none exists. Blinkered by self-love, it indulges in ego-inflating vanities. In short, your brain is vainglorious. It is emotional and immoral. It deludes you. This book describes the extent to which the truth-stretching, ego-boosting tactics of the brain keep us well insulated from reality.

Assumptions, Beliefs, Mindsets and Blind Spots

To assume is to make an ass out of you and me.

To possess unshakable assumptions and beliefs is another important reason for failures, closely related to arrogance.

Our assumptions and beliefs start very early when parents start telling us what to do or not. This behavior gets reinforced in schools where teachers follow the parents. When we join organizations, we already have an untested pool of behavior that follows us into adulthood.

At a gurukul (schools in ancient times), an acharya (esteemed teacher) taught students under a tree. The acharya had a pet cat that would come and play in the class disturbing the lessons. He asked a student to tie up the cat for the duration of the class, and this became the duty of a student. When the acharya died, they continued the practice, and when the cat died, the gurukul brought another cat and started restraining it. Over time, the original reason was lost and a belief grew in the power of the cat on study, and both teachers and pupils started assuming that tying of the cat is essential for learning. The cat survives in our organizations in the form of untested beliefs and assumptions. Assumptions should not be treated as knowledge.

Successful people are more prone to assumptions as they start believing that they have somehow discovered the formula for success. They continue to carry out strategies and practices that brought them success in the past. They don't pause to test these assumptions and create new knowledge.

Unshakable assumptions and beliefs are a result of a successful past. Mr. Chaturvedi tried to expand the old Dhanlaxmi Bank at the same scorching pace he was used to at ICICI Bank and

Reliance Finance without taking stock of the culture of this old Southern Bank and without carrying the organization with him. Mr. Mallya too assumed what worked in the past in taking his beverage business to great heights, that is, leveraging debt for acquisition, would work in the airline industry also.

Tim Irwin in his book *Derailed* discusses the causes for the failure of Mr. Nardelli as CEO of Home Depot. He suffered from untested assumptions and a fixed mindset, something he shared with Mr. Chaturvedi at Dhanlaxmi Bank and with Mr. Mallya at Kingfisher.

It is important to look at the behavior of Mr. Nardelli, whom Jack Welch called his ablest executive at GE, contrasting with another GE executive Dave Cote, who took over Honeywell at the same time, to understand the corrosive effects of assumptions and fixed mindsets.

Jack Nardelli along with Dave Cote were bypassed for the post of GE CEO and successor to Jack Welch. Jack Nardelli accepted the position of CEO at Home Depot, the largest chain of Do-It-Yourself Shops in the United States. In six years on the job, he doubled Home Depot's sales and more than doubled its earnings. Still he was fired. At GE, under the six-sigma command and control structure of Jack Welch, he was 'too focused on the idea that you do your job, you take care of your numbers, and the rest will take care of itself.' He brought the same mechanical mindset at Home Depot. He kept himself aloof from employees and did not even talk to Home Depot's retired founders upon taking over. He did not understand the freewheeling work culture at Home Depot where employees are empowered at front end and a pro-consumer culture. From day one he knew how to run Home Depot, just like his days at GE. Unlike GE, which is a systems oriented company, Home Depot is a marketing company with low margins operating in a very competitive environment. Here, empowering managers is essential to adapt to fast changing market realities. Mr. Nardelli even had a separate elevator installed for himself so that he did not have to be in close proximity with his employees. Instead of having his feet on the ground, Nardelli made decision based exclusively on tonnes of data.

Author Seth Godin gets it right when he says that consumer complaints about Home Depot soared under Nardelli. He alienated his customers, his employees and, ultimately, his shareholders, who were infuriated at his huge compensation while the stock languished. His compliant board, which gave him so much money despite that lagging stock price, finally bought him out with an outrageous package. They really should be following Nardelli out the door themselves. Partnering with your consumers, innovating with them, managing insights, raising the level of risk-taking, pursuing high-margin, new products, leading collectively and through example – these are some of the traits for twenty-first-century CEOs. Nardelli had few of them.[29]

Dave Cote, the other GE executive who was passed over for Jack Welch's successor, took over as CEO of Honeywell. The 59-year-old fills a room not because he's an imperial type who prizes pomp, but because he's a rough-hewn leader who demands accountability. Says Honeywell director Gordon Bethune, former CEO of Continental Airlines: 'He took us from a disaster to a hell of a company. And he never beat his chest while he was doing it.' Indeed, Cote, who recently logged his tenth anniversary as CEO, has orchestrated one of the best corporate comebacks in recent memory. Today, Honeywell ranks as a top performer among the diversified industrials, starting with how it has rewarded shareholders. Since the start of 2003, Honeywell's stock has surged from $24 to $60. Investors have reaped a total return, including dividends, of 215 percent. That puts Honeywell in second place among industrial conglomerates.

Cote's great accomplishment is unifying Honeywell's formerly fractured, dispirited culture, and at the same time charting a fresh strategy. He had no qualms about learning from others and sent executives to Toyota to learn from their famed manufacturing systems. Not following the usual practice during recession, especially favored by his mentor Jack Welch, he did not simply slash the workforce but sent them on unpaid leave. The purpose was 'to preserve our industrial base for the recovery, and huge layoffs will destroy it.' Every few months, Cote sets aside a day to sit alone in his office for reflection.[30]

Getting 114,000+ employees moving in the same direction, adopting the same values and behaviors and working like one cohesive team takes time and leadership. Building a new, fresh culture in a broad mix of corporate divisions takes drive and coordination, mixing in the cultural aspects that are unique to each business and driving new attitudes into every aspect of the total business. Dave Cote and his team have spent a lot of time and energy cultivating key initiatives throughout the entire corporation and have remained laser-focused on them. For example, people – Honeywell's people are its greatest assets. They recognize themselves as a global team of individuals, proud to be associated with Honeywell's heritage as an automation pioneer, with a common commitment to uphold that tradition. They take great pride in working among the best in the business, learning from each other and delivering as a team.[31]

Probably Jack Welch saw in Nardelli a little bit of himself and realized that his leadership style was obsolete even at GE and new age does not need a command and control leader like himself but a consultative, humble person like Mr. Immelt. Immelt apparently demonstrated a superior capacity to grow, which was the most important criterion in the choice. Welch and the directors knew they could never envision the challenges a CEO might face 15 years into the job. They just knew he would have to rethink and reinvent GE. Immelt demonstrated the 'most expansive thinking.' However, it seems Jack Welch wrote off Dave Cote too soon.[32]

Neuroscience research suggests that an assumption that what worked in the past would also work in the future can become a major obstacle to high performance. As Steven Snyder explains in his book *Leadership and the Art of Struggle*, the real secret of success resides in people's mind-set. He shows how a 'fixed' mind-set that ascribes success to innate qualities is less resilient and adaptable than a 'growth' mind-set that connects achievement to continuous learning and persistence.[33]

Further, Snyder writes, 'We tend to think of capabilities such as problem solving, communication skills and leadership as fixed and stable over time, hardwired by our genes. This mental model is a proven recipe for suboptimal performance over the long term. It becomes especially problematic when individuals with a fixed mind-set suffer a setback or make a mistake. They automatically associate their disappointing performance with an immutable deficit in abilities. This can diminish their confidence and spark an escalating spiral of negative emotion as they compare themselves unfavorably with others. More time spent in negative ideation means less time thinking about creative ways to improve performance.'

Research shows that a fixed mind-set can also be detrimental when things are going well. When people attribute their *good* performance to their innate ability, they tell themselves that effort and learning don't make much of a difference. Consequently, they select safer, less challenging routes where they can be assured of success, a pattern that further stagnates their growth, explains Snyder.

During the financial crisis, Lehman CEO Richard Fuld refused to recognize that Lehman was undercapitalized. His denial turned balance sheet misjudgments into catastrophe for the entire financial system. Fuld persistently rejected advice to seek added capital, deluding himself into the assumption that the federal government would bail him out. When the crisis hit, he had run out of options other than bankruptcy.[34] Jamie Dimon was sacked as President of Citigroup by then Chairman Sandy Weill following 16 years of partnership in building the institution. He did not dwell on his disappointment or sense of injustice. After a year of this, Dimon decided he needed closure, so he invited Weill to lunch. 'I had mellowed by then ... I knew I was ready to say thank you for what he did for me.'[35] Learning from that experience, Dimon bounced back and became the world's leading financial services CEO.

Why do companies continue to hire poor leaders? There's a reason we hire poor leaders. It's not because of incompetent HR departments or poor competency frameworks. According to a study in the *Journal of Applied Social Psychology*, narcissism increases one's chance of acing a job interview. And the more extroverted someone is, the more likely, they will be hired. In short, we hire poor leaders because they interview better. There is a widespread assumption in organizations that extroverts make better leaders.[36]

According to Susan Cain, the author of *Quiet: The Power of Introverts*, it is no surprise that extroverts are more likely to have serious road accidents, participate in extreme sports and to place large financial bets. Extroverts have more sex partners than introverts do – a boon to any species wanting to reproduce itself – but they commit more adultery and divorce more frequently, which is not a good thing for the children of all those couplings. Extroverts exercise more, but introverts suffer fewer accidents and traumatic injuries. Extroverts enjoy wider networks of social support, but commit more crimes. As Jung speculated almost a century ago about the two types, '[T]he one [extroversion] consists in a high rate of fertility, with low powers of defense and short duration of life for the single individual; the other [introversion] consists in equipping the individual with numerous means of self-preservation plus a low fertility rate.'[37] The extrovert's overconfidence and desire to outsmart their peers overtakes prudence.

According to a team of researchers led by the Wharton management professor Adam Grant, introverted leaders typically deliver better outcomes than extroverts, because they're more likely to let proactive employees run with their ideas. Extroverted leaders, who like to be at the center of attention, may feel threatened by employees who take too much initiative (but outperform introverts when managing less proactive workers who rely on their leader for inspiration).

Grant's research echoes other findings on the power of introverts. They're persistent – give them a difficult puzzle to solve, and they'll analyze it before diving in, then work at it diligently. ('It's not that I'm so smart,' said Einstein. 'It's that I stay with problems longer.') Warren Buffett is a self-described introvert who attributes his success to his temperament.[38]

After a tumultuous few years, the banking sector is actively seeking CEOs who can bring a bit of stability, and even downright boredom, to their institutions. While it's still important for leaders to inspire their workers, banking CEOs now also need to be able to project a dull, dependable air, at least in public, experts say. 'Humility and high levels of self-awareness are now desirable. Five years ago they were not necessarily sought-after attributes.'[39]

The Talent Mindset

Alfred Binet, the inventor of the IQ test, said, 'It is not always the people who start out the smartest who end up the smartest.' These are people whom Carol Dweck in her book *Mindset*[40] termed as those with fixed mindsets, also sometimes called the CEO disease suffered by a majority of CEOs in our case studies, as against those with learning mindsets.

Those with fixed mindsets live in a world with fixed traits and success is about proving you're smart or talented, validating yourself. In the other – the world of changing qualities – it's about stretching yourself to learn something new, to develop yourself. To people with fixed mindsets, failure is a setback, showing that you are not smart or talented. In other words, failure is about not growing, not reaching for the things you value, not fulfilling your potential. When people focus on improvement rather than on whether they're smart, they learn a lot more. Scientists are learning that people have more capacity for life-long learning and brain development than they ever thought. Of course, each person has a unique genetic endowment. People may start with different temperaments and different aptitudes, but it is clear that experience, training and personal effort take them the rest of the way.

Executives long understood that capital was scarce and talented people abundant. Neither is true now. Today, businesses must hoard talent while the world is awash in capital.

Assumptions about talent 'mindset' also abound in our companies, which see the long lines at our IIMs to hire the best and the brightest. It is the intellectual justification for why such a high premium is placed on degrees from first-tier business schools, and why the compensation packages for top executives have become so lavish. In the modern corporation, the system is considered only as strong as its stars, and, in the past few years, this message has been preached by consultants and management gurus all over the world. During the nineties, Enron was bringing in two hundred and fifty newly minted MBAs a year. 'We had these things called Super Saturdays,' one former Enron manager recalls. 'I'd interview some of these guys who were fresh out of Harvard, and these kids could blow me out of the water. They knew things I'd never heard of.' Once at Enron, the top performers were rewarded inordinately, and promoted without regard for seniority or experience. Enron was a star system. The management of Enron, in other words, did exactly what their consultants at McKinsey said that companies ought to do in order to succeed in the modern economy. It hired and rewarded the very best and the very brightest – and it is now in bankruptcy. The reasons for its collapse are complex, needless to say. But what if Enron failed not in spite of its talent mind-set but because of it? What if smart people are overrated? The broader failing of McKinsey and its acolytes at Enron is their assumption that an organization's intelligence is simply a function of the intelligence of its employees. They believe in stars, because they don't believe in systems. In a way, that's understandable, because our lives are so obviously enriched by individual brilliance.

Groups don't write great novels, and a committee didn't come up with the theory of relativity. But companies work by different rules. They don't just create; they execute and compete and co-ordinate the efforts of many different people, and the organizations that are most successful at that task are the ones where the system is the star. Southwest Airlines hires very few MBAs, pays its managers modestly and gives raises according to seniority, not 'rank and yank.' Yet it is by far the most successful of all US airlines, because it has created a vastly more efficient organization than its competitors have. [41]

Captain Gopinath's many ventures after selling Deccan Airways (which never made a profit), such as Deccan Charters, 360 Cargo, all resulted in insolvency. Mohammad Ali once said that '[a] man who views the world the same at 50 as he did at 20 has wasted 30 years of his life.' Mahatma Gandhi also said that 'I change my opinion every few years.'

Assumptions and mindsets can undermine performance not only at individual levels but also ingrain itself in the collective psyche. Over a period, the CEO, as described in this book, selects senior managers and board members who have attitudes and behavior similar to his own and deny access to contrary thinkers. They tend to think alike and develop same sets of assumptions and beliefs as the CEO, and this mindset percolates downwards in the organizational culture. Such CEOs also bring their former colleagues into the new jobs as we have seen in the case of Dhanlaxmi Bank. Richard Fuld as CEO of Lehman Brothers systematically brought to the top management like-minded executives, and those who showed independence were either asked to go or removed from positions of influence.

For example, one key executive sidelined was CFO Chris O'Meara, who was finding it more and more difficult hiding the truth from the media and from Wall Street. She was replaced by Erin Callen, a lawyer and investment banker. As Lawrence McDonald, one of the authors on the Lehman Brothers expose, *A Colossal Failure of Common Sense,* who worked as a Vice President in the firm writes,

> zero experience in the office of the comptroller in the corporate treasury department, which is an almost unheard-of omission on the resume of a Chief Financial Officer. Erin enjoyed the attention more than most of us had anticipated. And she quickly became a business celebrity. Her good looks and fast mind enabled her to capture the television audience.

This was something Lehmann Brothers was looking for to divert attention from increasingly toxic financial reports. Even more bizarre was sidelining of Chief Risk Officer Madelyn Antoncic, a woman with sterling education and experience and who was known as 'Wall Street's Queen of Risk Management.'

McDonald writes,

> [...] she found it difficult to accept being asked to leave the room whenever there were tense issues involving risk being aired in front of the executive committee. This was presumably because of her whipsmart, cautious mind, which dealt with the risk rather than with the maximum profits that might accrue. Madelyn was a bear by late 2006, advising caution, pullback and extra study. So they just threw her out, on the grounds that it saved a lot of trouble because it was obvious to anyone they would only discuss what they thought the firm could make. Not the possibility of loss.

The author was further shocked into remarking that 'I have been told by two close friends who were in attendance at one of those meetings that Dick Fuld, irritated beyond reasonable endurance by Madelyn's warnings, resolutely told her to *shut up*, which was a somewhat eccentric way to treat Wall Street's acknowledged authority on risk.'[42]

This collective mindset makes itself visible in many ways. The attitude of large companies when entering a new market is to think big – this is a mindset that is difficult to shake. They have many assumptions, principal being that you can use the same strategies to succeed here as in their home markets, principally the United States, Europe and Japan. In a new market, even a large company should start small in niche or segments where market leaders are weak. P&G has been struggling for years, suffering heavy losses, with Ariel by going into head-on competition with Hindustan Lever's Surf. A.G. Lafley, who recently returned as the CEO of Procter & Gamble after a gap of four years, observes that it was a mistake to take big rivals such as Hindustan Unilever head on when P&G first entered India. It would have been much easier to build a beachhead in the market if it had first attacked segments where big rivals were not present in, such as baby care and skin care.[43]

Similarly, large international commercial vehicles companies such as Scania, SML Isuzu, Daimler India and even M&M's Navistar have struggled for years as they gave direct competition to entrenched Tata Motors (TML) and Ashok Leyland (AL) and failed. They were misled by untested assumptions like what works there will work here. In contrast, an unknown entity, AMW, chose a niche construction and mining segment to introduce its vehicles, rather than general goods carriers, and quickly made a success to become the third largest heavy duty vehicle manufacturer. Eicher, competing head on with TML and AL, slipped from third in a three horse race to fourth place in a four horse race.

In dynamic internal and external business environments, leaders must be able to interpret cues and make decisions. But decision making is increasingly complex and success uncertain. Smart choices are often incompatible with existing knowledge and past experience, so managers may feel they are traveling without guideposts. Decision making is an art and a science, with no simple rules. A decision maker might need to use intuitive assessment in addition to analytic tools and research. As human beings, we often misperceive the commonness of our beliefs, values and behavior. Most often, we overestimate the proportion of others who share our beliefs. So we come to see our own values and choices as relatively typical and appropriate – and we view alternative responses as unusual and even deviant. Because of our bias, we assume that the beliefs and behavior of others will be like ours.[44]

Misperception of the commonness of one's beliefs has five primary sources:

1. Surrounding oneself with similar others

2. Attending to one's own views the most

3. Believing one's own behavior is based on the situation and others' is not

4. Filling in the gaps in ambiguous situations

5. Needing to validate one's own beliefs[45]

'In order to grow, a business must have a systematic policy to get rid of the outgrown, the obsolete, and the unproductive,' said Peter Drucker. In the end, mindsets are just beliefs that can be changed as readily as assumptions.

SYSTEMIC OR ORGANIZATIONAL CAUSES

> Business success contains the seeds of its own destruction.
>
> –Andy Grove

Too Fast Too Furious – Uncontrolled and Speedy Growth

Author Jim Collins noted undisciplined pursuit of more as one of the major causes of corporate failures. Many companies in case studies highlighted in this work have suffered due to their fast and reckless expansion in new industries leveraging debts, which are easily available today, in several forms and from diverse sources. Some banks even funded power distribution companies with negative net worth.[46]

Some have gone bankrupt; others are struggling to recast debts and selling assets to repay loans. In fact, applying for CDR (corporate debt reorganization) has reached epidemic proportions since 2012, primarily due to this quest. As against 433 cases referred to CDR in Q1 2012–2013, 522 cases have been sent Q4 of the same financial year. Weak economy has a role to play in this state of affairs, but that is not the whole case.

International investment banks beguile the local elite with stories of how their country and the world have changed, so it makes sense to borrow more. That is not a hard sell. Policymakers want to believe they have found the special elixir of economic growth and, in recent years, to believe they have 'decoupled' from the prolonged recessions and slow growth in the United States and Western Europe.

Issuing debt – 'increasing leverage,' in the jargon – feels like alchemy during good times. If you put less money down to buy an asset (i.e., less equity and more debt in your purchase) and the asset appreciates in value – then you have made a great return on your equity. But you are almost certainly not thinking about VUCA environment, in this case, risk-adjusted returns – that is, what happens when asset prices fall. Less equity means the value of your debt will exceed the value of your asset that much sooner. Put all of that together, and you have a classic recipe for vulnerability. That is sustainable as long as the capital continues to flow in – particularly as long as companies can issue debt in dollars but private capital flows are typically volatile for all countries, advanced or emerging, across all points in time.[47]

Rapid expansion also brings stress in internal operations such as:

Synergy Failures: There has to be a synergy between what the organization is gearing for delivering to its customers vis-à-vis its internal capability.

Resource Management Failures: Organizations have failed miserably since they could not measure the 'resources they possessed' and the 'resources required' to be in business. Famously saying, 'what business were they in,' to 'what business they are in' and leading to 'what business they must be in' desired the firm to have an internal appraisal on resources. Emotionally ambitious without fair track of what the market desires and what could be delivered have been the cause of many firms failing, despite their strengths.

Dynamic Capabilities Acquisition Failures: Firms need not only innovate, but innovate continuously and keep on acquiring dynamic capabilities to withstand competitiveness. There is no fixed path or remedy to do so. Dynamic capabilities must be acquired at each stage of the competence. It may be in process, services, products, supply chain, customer experience and so on.

Henry Mintzberg, the strategy guru, advocates The Learning School,[48] where strategy formation is an emergent process, that is, crafting strategy as opposed to planning strategy.

In planning strategy, the keynote is reason – rational control, the systematic analysis of competitors and markets, of company strengths and weaknesses, the combination of these analyses producing clear, explicit, full-blown strategies. When attempting new businesses such as buying coal mines abroad, knowledge is passively acquired, which is typically brought in from outside.

Now imagine someone crafting strategy. A wholly different image likely results, as different from planning as craft is from mechanization. Craft evokes traditional skill, dedication, perfection through the mastery of detail. What springs to mind is not so much thinking and reason as involvement, a feeling of intimacy and harmony with the materials at hand, developed through long experience and commitment. Formulation and implementation merge into a fluid process of learning through which creative strategies evolve. Strategies emerge as people, sometimes acting individually but more often collectively, come to learn about a situation as well as their organization's capability of dealing with it. Eventually, they converge on patterns of behavior that work.[49]

Crafting, Operationalizing and Implementing Strategy (COIS): Each component of COIS needs to be threaded, aligned and honed to suit market conditions. It's warfare in business, and the most competent organization with alternate plans – will emerge victorious. This necessitates deeper understanding on systemic, synergy, resource management and dynamic capabilities acquisition.

Many other companies, though not yet in the mess that Subhiksha and Kingfisher find themselves in, definitely are driving on the same road. Leela Venture and HCC have already asked banks for debt restructuring and others such as GMR, Lanco and HCC, and Shri Renuka Sugars, retailers such as Future Group, a host of real estate leaders such as DLF and Unitech, very recently pharma companies such as Wockhardt and diversified groups such as the Anil Ambani Group have followed suit. There is one thing common to all of them. All are highly leveraged companies fast moving companies with huge debts on their books, and these debts are dragging down their shareholders' wealth.

Many of these high leverage failures are also due to the copycat nature of entrepreneurship. From FCCB to Special Economic Zone (SEZ), and now we are seeing this phenomenon being played out in the Australian coal mining scenario. Companies follow the first mover in the hope that since he has already done the due diligence and built his strategy on sound data and forecast, the next one and so on can just follow in his footsteps and reap the rewards. There is no need to build organizational knowledge through the crafting strategy route. This again is a recipe for failure, especially when entering new businesses, according to Henry Mintzberg as described earlier. A large number of companies of all colors and shades took up SEZ projects. In spite of tweaking the norms, there is now a long queue for denotification or surrender. Till now, 576 SEZs have been approved, out of which 392 have been notified. A total of 173 SEZs have commenced export, of which 20 are multi-product SEZs. Till 31 July 2013, 58 had been denotified, most of which happened in the past two years because of the imposition of a new tax regime. The reasons given by the developers for de-notification include a global economic slowdown, poor market response, nonavailability of skilled labor force, lack of demand for space and a changed fiscal incentive regime for SEZs.[50]

The problem with all these companies can be traced to one word: *Learning*. All these companies went into new businesses and straightaway plunged into reckless expansion and growth using easily available debt. Some of these new instruments such as FCCB were widely used even though the effect of such loans in a volatile global business environment was not widely understood.

Now they are selling those assets that they acquired using debts to retire the same debts. The real estate companies are selling land, malls and hotels, pharma companies selling foreign subsidiaries and hotels and infrastructure companies are selling various assets and so on.

As we shall see in the following chapter, 'slow is fast.'

THE VUCA WORLD

> We don't believe the world we see; we see the world we believe.
>
> —Steven Covey

There are few certainties about the future other than the fact that it is uncertain. Most of the problems we face in business are ill-defined and open-ended. We often do not really know the answers even after the event. We cannot envisage the full range of possible outcomes or the options available. Nassim Nicholas Taleb (author of *Black Swan*) famously characterized this world as populated by 'black swans.' People crave specific knowledge of the evolution of complex systems, paying good money for the services of clairvoyants and economic forecasters. But such knowledge is rarely available. Nor, even if it were available would it often be useful. Physicists studying sport have established that many fieldsmen are very good at catching balls, but bad at answering the question: 'Where in the park will the ball land?'[51]

Good players don't forecast the future, but adapt to it. That is the origin of the saying 'keep your eye on the ball.' Managers who know the future are more often dangerous fools than great visionaries.[52] Many well-known economists, institutions and other smart people have bitten the dust in trying to forecast the future. Thomson Reuters Starmine Data, which places great emphasis on forecasts by top-rated analysts, expected Ranbaxy to report a profit of ₹1,560 crores for the 1Q 2013.[53] However, when the company announced results, its net had dipped 90 percent to ₹126 crores.[54]

Recently, Russia, Turkey, Azerbaijan and Kazakhstan all boosted their gold holdings in March 2013 (no doubt, advised by their Central Bank's economists) in a bet on a long-term appreciation in the precious metal's price just before it slumped by more than $270 an ounce.[55]

Mark Mobius is one of the world's most astute investors. When his Templeton Asset Management (TAML) announced an investment of $20.6 million in shares of Shiv-Vani Oil and Gas Exploration Services on 29 March 2010, it joined other astute investors such as Citi Venture, Reliance Capital, Aviva Life and Religare Finvest. When Mark Mobius's TAML announced the investment, the share was trading at ₹412.

Soon after the deal, Mobius, Executive Chairman of TAML, said: 'We are impressed with Shiv-Vani's oil and gas exploration services capabilities and are confident these can be leveraged to assist oil & gas companies around the world.' Circa July 2013, the share is trading at ₹28. Fund managers with exposure to the company said Shiv-Vani has been facing trouble on multiple fronts over several months and has not done enough to fight these. While the business outlook became grim following lower government spending, several operational issues erupted as the company found it difficult to service high-cost debt.[56] In February 2014, the company defaulted on its FCCB payments.

All these examples are primarily the result of a poor understanding of the complex, uncertain and chaotic business ecology. The reality is that the world is a complex ecosystem where the future is unpredictable and chaotic. As noted earlier, companies that mimic living system are more likely to survive than the traditionally managed firms, which generally model themselves on mechanical systems. The mechanistic model is deeply embedded in traditional business practices because it has produced so many successes. It is rooted in successes of the Industrial Age and heavily influenced by Taylor's scientific management to move the modern world out of a feudal agrarian past and into the prosperity of the scientific/industrial age.[57]

We know from the natural world that systems – biological or social – and entities that lack effective feedback loops do not survive. Slow adaptors fail in any evolutionary and competitive environment. This is also the case with man-made organizations. The fall of Lehman Brothers, General Motors and Kodak have only underlined this principle.

Strategic planning assumes one can predict the outcome and control the process. When there is ambiguity and uncertainty, there is no ability to predict and control. This is the business environment we are facing now. Tata Power won the Mundra Project in a competitive bidding process in 2006. The project was to get coal from Tata Power's coal mines in Indonesia. A couple of years ago, the Indonesian Government made it mandatory to link the Indonesian coal prices to international prices of coal. The resultant increase in fuel prices made it unviable for Tata Power to sell electricity at the mandated price.[58] Though the regulators saved the future of Tata Power by allowing it to increase price, it underlines the risk of taking decisions under uncertain business conditions. The mine has since been sold.

Harish Manwani, then Hindustan Unilever CEO, said,

> As far as businesses are concerned, the most important thing for us to ensure is that we build enough flexibility in our plans to manage and tackle any scenario. The days of long-term planning and plans cast in stone are over. It can provide a context, but if you're operating a business on the basis of long-term business plans, that model is not valid any more. You have to have clarity in terms of destination, be clear about strategic thrusts, but operating plans have to be really flexible.[59]

Nitin Paranjpe, another former HUL CEO and present global President of the Home Care Business of Unilever, at a keynote address to Insead India Business Dialogue said that '[i]n a volatile, uncertain, complex and ambiguous (VUCA) world, organizations would increasingly have to push the boundaries in their endeavor to adapt to this new reality and organizations needed to build capabilities that could future-proof their business.'[60]

The ratings agencies ought to have been just about the first ones to detect problems in the US housing market. They had better information than anyone else: fresh data on whether thousands of borrowers were making their mortgage payments on time. But they did not begin to downgrade large batches of mortgage-backed securities until 2007 – at which point the problems had become manifest and foreclosure rates had already doubled.[61] Why did the rating agencies, especially S&P, not raise an alarm. They were too busy earning enormous profits through granting top ratings to below par instruments.[62]

Kaushik Basu, Senior Vice President and Chief Economist of the World Bank, notes,

> Very long-run forecasting is a hazardous activity because the uncertainties and imponderables of life have plenty of time to intrude, and bend and buck the charted path. At the same time, to craft policy that is rooted in reason and reality, we need to peer into the future with the best information, statistics, and models that we have.[63]

Predicting the future is a tricky business – especially when based on assumptions that need not be true. 'The quest for certainty blinds us to this possibility. Giving up this quest lets us co-create new futures, even if none of us can know or imagine them ahead of time.'[64]

According to research on the psychology and efficacy of predictions, long-term expert predictions have been found to be about as accurate as monkeys tossing darts at a board labeled with potential future outcomes. And yet forecasting remains a growth industry.

The predictions from experts, both internal and external and that includes top management consultants, investment bankers, TV luminaries and so on, should always be validated with information coming from other sources, especially those having contrary opinion and assumptions and biases checked thoroughly. Refusal to see both sides of the coin can result in losses as Henry Ford's lawyer learnt to his cost when the President of the Michigan Savings Bank advised him not to invest in the Ford Motor Co. in 1903 saying, 'The horse is here to stay but the automobile is only a novelty, a fad.'[65]

Nate Silver in his book *The Signal and the Noise* further states that data-driven predictions can succeed – and they can fail. It is when we deny our role in the process that the odds of failure rise. Before we demand more of our data, we need to demand more of ourselves. There were the widespread failures of prediction that accompanied the recent global financial crisis. Our naïve trust in models, and our failure to realize how fragile they were to our choice of assumptions, yielded disastrous results. Human beings do not have very many natural defenses. We survive by means of our wits. Our minds are quick. We are wired to detect patterns and respond to opportunities and threats without much hesitation. 'This need of finding patterns, humans have this more than other animals, recognizing objects in difficult situations means generalizing. A newborn baby can recognize the basic pattern of a face. It has been learned by evolution, not by the individual.' The problem is that these evolutionary instincts sometimes lead us to see patterns when there are none there. 'People have been doing that all the time, finding patterns in random noise.'[66]

Business leaders should review their strategic planning processes, especially the various assumptions that come into play. They can also anticipate change by understanding that a lot of what seems like uncertainty is actually unfamiliarity. This distinction means that old ways can be adjusted and new methods acquired in pursuit of real opportunities that never have been seen before. Many of our leaders in the case studies slipped, like

Venky's, by venturing fast into unknown territory without familiarizing themselves with the business in question.

Board Composition

All the issues that been discussed earlier about failure in companies, both behavioral and systemic, are played out in the boardroom. Corporate governance is a large and evolving discipline in India, and here, we will touch on a few areas that have a direct bearing on the subject of failure as illustrated in the cases.

As we have seen in the case of Subhiksha, even the presence of business luminaries such as Azim Premji and Renuka Ramanathan on the board could not prevent the slide of this once very promising company into bankruptcy. The board should be constituted of persons who can contribute meaningfully to the discussions at board meetings. Mr. Premji, who runs a ₹30,000 crore global empire, cannot be expected to devote significant time and attention to study strategic and financial papers of a tiny company like Subhiksha with a turnover of 3 percent of aforementioned turnover. Same goes for Renuka Ramanathan. It is inconceivable to accept such corporate and financial giants to their agreeing of using short-term funds for capital expansion, even that for expanding number of stores by three times in one and a half years except through neglect. They could have nominated other colleagues who could devote more time and effort on this fledging company and perhaps save it. Luminaries such as the well-known tennis star Vijay Amritraj, management gurus and so on can certainly bring glamor to the boardroom and can impress certain investors, but before appointing them, the company management should see whether they have the time and energy to bring a strong outside perspective and, more important, also whether they have the courage to stand up to any weaknesses in the company's strategy. For example, Mr. Ajay Piramal, Chairman of Piramal Enterprises Limited, takes intense efforts to choose outside board members such as S. Ramadorai, former CEO of TCS; Keki Dadiseth, former CEO of Hindustan Unilever; N. Vaghul, former Chairman of ICICI Bank; and Dr. R.A. Mashelkar, former Director-General of Council of Scientific and Industrial Research (CSIR),[67] who not only bring in insightful outside perspectives but also have the courage to stand up to family members on the board to make their point.

The boards of many family companies are heavily populated by family members and their close associates. For example, the Board of Venkateshwara Hatcheries consists of two brothers, a sister and one close associate. No doubt, they are astute business persons in the field of poultry business and therefore are likely to have similar opinion on most issues. However, like Piramal, the board could have benefited from the advice of an outsider who could have cautioned them on the bizarre acquisition of Blackburn Rover Club, an area totally different from poultry business.

Infobesity

An epidemic is plaguing the corporate world, and people have already coined a word to describe it – infobesity. Companies have overindulged in information. Some are finding it more difficult than ever to decide and deliver. Useful information creates opportunities and makes for better decisions. But the torrent of information termed as *infobesity*, which flows through most organizations today, acts like so much bad cholesterol, clogging their arteries and slowing their reactions. Due to shortage of time and quantity of information to process, we tend to take shortcuts. Infobesity affects the boards too. More and more members and other senior leaders rely on power-point bullets to make decisions. The assumptions and biases of the deliverer is usually reflected in these summaries. All assumptions should be thoroughly revisited and divergent views should be sought, which again means a slower development of strategy.

The Chairman of a group like GMR has to process a huge amount of information in diverse business interests such as airport development and management, highways construction, power plant projects and operations, national and international subsidiary companies and so on. He may have an army of smart MBAs of premier business school to process this information along with external experts and consultants but the larger the army, the more the assumptions and mindsets that come into play, and these have a bearing on the decision making.

In the following chapters, we will discuss how to minimize the effects of these and other factors that lead to failure in organizations and further and also how to create organizations where failures are nipped in the bud.

NOTES

1. Jim Collins, *How the Mighty Fall ... and Why Some Companies Never Give In* (Harper Collins, 2009).
2. 'Taking on Tyson,' TV serial part 1 (Animal Planet).
3. Mike Tyson, interview (www.details.com), 16 August 2010.
4. Larry King Live, CNN, 2 December 2010.

5. 'Zeroes: Vinod Kambli,' The Reverse Sweep, October 2010.

6. 'My Lifestyle Was Different from Vinod Kambli's,' says Sachin Tendulkar, IBN Live, 13 November 2014.

7. Johnny Lever, 'The Missing Comic in Hindi Films,' *DNA*, Sunday, 9 October 2011.

8. 'Kambli the Rising Star Who Ran Himself Out,' *The Telegraph*, 8 August 2007.

9. Mark Kroll et al., 'Napoleon's Tragic March Home from Moscow: Lessons in Hubris,' *Academy of Management Executive*, II (1), 2000.

10. 'Perspectives on Merger Integration,' McKinsey & Co., June 2010.

11. 'BP: An Accident Waiting to Happen,' *Fortune*, 24 January 2011.

12. Ibid., 11.

13. Robert Perkins and Henry Edwardes-Evans, 'US Energy Boom Takes Center Stage,' *Insight*, October 2013.

14. Hubert I. London, 'The Dangers of Hubris,' *American Outlook*, 7 April 2002.

15. Tim Irwin, *Derailed: Five Lessons Learned from Catastrophic Failures of Leadership* (Thomas Nelson, 2009).

16. 'A Man of Minimal Needs,' *Financial Express*, 20 April 2011.

17. 'The Success Story of Shriram Transport Finance,' *Forbes India*, 18 April 2013.

18. Ibid., 16.

19. Steven Snyder, *Leadership and the Art of Struggle: How Great Leaders Grow through Challenge and Adversity* (Berrett-Koehler Publishers, 2013).

20. 'Setbacks to Success: 20 Lessons,' *Economic Times*, 22 July 2011.

21. 'Thyrocare's Velumani: Owns No Car, Lives in a Small Quarter, but Helms a Rs 1,320-Crore Company,' *Economic Times*, 23 October 2013.

22. 'Diversifying into Unknown Areas without Management Bandwidth Is Not Sustainable: Bhavarlal H. Jain,' *Business Today*, 17 July 2012.

23. Ibid., 15.

24. Ibid., 1.

25. Hogan et al., 'The Dark Side of Charisma,' in *In Measures of Leadership* (Leadership Library of America, Inc., 1990), 343–354.

26. Christian Stadler and Davis Dyer, 'Why Good Leaders Don't Need Charisma,' *Sloan Management Review*, 19 March 2013.

27. 'Vijay Mallya Warns Striking Staff He'll Stop Funding Kingfisher Airlines,' *Times of India*, 10 August 2012.

28. Cordelia Fine, *A Mind of Its Own* (W.W. Norton, 2008).

29. 'Lessons from Home Depot's Bob Nardelli – Why Command and Control Is So Bad,' *Business Week*, 4 January 2007.

30. 'How Dave Cote Got Honeywell's Groove Back,' *Fortune*, 14 May 2012.

31. http://www.jimpinto.com/commentary/honeywellculture.html.

32. 'Changing of the Guard Some People Think Jack Welch Is Irreplaceable,' *Fortune*, 8 January 2001.

33. Ibid., 19.

34. Bill George, 'Why Leaders Lose Their Way' HBR Blogs, 8 June 2011.

35. Jeffrey A. Sonnenfeld and Andrew J. Ward, 'Firing Back: How Great Leaders Rebound after Career Disasters,' *Harvard Business Review*, January 2007.

36. '5 Big Discoveries about Leadership in 2012,' *Psychology Today*, 28 December 2012.

37. Susan Cain, *Quiet: The Power of Introverts in a World That Can't Stop Talking* (Crown Publishers, 2012).

38. Susan Cain, 'Hire Introverts,' *The Atlantic*, 19 June 2012.

39. 'New Breed of Bank Chief Can Spin a Yawn,' *Wall Street Journal*, 12 August 2013.

40. Carol Dweck, *Mindset: The New Psychology of Success* (Ballantine Books, 2008).

41. Michael Gladwell, 'The Talent Myth,' *The New Yorker*, 22 July 2002.

42. Lawrence G. McDonald and Patrick Robinson, *A Colossal Failure of Commonsense* (Crown Publishing, 2009), 274.

43. 'It Was a Mistake to Take HUL Head On When We First Entered India: AG Lafley, CEO, P&G,' *Economic Times*, 27 May 2013.

44. Robert L. Cross and Susan E. Brodt, 'How Assumptions of Consensus Undermine Decision Making,' *Sloan Management Review*, Winter, 15 January 2001.

45. Ibid., 44.

46. 'India Inc. Sitting on Debt Bomb,' *Economic Times*, 25 August 2013.

47. Simon Johnson, 'Lesson from India's Mess: Capital Flows Are Fickle,' *Deccan Chronicle*, 29 August 2013.

48. Henry Mintzberg et al., *Strategy Safari* (The Free Press, 1998).

49. Henry Mintzberg, 'Crafting Strategy,' *Harvard Business Review*, July 1987.

50. 'Easier Norms Fail to Kill SEZ Denotification Queue,' *Financial Express*, 29 August 2013.

51. Nassim Taleb, *Black Swan* (Penguin Books, 2008).

52. John Kay, 'Only Fools Claim to Know the Future,' *Financial Times*, 1 January 2013.

53. 'India's Ranbaxy Earnings May Beat Estimates – StarMine,' *Reuters*, Tuesday, 7 May 2013.

54. 'Ranbaxy Q1 Net Dips 90% to Rs 126 Crore,' *Times of India*, 8 May 2013.

55. 'Russia, Turkey, Kazakhstan Caught Out by Gold Rout,' *Wall Street Journal*, 25 April 2013.

56. 'The Mark Mobius Pick That Bombed,' *Business Standard*, 10 July 2013.

57. Joseph H. (Jay) Bragdon and Jeanne V. Bragdon, 'Companies That Mimic Life, Reflections,' *The SOL Journal* 8 (2), 2007.

58. 'Electricity Regulator Allows Tata Power to Raise Tariff at Mundra Plant,' *Economic Times*, 15 April 2013.

59. '70% of Our Business Will Come from Developing Markets: Harish Manwani, Unilever,' *Economic Times*, 20 February 2012.

60. 'Volatility Is the New Normal,' *Business Standard*, 20 April 2013.

61. Nate Silver, *The Signal and the Noise: Why Most Predictions Fail but Some Don't* (Penguin Books, 2012).

62. 'Rating Agencies Come Under Fire from EU Watchdog,' *First Post*, 19 March 2013.

63. 'Capital for the Future: Saving and Investment in an Interdependent World,' accessed at www.worldbank.org.

64. Saras Sarasvathy, 'Of Maps & Paths,' *Corporate Dossier*, 9 August 2013.

65. '20 Predictions from Smart People That Were Completely Wrong,' *Business Insider*, 3 May 2012.

66. Ibid., 61.

67. http://www.piramal.com/our-leadership/bod-piramal-enterprises.

FAILURE OF PERFORMANCE IS FAILURE OF LEARNING

We are in a new world, using old tools.

–Thomas Friedman, *The World Is Flat*

We are increasingly passing through a very unstable and fast-changing world, and leaders increasingly have to deal with complexity and ambiguity. In the past, leaders could see far ahead and make their strategic decisions while today they largely see a foggy road. Therefore, assessing micro and macro changes is not easy, to say the least. As most people are painfully aware, few leaders – business or other – were able to foresee the chain of events in 2008 that plunged the world into recession. Of those who did foresee the meltdown, still fewer were able to draw a strategy to mitigate relevant risks, or the recent sharp drop in crude oil prices. What is the way forward for organizations to maintain growth and manage risks in this VUCA world, which is a veritable minefield of disruptive and potentially discontinuous political, social, economic, and business changes that would exasperate even the most competent and alert CEOs, without rearming themselves with new behavior and techniques, both at individual and corporate levels?

The VUCA world offers tremendous opportunities to those who are prepared. The nineteenth-century British banker and financier Nathan Rothschild noted that great fortunes are made when cannonballs fall in the harbor, not when violins play in the ballroom. Rothschild understood that the more unpredictable the environment, the greater the opportunity – if you have the leadership skills to capitalize on.

We have seen myriad causes attributed to failures of VUCA companies as discussed in this book. These are shown in Table 4.1.

Case	Apparent Cause of Failure
Kingfisher Airlines	Excessive debt for acquisition; lack of professional management
Dhanlaxmi Bank	New CEO's eagerness to join running and start showing results; his failure to read organization's culture and its ability to move at his pace
SKS Microfinance	Change of vision to incorporate founder's bloated ego
Wockhardt Limited	Series of quick acquisitions in new markets; did not fully understand new financial debt instruments
Jain Irrigation Systems	Ill advised and ill prepared for diversifications into unknown areas
Shree Renuka Sugars	Series of acquisitions in an unfamiliar business environment
Venky's	No clarity regarding acquisition in business strategy; quick changes in new acquisition
Suzlon and GMR	Huge debt-based acquisitions in new markets and verticals
Aakash Tablet and Nano Car	Large gap between developers' and customers' perceptions of new products

Case	Apparent Cause of Failure
Subhiksha and Vishal Retail	Spurt in expansion; ran out of working capital
Arvind Mills	Huge investments in a single product due to inaccurate forecast
Ranbaxy Laboratories	'Chalta hai' attitude toward serious quality issues; failure of corporate governance

These failures were primarily due to a poor understanding of the complex, uncertain and chaotic business ecology. Our understanding of the business environment has to change from a mechanistic one where future is calculable, plan-able, predictable and engineer-able to one that mimics the natural world that adapts to changing circumstances or vanish like once great companies such as Kodak, HMV and Nirlon and NOCIL in India.

All these cases, whatever the apparent causes of failures, have one thing in common. They have a dysfunctional learning environment. To succeed consistently in a VUCA world, one has to look at all aspects of leadership and organizational behavior in a new light, which, at times, looks diametrically opposite to what we are led to believe as successful behavior in an industrial society.

This dysfunctional learning environment in our organizations can also be seen as responsible for failure to implement new management tools such as Balanced Scorecard, Re-engineering, Lean organizations, various quality management processes, knowledge management and so on. These are seen as fads that

CEOs like to talk about at various forums but which refuse to take roots and are discarded as soon as a new magic tool is announced.

To lead in the VUCA world, first we have to unlearn whatever practices we were led to believe were essential in the industrial world. For example, some of the existing assumptions that can be tossed out of the window are:

Join new company running? How many times we have heard that '[w]e want to hire people who can join running.' This assumes that all organizations are clones and a person only requires his competency to make a success. However, this does not seem to be the best way to lead, as Mr. Chaturvedi learnt at his cost at Laxmi Commercial Bank and Mr. Nardelli at Home Depot. The leader should take time to understand the organizational culture, to be able to leverage it, before making crucial moves.

Decisive leader or doubting leader? Most people would vote for the first. We are not impressed with leaders who show doubt, are not sure, keep saying possibly, maybe, listen extensively and take time to arrive at decisions. Narasimha Rao, who had all these 'limitations,' was one of our most effective Prime Ministers. Doubt and deliberation are signs of the enlightened mind but are seen as indecision when we are assessing leadership. In a VUCA world, the second captain is more likely to ensure the ship moves safely in a turbulent world.

Pay for performance pays for the organization. This is usually the case. However, CEOs with high pay for performance are more likely to take their organizations down the failure path, especially where corporate governance is weak. Remember Fuld at Lehman Brothers. His vision, and those of many other top bankers, was solely limited to increasing topline by whatever means possible as the management bonuses were solely linked to topline growth.

New research by Wharton Business School sheds some light on how an incentive plan can backfire. It shows how an approaching vesting of stock options can cause a CEO to pump up the firm's earnings, and thus its stock price, by slashing critical long-term investment in research and development, advertising and capital expenditures. This behavior puts the CEO's interests at odds with that of the firm.[1] American Airlines, which has been consistently profitable during ups and downs of the travel industry, does not believe in pay for performance.

Extrovert or introvert leader. Once again the majority would vote for extrovert. Eminent psychologist Susan Cain in her book *Quiet: The Power of Introverts in a World That Can't Stop Talking* says,

> We live with a value system that I call the Extrovert Ideal – the omnipresent belief that the ideal self is gregarious, alpha, and comfortable in the spotlight. The archetypal extrovert prefers action to contemplation, risk-taking to heed-taking, certainty to doubt… In an interview, it is the extroverts who excel. Introversion is now a second-class personality trait. Even in less obviously introverted occupations, like finance, politics, and activism, some of the greatest leaps forward were made by introverts…figures like Warren Buffett and Mahatma Gandhi achieved what they did, not in spite of but because of their introversion. Make the most of introverts' strengths – these are the people who can help you think deeply, strategize, solve complex problems, and spot canaries in your coal mine.[2]

Research has shown that extroverts are more likely to have serious accidents on the road due to their overconfidence. Many banks after burning their fingers with towering extrovert figures are now combing for introvert boring leaders who can put safety above growth.

Open plan office or cubicles. The trend today is for open plan, where, like a zoo, everybody is visible, an environment conducive for open communication, networking and teamwork. Those who have not yet converted their offices to open plan should take relief in the evidence that '[o]pen-plan workers are more likely to suffer from high blood pressure and elevated stress levels and get the flu; they argue more with their colleagues...'[3]

Fast growth or slow growth? All companies showcased in this book registered failure largely due their scorching growth strategy regardless of their competencies and business environment.

In *The Fifth Discipline*, the path-breaking work on organizational learning, author Peter Senge says,

> The irony is that to do things faster, you often have to go slower. You have to be more reflective. You have to develop real trust. You have to develop the abilities of people to think together. Why? Because it requires you to go through basic redesigns. You need to build a shared understanding of how the present system works ... People must trust one another through difficult systemic changes ...[4]

These are only some of the assumptions and mindsets that plague our organizations and since the leaders believes so, the same set of behaviors percolate down till we all begin to think alike.

To develop leaders for the VUCA environment, VUCA Prime was developed by Bob Johansen, distinguished fellow at the Institute for the Future and the author of *Leaders Make the Future: Ten New Leadership Skills for an Uncertain World*. Johansen proposes that the best VUCA leaders are characterized by four anchors of vision, understanding, clarity and agility – the 'flips' to the VUCA model.[5]

In the VUCA Prime, volatility can be countered with vision because vision is even more vital in turbulent times. As we have seen with SKS Microfinance, when vision is ditched, failure follows. Leaders with a clear vision of where they want their organizations to be in three – five years can better weather volatile environmental changes such as economic downturns or new competition in their markets, for example, by making business decisions to counter the turbulence while keeping the organization's vision in mind. In SKS Microfinance, the promoters changed the vision from a microfinance company to an NBFC from serving the very poor to maximizing profits for shareholders.

Uncertainty can be countered with understanding, the ability of a leader to stop, look and listen. To be effective in a VUCA environment, leaders must learn to look and listen beyond their functional areas of expertise to make sense of the volatility and to lead with vision. This requires leaders to communicate with all levels of employees in their organization and to develop and demonstrate teamwork and collaboration skills. We have already seen Mr. R. Thyagarajan, founder of Shriram Capital, who fits these qualities to a tee.

Complexity can be countered with clarity, the deliberative process to make sense of the chaos. In a VUCA world, chaos comes swift and hard. Leaders, who can quickly and clearly tune into all of the minutiae associated with the chaos, can make better, more informed business decisions.

Finally, ambiguity can be countered with agility, the ability to communicate across the organization and to move quickly to apply solutions. The great nineteenth-century Prussian military strategist Helmuth von Moltke said,

> Certainly the commander in chief will keep his great objective continuously in mind, undisturbed by the vicissitudes of events. But the path on which he hopes to reach it can never be firmly established in advance. Throughout the campaign he must make a series of decisions on the basis of situations that cannot be foreseen ... Everything depends on penetrating the uncertainty of veiled situations to evaluate the facts, to clarify the unknown, to make decisions rapidly, and then to carry them out with strength and constancy.[6]

VUCA Prime presupposes that the leader is ready to jettison his old assumptions and mindsets, and this requires an individual who treats lifelong learning as an anchor to change. How does one go about becoming a lifelong learner? This is dealt with in the following chapter.

The organization must also take stock of the new realities of the VUCA world and align its processes and systems. Some of the key areas that require strengthening and changes are discussed in the sections that follow.

STRATEGY

Peter Senge further destroys the illusion that the world is created of separate, unrelated forces.

When we give up this illusion – we can then build 'learning organizations,' organizations where people continually expand their capacity to create the results they truly desire, where new and expansive patterns of thinking are nurtured, where collective aspiration is set free, and where people are continually learning how to learn together... As the world becomes more interconnected and business becomes more complex and dynamic, work must become more 'learningful.' It is no longer sufficient to have one person learning for the organization... It's just not possible any longer to 'figure it out' from the top, and have everyone else following the orders of the 'grand strategist.' The organizations that will truly excel in the future will be the organizations that discover how to tap people's commitment and capacity to learn at all levels in an organization.[7]

Slow Is Fast Strategy

> Follow effective action with quiet reflection. From the quiet reflection will come even more effective action.
>
> –Peter Drucker

We have seen in the cases discussed in this book that most of the slippages occurred due to the speed of growth. High growth, vertical, horizontal and whichever direction available through huge deployment of debt.

In a VUCA world, since the way ahead is not clear, one has to start slow, build up the necessary speed and use variability of speed as a strategy of growth, whether through M&A, greenfield or brownfield expansion. This is just like driving a vehicle. One starts in first gear and slowly moves to fourth. As one drives, the speed varies depending on the road driving condition, traffic and other factors. If one drives fast, disregarding the condition of the vehicle, the skill of the driver and road conditions, the risk to driver and others increases.

Similarly, in a VUCA world, when business environment is hazy, the company should conserve capital and reserves that can be deployed when future assessment is clearer and opportunities become available, especially cheap acquisitions of assets. Most of the companies studied here suffer from fixed mindsets of scarcity, which is a follow-up of the license raj.

Prior to the opening of the economy in the 1990s, the government gave out licenses for new businesses or capacity expansion. For example, in 1985, four companies, Eicher Mitsubishi, Swaraj Mazda, DCM Toyota and Allwyn (now Mahindra) Nissan, were given licenses to manufacture light commercial vehicles (LCVs), and each was given a license to manufacture 10,000 LCVs. Of these, two had no prior experience in automotive industry, and the other two were producing tractors. In time, all four closed down operations or were acquired by other companies or reduced operations significantly. These Japanese joint-venture undertakings had been adversely affected by delays in the phased manufacture program, as well as by their dependence, to a greater extent, on imported components and their susceptibility to the devaluation of the rupee.[8] It is surprising that all four went in for identical copycat strategy, which failed, while latecomer Tata Motors took the lead with its LCVs. Why did they set up the plants? One reason could be that licenses were available and the opportunistic businessman took whatever licenses were doled out. The same scarcity mindset persists today in telecom, infrastructure, retail and so on.

Many of our companies that are in deep trouble today, such as infrastructure or real estate companies, have set up new businesses or expanded fast in a VUCA environment only because opportunity was available, and the strategy was that if one does not act now, the opportunity will be lost forever.

DLF and Unitech, leaders in real estate, are till date carrying huge debts on their books. They are disposing off land, hotels and other assets bought through the very same debts to retire these debts. On the other hand, companies such as Oberoi Realty and Mantri Developers are not facing debt problems because there is zero debt on their books. Despite a sharp decline in property values and having around ₹1,400 crore cash on its books, Oberoi says the company is in no hurry to buy new land and is waiting for good deals to come up. Oberoi Realty recently jumped three places to become the second largest real estate company by market capitalization, overtaking Unitech.

The 'patient' strategy also helped it to preserve cash during the property boom of 2005–2008. When most of these companies aggressively bought land and piled on huge debt on their books, Oberoi remained largely conservative in buying land, similar to a strategy followed by other developers such as Peninsula Land and Hiranandani in Mumbai. At a time when developers such as DLF and HDIL are selling land parcels and development rights to reduce debt, Oberoi is well poised to 'deploy cash in right acquisitions.'

'It all depends on how disciplined you are. Cash is the king now when banks are not lending and equity markets are down. Many realty companies had money but deployed money wrongly. Most of his (Oberoi's) acquisitions have been right,' says a senior executive of a foreign investor who has invested in the company.[9]

JP Morgan's CEO Jamie Demon says that

[a] 'fortress balance sheet' to us is strong capital, liquidity and margins. We also believe in conservative accounting,

rapid recognition of problems and strong risk management, including quality clients and good underwriting, among other criteria. Policies and principles like these protect the company in all types of weather. Our fortress balance sheet, including our strong return on capital, provides us with excess capital to invest, and we always are thinking way ahead about the best ways to deploy it.[10]

Warren Buffet says,

Of course, the immediate future is uncertain; America has faced the unknown since 1776. It's just that sometimes people focus on the myriad of uncertainties that always exist while at other times they ignore them (usually because the recent past has been uneventful). Periodic setbacks will occur, yes, but investors and managers are in a game that is heavily stacked in their favor. I believe it's a terrible mistake to try to dance in and out of it based upon the turn of tarot cards, the predictions of 'experts,' or the ebb and flow of business activity. The risks of being out of the game are huge compared to the risks of being in it. What needs to be done: There will be uncertainty in business and in the world around you, some days more than the others. Focus on performance and making sure that your long-term fundamentals are in place. Of course don't totally ignore immediate business considerations but make sure you aren't doing it by putting the very survival of your business at stake.[11]

Less Is More Strategy

The biggest problem in the business world is not too little but too much – too many distractions and interruptions, too many things done for the sake of form, and altogether too much busyness. The Dutch seem to believe that an excess of meetings is the biggest devourer of time: they talk of vergaderziekte, 'meeting sickness.'

A majority of employees today are knowledge workers and creative people's most important resource is their time – particularly big chunks of uninterrupted time. Indeed, creative people may be at their most productive when, to the manager's untutored eye, they appear to be doing nothing. When he was boss of General Electric (GE), Jack Welch used to spend an hour a day in what he called 'looking out of the window time.' Those at the top are best employed thinking about strategy rather than operations – about whether the company is doing the right thing rather than whether it is sticking to its plans.[12]

EXECUTION

Early detection is key to survival during economic downturns. Genpact's international exposure and long association with GE – it started as the captive business process outsourcing (BPO) arm of the US conglomerate – may have helped it foresee the trouble, much before it became an everyday reality. The company, a pioneer of the BPO industry in India, continues to surge ahead of its rivals, despite serious economic problems in its major markets. 'We can't control the economic environment. We learnt from GE to try and focus on things we can control – internal cost and expenditure,' said Pramod Bhasin, former President and Chief Executive of Genpact. 'We talked to clients, suppliers and advisors and put all that information together in a cohesive way,' he said.[13]

Bob Johansen, a Distinguished Fellow at the Institute for the Future, says,

I think your focus, with strategic speed, is to figure out how to regulate your speed to play into that VUCA world in a positive way. You can't just run at your peak level all the time. What's going to win is not constant speed, it's variable speed. There will be times to reflect, and there will be times to run, there will be time to push, there will be times to pause. It's not just running fast all the time. Those that run fast all the time will wear out. It's variable speed and flexible speed that will win in the VUCA world.[14]

Our set of failures believed otherwise drive at constant speed, which is fast. Therefore, aside of strategy, there are skills and knowledge that a company can acquire to ensure that changes in environment are regularly and widely discussed and the management has ample time to make course corrections. If not guaranteed to avoid failures, it will at least ensure quick recovery.

Develop Organization IQ

We know that teams of smart people from different backgrounds are more likely to come up with fresh ideas more quickly than individuals or like-minded groups do. When a diverse range of experts – game theorists to economists to psychologists – interact, their approach to problems is different from those that individuals use.[15]

A striking study led by an MIT Sloan School of Management professor showed that teams of people display a collective intelligence that has surprisingly little to do with the intelligence of the team's individual members. Group intelligence, the researchers discovered, is not strongly tied to either the average intelligence of the members or the team's smartest member. And this collective intelligence was more than just an arbitrary score: When the group grappled with a complex task, the researchers found it was an excellent predictor of how well the team performed.

The new work is part of a growing body of research that focuses on understanding collective behavior and intelligence – an increasingly relevant topic of research in an age where everything from scientific progress to entrepreneurial success hinges on collaboration. Says Thomas W. Malone, director of the MIT Center for Collective Intelligence and senior author of the study:

> Intuitively, we still attribute too much to individuals and not enough to groups. Part of that may just be that it's simpler; it's simpler to say the success of a company depended on the CEO for good or bad, but in reality the success of a company depends on a whole lot more.[16]

This study counters an assumption, a fallacy that star performers perform and others only support them. Your experts needn't be the most famous people in their fields. Sometimes a talented team of young and forward-looking researchers can be more effective. Eminent experts who are the source of dominant assumptions may be less likely than up-and-comers to challenge those assumptions.[17]

Dialogue, Not Discussion or Debate

Robust dialogue starts when people go in with open minds. They're not trapped by preconceptions or armed with a private agenda. They want to hear new information and choose the best alternatives, so they listen to all sides of the debate and make their own contributions.

You cannot have an execution culture without robust dialogue – one that brings reality to the surface through openness, candor, and informality. Robust dialogue makes an organization effective in gathering information, understanding the information, and reshaping it to produce decisions. It fosters creativity – most innovations and inventions are incubated through robust dialogue. Ultimately, it creates more competitive advantage and shareholder value.[18]

Margaret Heffernan in her book *Wilful Blindness* advises us to 'endure the noise.' Silence – fear of debate – becomes self-perpetuating. 'Without conflict, everyone remains afraid and blind… We need to celebrate those that make the noise, heroes more inspiring than talent contest winners and drunken movie stars.'[19]

Those who have endured hours of meetings, with never ending power-point slides by colleagues who have not learnt brevity, would agree that most meetings end in one of two ways.

One ends with disagreement, frustration and confusion. There is polarization on all issues, and everyone tends to safeguard their turf instead of finding optimal solutions.

In the other, the participants keep a sharp ear on what the boss wants. The tendency is to accept the boss's views and any disagreement is couched in language that will not adversely affect the next performance review.

The meetings may often have free and frank debates or discussions but rarely dialogue.

Dialogue requires a shift in mindset from telling others what you think, to inquiring as to what they think. It requires a deeper level of listening and a more active approach to demonstrating that you are listening to others. I used to attend meetings where the leader was always texting during presentations and deliberations. It gave the impression that the leader's mind is already made up and he is only going through the motions. The most important ability is to look through the presenter's assumptions and mindset to uncover what governs their behavior, study the unspoken with the spoken.

We tend to associate meetings of long hours with heightened productivity.

> The sooner we associate long hours and multitasking with incompetence and carelessness the better. The next time you hear boasts of executives pulling an all-nighter or holding conference calls in their cars, be sure to offer your condolences; it's grim being stuck in sweatshops run by managers too ignorant to understand productivity and risk. Working people like this is as smart as running your factory without maintenance. In manufacturing and engineering businesses, everyone learns that the top priority is asset integrity: protecting the machinery on which the business depends. In knowledge-based economies, that machinery is the mind. When we are tired or preoccupied—what psychologists call 'resource-depleted' – we start to economise, to conserve those resources. 'Because it takes less brain power to believe than to doubt, we are, when tired or distracted, gullible. Because we are all biased, and biases are quick and effortless, exhaustion tends to make us prefer the information we know and are comfortable with. We are too tired to do the heavier lifting of examining new or contradictory information, so we fall back on our biases the opinions and the people we already trust.'[20]

Unlike discussion and debate that have speaking and listening processes, dialogue brings in another element – 'silence.' A person, even top leaders with outstanding capabilities, has limited capacity to process information at any one time, which is being acquired by sight and sound. In a long meeting, it would be beneficial to have a few minutes' pause with overhead lights dimmed after decent intervals for the mind to process information and ready the response. Margaret Heffernan further states that '[h]umans do not have enough mental capacity to do all the things that we think we can do. As attentional load increases, attentional capacity gradually diminishes.'[21]

Fostering dialogue is a key competency for leaders to prepare them for a tougher future because the ability to welcome and channel dialogue and conflict requires practice and protection.

PERIPHERAL VISION: DETECTING WEAK SIGNALS

> When spring comes, snow melts first at the periphery, because that's where it's most exposed.
>
> –Andrew Grove,
> Former CEO and Chairman, Intel

Most managers are good at focusing on the immediate task, next quarter's results and moves and countermoves of direct competitors.

In a survey of 140 corporate strategists, two-thirds admitted their firms were surprised by three or more high-impact events in the past five years. Moreover, 97 percent of the respondents said their companies lacked any early warning system to prevent such future surprises.[22] Jack Welch included among his top five capabilities of leaders the ability to see around corners: the need for leaders to have a sixth sense of what lurks at the periphery (as a threat or opportunity) and even a seventh sense as to what the future may bring.

In the movie *The Anderson Tapes* (1971), Anderson, a burglar, is planning a large house-break. Several law enforcement and private agencies are electronically eavesdropping on him, and data is being collected through security cameras in public places. This pervasive surveillance – the agents, cameras, bugs and tracking devices – see almost the entire operation from the earliest planning to the execution. Still Anderson was able to conduct the entire operation, but at the end was thwarted, not by these agencies but by the police, who were alerted by an amateur radio operator in the building with the help of other radio amateurs.

Law enforcement had failed to discover the robbery despite having Anderson on tape in several surveillance operations. The reason was that different agencies were tapping Anderson for different objectives and each had bits and pieces of data. In the final scene, the government agencies, still unaware of each other, become aware that the crime has been foiled by reading the newspaper the next day. Finally, to cover up for themselves, each agency erases its tapes.

In the Kargil War,[23] as well as in the 9/11 bombing of the World Trade Centre,[24] different agencies had pieces of information but could not connect the dots. In the United States, there were 17 intelligence agencies keeping tabs on Al-Qaeda. In the business environment too, relevant information is available as weak signals from diverse sources, but without conscious efforts in collation, analysis and sharing, data is not converted into actionable information or knowledge.

The global meltdown led by US housing subprime crisis stunned Wall Street and resulted in the spectacular bankruptcy of Lehman Brothers, which was visible for at least three – five years prior to the tsunami. There were ample warning signs that a financial time bomb in the form of subprime mortgages was ticking quietly for months, if not years. Among the sound sleepers was Mr. Greenspan, then Chairman of Federal Reserve Board, an institution responsible for oversight of such a crisis.

Since 2001, concerns were growing that mortgage providers were making loans to borrowers who did not have the ability to repay. Many could not even make a down payment and provide any income documentation or assets; in short, banks were offering mortgages of dubious creditworthiness. In December 2007, the subprime lenders started failing as more borrowers began falling behind on payments even often shortly after obtaining the loans. Shortly, this slowly building wave became a tsunami in the global financial markets.

One of the earliest who voiced their concern was Christopher Wood, managing director and chief strategist of brokerage firm CLSA, who said in 2005 that investors should sell all exposure to the US mortgage securities market.[25]

On 7 September 2006, Nouriel Roubini, an economics professor at New York University, stood before an audience of economists at the International Monetary Fund and announced that a crisis was brewing. In the coming months and years, he warned, the United States was likely to face a once-in-a-lifetime housing bust, an oil shock, sharply declining consumer confidence and, ultimately, a deep recession. He laid out a bleak sequence of events: homeowners defaulting on mortgages, trillions of dollars of mortgage-backed securities unraveling worldwide and the global financial system shuddering to a halt. These developments, he went on, could cripple or destroy hedge funds, investment banks and other major financial institutions like Fannie Mae and Freddie Mac.

The audience seemed skeptical, even dismissive. As Roubini stepped down from the lectern after his talk, the moderator of the event quipped, 'I think perhaps we will need a stiff drink after that.' People laughed – and not without reason. At the time, unemployment and inflation remained low, and the economy, while weak, was still growing, despite rising oil prices and a softening housing market.[26]

The crisis was either not visible to many leading bankers such as Lehman Brothers or they were wilfully blind; some had anticipated it and made plans to profit from it. One was Jim Melcher of hedge fund Balestra Capital. So in October, as mortgage-backed bonds were still flying high, he bet $10 million that these bonds would plunge in value, using complex derivatives available to any institutional investor. As his gamble began to pay off in the first months of 2007, Mr. Melcher, a money manager based in New York, plowed the profits into ever bigger wagers that the mortgage crisis would worsen further, eventually risking some $60 million of the fund's money.

'We saw the opportunity of a lifetime, and since then events have unfolded on schedule,' he said. Mr. Melcher's flagship fund has since doubled in value, even as this summer's market turmoil cost other investors billions, forced the closing of several major hedge funds and pushed the stock market down 7 percent since mid-July.[27]

Long-term dangers and major opportunities may lie just outside the area of present focus. The challenge for all organizations is to see potential threats and opportunities sooner. There is need for developing peripheral vision just like a footballer whose focus may be on the opponent in front but his peripheral vision allows him to see various players around him.

The winter of 2013 was among the most severe in the United States when even the Niagara Falls froze over. The US weather Office predicted that

> the chances for normal temperatures were about even for much of the country and warm down south. Averaging it out: a moderately warmer than normal winter. Today we see that the Midwest is having one of its harshest winters in decades and that the Great Lakes are almost completely frozen over.

An exact opposite had occurred.[28]

On the other hand, a little known periodical named *The Farmers' Almanac* predicted that

> it was going to be a very, very cold winter. We used the words 'bitterly cold,' 'piercingly cold,' 'bitingly cold' and a lot of snow to go with it. And that was pretty much for the entire country, I would say, with the exception of the Northwest. As it turns out, that's exactly what it was, and it just keeps on coming. It's been an incredible winter for the cold. When we released the almanac back in August, the big deal was the Super Bowl prediction, where we said we thought there would be a storm during the Super Bowl. It started to snow about two hours after the game, and within 10 or 12 hours they shut down New Jersey with a state of emergency.[29]

The *Washington Post* had called this prediction 'outrageous.'[30]

A VUCA company should use all eyes, both inside and outside the organization, such as customers and channels, competitors, political, legal, social and economic forces, influencers and emerging scientific and technological developments, to develop and improve its peripheral vision.

The basic problem is one of distributed intelligence and organizational filtering.

Effective scanning is an active learning process: It is guided by 'good' questions, uses triangulation to reveal the meaning of ambiguous signals and flexibility of acquiring a portfolio of strategic options.

A superior peripheral vision capability requires:

- An inquisitive approach to strategy making

- A flexible and inquisitive culture

- Knowledge systems for detecting and sharing weak signals

- An organizational configuration that encourages the exploration of the periphery

Without these you are inviting trouble.[31]

SEE THROUGH THE FOG

Economics is an inexact science. Those who expect solid and reliable predictions will often be disappointed. In many situations, it is helpful to know what's going to happen or what needs to be done. Dr. Saras D. Sarasvathy, a professor at the University of Virginia's Darden School of Business, notes that the quest for certainty also blinds us to possibility. True, if we knew what to do and how things would turn out, we could act and achieve, without surprise, the results we'd expected. First, it encourages a bias for focusing on what we think we know. But knowing what we don't know is at least as useful. In accepting our ignorance, we are able to let ourselves rely on others and not waste what they might know.[32]

Awareness of our ignorance also helps overcome a second problem with the quest for certainty. This has to do with a bias in the way we see opportunity costs. More certain outcomes are given more value than less certain ones. Does this mean that we should always choose the unknown, always embrace uncertainty? Of course not. The idea here is to understand the Socratic maxim, common to all ancient civilizations, that a recognition of ignorance is the beginning of wisdom. Wisdom, here, means not to undervalue something simply because it has an uncertain reward.[33]

The key to making a good forecast is not in limiting yourself to quantitative information. Rather, it's having a good process for weighing the information appropriately. This is the essence of Beane's philosophy: collect as much information as possible, but then be as rigorous and disciplined as possible when analyzing it.[34] Alvin Toffler foresaw the future when writing *Future Shock* (Random House, 1970). Many of his predictions have proved right 40 years on, challenging and bewildering a society with vision of a society being torn apart by the 'premature arrival of the future.'[35] Toffler was not an astrologer or an oracle. He was observing early trends that were not visible to others. Future comes slowly, and it only looks fast and imminent because we were unable to spot early trends. The two words he is most associated with, 'predict' and 'trends,' are not there in his vocabulary.

An organized approach to developing Group IQ, internal expertise and peripheral vision enables the organization to develop capabilities to see through the fog with less probability of massive failures rather than relying on the expertise or gut feeling of one or few people.

Take Experts Predictions and Insights with a Pinch of Salt

'We believe nobody can predict the future,' says Alvin Toffler. 'We'll read the stuff that comes out of mathematical models, but we'll read it with a degree of skepticism.'[36] These experts who predict on a regular basis include management consultants, domain experts, television personalities, eminent economists such as Mr. Greenspan, former Chairman of Federal Reserve Board, whose advise is sought either on an organizational basis or through media.

In 2006, Philip Tetlock published his answers in 'Expert Political Judgment: How Good Is It? How Can We Know?' The book – which includes a 20-year study of 284 experts from a variety of fields making roughly 28,000 predictions about the future – was both revelatory and much-discussed, finding that political analysts:

- are less accurate than simple extrapolation algorithms;

- are only slightly more accurate than chance;

- become significantly less accurate—less likely to better the dart-throwing monkey—when their predictions project more than one year into the future;

- are overconfident, believing they know much more about the future than they actually do—for example, when they reported themselves as 80 or 90 percent confident about a particular prediction, they often were correct only 60 or 70 percent of the time;

- are strongly disinclined to change their minds even after being proven wrong, preferring instead to justify their failed predictions or shoehorn them into their cognitive biases and preferred ways of thinking about and understanding the world.[37]

People who make prediction their business – people who appear as experts on television, get quoted in newspaper articles, advise governments and businesses, and participate in punditry roundtables – are no better than the rest of us. When they're wrong, they're rarely held accountable, and they rarely admit it, either. They insist that they were just off on timing, or blindsided by an improbable event, or almost right or wrong for the right reasons. They have the same repertoire of self-justifications that everyone has and are no more inclined than anyone else to revise their beliefs about the way the world works, or ought to work, just because they made a mistake. No one is paying you for your gratuitous opinions about other people, but the experts are being paid, and Tetlock claims that the better known and more frequently quoted they are, the less reliable their guesses about the future are likely to be. The accuracy of an expert's predictions actually has an inverse relationship to his or her self-confidence, renown and, beyond a certain point, depth of knowledge. People who follow current events by reading the papers and newsmagazines regularly can guess what is likely to happen about as accurately as the specialists whom the papers quote. Our system of expertise is completely inside out: it rewards bad judgments over good ones.[38]

Mr. Tetlock divided forecasters into two types of thinking styles: hedgehogs, who are deeply knowledgeable about and devoted to a particular subject or body of knowledge; and foxes, who have eclectic interests and know a little about a lot of things. Fox-style thinkers, he discovered, were more successful at predicting than hedgehogs – a counterintuitive finding that cuts against the whole notion of expertise.

'You find serious overconfidence by hedgehogs,' Mr. Tetlock said. 'With a rigid, self-justifying style of thinking, combined with a lot of content knowledge, combined with trying to see far in the future – well, you are more likely to go off a cliff.'[39]

> On the other hand, a key factor underlying superior fox performance was that they were more modest about what they could predict. The longer you try to see into the future, the more advantageous it is to be modest. I think they also derive some befits by being more self-critical and aware of alternative possibilities.[40]

Specialists are not significantly more reliable than non-specialists in guessing what is going to happen in the region they study. Knowing a little might make someone a more reliable forecaster, but Tetlock found that knowing a lot can actually make a person less reliable. 'We reach the point of diminishing marginal predictive returns for knowledge disconcertingly quickly,' he reports.[41]

'Global Trends 2030: Alternative Worlds' is the latest edition of a quadrennial report released by the National Intelligence Council, which serves under the US Director of National Intelligence and is intended to help new or returning presidential administrations make forward-thinking policy decisions, the document is the intelligence community's collective and expert best guess at what the long-term future holds.

The most common problem with forecasts like the Global Trends report, Mr. Michael Horowitz, a professor of political science at the University of Pennsylvania, said, is that

> they fall into a hedgehog-style trap of treating current conventional wisdom as a blueprint for the long-term future. For example, extrapolating from the late 1990s economic boom, the 2001 Global Trends report predicted that the

global economy of 2015 would 'return to the high levels of growth reached in the 1960s and early 1970s.' The most natural thing to do intellectually is look at the present. What is going on now is going on for a reason, and therefore it is most likely to continue. There's nothing wrong with that. To do better is difficult. It requires both being more aware of your own biases and being forced out of your intellectual comfort zone.[42]

Assess People Psychologically

Organizational psychologist and professor Stanley Silverman of the University of Akron and Michigan State University developed a measure of arrogance, called the Workplace Arrogance Scale (WARS), to help organizations differentiate between narcissism and competence before they experience a costly impact. If overconfidence is a natural tendency for some, employers must recognize this as a potential flaw rather than an asset. Good interviewers look out for these traits, and know how to look past them.

Silverman says that arrogance is less a personality trait than a series of behaviors, which can be addressed through coaching if the arrogant boss is willing to change. He recommends that organizations incorporate an assessment of arrogance into the employee review and performance management process. Silverman emphasizes that cultivating humility among leaders and promoting a learning-oriented work climate go far in reducing arrogance and increasing productive leadership and employee social interaction.[43] Psychological assessment also, to a certain extent, downplays the bias of recruiters towards extrovert personalities who are better at facing interviews and if interviews are the only way to judge a person, the company is taking a big risk, especially if the post is senior such as that of the CEO. Psychological assessments may bring out dark personality flaws that are overshadowed by high competency and skills. If such a person has to be selected, make sure that certain safeguards are in place to neutralize the personality deficiencies.

In a VUCA world, present competency and skills and past achievements may not result in future success, and therefore, promotion process at higher levels must include a strong element of psychological profiling. However, the aim should be to get people to change. It should be about development, not selection.

Assess and Manage Risk

The forced exit of GMR Infrastructure from Maldives in December 2012 caused a huge loss to the Indian company, but GMR, which has claimed a compensation of $800 million from the Maldives government, could have easily cut its losses had it purchased a political risk cover.[44]

Indian companies rarely buy risk assessment cover, which is a Standard Operating Procedure with multinationals.

All social sciences are based on the assumption that human beings have agency and that they can choose from a variety of behavioral options. Agency presupposes that human beings are capable of acting in a strategic fashion by linking decisions with outcomes. Humans are goal oriented; they have options for action available and select options that they consider appropriate to reach their goals. Selecting options implies that humans consider and weigh the opportunities and risks that are linked with each option. Thinking about 'what could happen' is one of the major distinctions between instinctive and deliberate actions.[45]

So far, in Indian companies, risk has been seen from balance sheet point of view only.

Risk is a truly inter-disciplinary, if not trans-disciplinary, phenomenon. Risk is a popular topic in many sciences: aspects of risk are studied in the natural, medical, engineering, social, cultural, economic and legal disciplines. Yet, none of these disciplines can grasp the entire substance of this issue; only if they combine forces can one expect an adequate approach to understanding and managing risks. Investigating risks necessitates a multidisciplinary approach. Risk is like a polished gem with different facets: each facet reflects the light in different colors; but the whole gem can be appreciated only if the images of all the facets are being absorbed.[46]

A 2012 Booz & Co. study[47] found that underestimating strategic risk is the number one cause of shareholder value destruction. The study determined that, contrary to prevailing wisdom, it was not compliance issues that were most responsible for destroying shareholder value. That distinction went to the mismanagement of strategic risks – those risks embedded in the top-level decisions made by the executive team, such as what products and services to offer, whether to outsource manufacturing or what acquisitions to make.

No doubt, GMR too possesses a functional ERM process. But although ERM teams can identify and hedge risks related to relatively narrow business decisions, they do not have the mandate to evaluate the strategic risks rooted in the decisions made by senior management. An ERM team must assume that the strategic course set by senior management is sound. The results are unambiguous. Among the 103 companies studied, strategic blunders were the primary culprit a remarkable 81 percent of the time.

How should management respond to the threat posed by strategic risks? Senior leaders can't rely on ERM teams to make the enterprise more strategically resilient, because ERM teams do not have the scope to question the strategic decisions that set the company's course and undergird its operations. Make no mistake, the ERM function is vital: Once handed a strategic plan, these teams identify and quantify risks and then assign people to build continuity plans. Thus, ERM groups play an essential role in addressing frequently encountered risks in areas such as compliance, ethics, finance and accounting, as well as safety. However, ERM groups can't be the only source of protection, especially when it comes to the most potentially disruptive issues.[48]

The emergence of Indian companies operating in foreign countries, through M&A and new projects, have put the spotlight on managing their risk in these countries. Such investments have a long gestation period and the risk associated should also be evaluated on a long term, from all angles, such as political, social and economic and financial.

Large companies manage risks through ERM tools and practices. Over-reliance on modeling tools can blind the company to unknown risks. In the aftermath of the global financial crisis, companies worldwide have become more focused on risk management. What was once a concern primarily of senior executives in the financial services sector has now become a top-management priority in nearly every industry.[49]

To improve their risk management capabilities, executives should add the following three steps to their decision-making process – all of which are outside the scope of most ERM teams.

1. Broaden awareness about uncertainty and risk. Management teams need to think broadly about what could occur and

constantly layer new risks into their calculations as these risks emerge.

2. Integrate risk awareness directly into strategic decision making. By conducting more conversations about risk at the top levels of the company, looping in key individuals as needed, management acquires a full understanding of the uncertainties – both upside and downside – inherent in strategic decision making.

3. Focus on strategic resiliency. Managers need to consider how strategic decisions can affect resiliency, incorporate resiliency into all decision making and always be on the lookout for more strategically resilient alternatives in order to build greater corporate agility.[50]

THE LIMITS OF TRADITIONAL RISK MANAGEMENT

The financial firms that took dangerous risks before the financial crisis often had some of the most sophisticated risk-management operations. Today, many companies are making the same mistakes: pursuing a highly technical approach to risk management – characterized by complex financial models and elaborate, formal risk-management systems – in isolation from the day-to-day activities of the broader organization.

Companies need a different approach. They need to stop thinking of risk management as a regulatory issue and to reconceive risk management as a value-creating activity that is essential to the strategic debate inside the company. Creating a more dynamic managerial system for risk management is as much an art as it is a science. Boston Consultancy Group has identified 10 principles of risk management.

1. Risk management starts at the top.

2. Risk cannot be managed from an ivory tower.

3. Avoid relying on black boxes.

4. Risk management is strategy, and strategy is risk management.

5. Risk management is more than a policy; it is a culture.

6. A risk-aware culture requires the free flow of information.

7. What matters is the 'talk,' not the 'report.'

8. The path is the goal.

9. It is possible to prepare for unknown risks.

10. Avoid the downside, but don't forget the upside.[51]

CORPORATE GOVERNANCE

Companies spend over $1 trillion on mergers and acquisition every year. Yet study after study puts the failure rate of mergers and acquisitions somewhere between 70 and 90 percent.[52] These and many other drama are played out in boardrooms daily. Our study of 12 organizations also place decisions taken at this highest decision making body in any company for a majority of failures.

Corporate misbehavior can be curbed, at least in part, by having a strong oversight structure and a directly involved board. Boards and shareholders should increase their vigilance when their company is doing well. Leaders – especially those with pay-for-performance incentives – are more likely to act in ways that are at odds with shareholders' interests.

SELECTION OF CEO

One of the most important functions of the board is appointment of CEO. There is little doubt that those who reach this space possess the competence, skills and experience required of the job. However, the CEO and other senior officers must also be evaluated on soft skills such as cultural fit, attitude and blind spots. For example, Mr. Chaturvedi as CEO of Dhanlaxmi Bank was certainly a cultural misfit, a highly competent person with an outstanding track record at fast moving empowered banking organizations, he could not carry the managers and employees of the conservative Southern Bank along on his fast growth trajectory and had to part company in less than two years. In his eagerness to show results as soon as possible, he did not have the time or the inclination to study the organizational culture and leverage it, unlike Dave Cote at Honeywell who did this before attempting the transformation.

The selection of Mr. Apotheker as CEOs of Hewlett-Packard exemplifies the destructive role of boards. HP is a consumer products company with PCs, laptops and printers as its mainstay. Mr. Apotheker came as CEO in September 2010 and was fired in less than a year. Two previous CEOs were also summarily fired, one of them at an airport lounge. Apotheker, a former CEO of business software vendor SAP (where too he lasted less than a year as CEO), sought to change in a strategy of moving into value-added software, because that is a business he knew best. Tremors of his disastrous purchase of software firm Autonomy for $10 billion are still being felt today.

The potential sudden removal of Apotheker as CEO and the fact that such Board discussions were once again leaked to the press are likely to further undermine the Board's already fragile credibility. Our conversations with major shareholders also indicate that they have been disgruntled with the Board, given it has made and approved a series of decisions (Hurd's firing; Leo's hiring; approval of the Autonomy acquisition; the premature announcement of the exit of the PC business) that many shareholders believe were poor decisions and misaligned with their interests.[53]

'I was trying to think of another company that had tripped up that often in this many years and I found it impossible to come up with another example,' said Paul Hodgson, senior research associate at corporate governance advisers Governance Metrics International.[54]

Interviews with several current and former directors and people close to them involved in the search that resulted in the hiring of Mr. Apotheker reveal a board that, while composed of many accomplished individuals, as a group was rife with animosities, suspicion, distrust, personal ambitions and jockeying for power that rendered it nearly dysfunctional. When the 12-member board voted to name Mr. Apotheker as the successor to the recently ousted chief executive, Mark Hurd, most board members had never even met Mr. Apotheker. 'I admit it was highly unusual,' one board member who hadn't met Mr. Apotheker told me. 'But we were just too exhausted from all the infighting.' During Mr. Apotheker's brief tenure, the once-proud HP has become a laughingstock in Silicon Valley.[55]

In the words of Harvard Professor Gary Hamel,

Never before has leadership been so critical, and never before has it seemed in such short supply. It takes extraordinary leadership to keep an organization relevant in a world of relentless change. When leaders come up short, as they often do, the problem may have less to do with them as individuals than with the top-down structures in which they operate. In most organizations, the responsibility for setting direction, developing strategy and allocating resources is highly centralized. What needs to be done: Businesses will have to look at innovative management structures they want to survive. A centralised, bureaucratic decision making process will sound the death knell for business in an environment where a premium is placed on speed. What's exciting is that there's no defined parameters as to what this new structure should look like. Go on, be creative, be innovative.[56]

Quit taking risks, be inflexible, isolated, assume infallibility, play the game close to the line, don't take time to think, put all your faith in outside experts, love your bureaucracy, send mixed messages and fear the future.[57] Failure is guaranteed.

NOTES

1. "Managerial Myopia': How CEOs Pump Up Earnings for Their Own Gain,' Knowledge@Wharton, 7 February 2014.

2. Susan Cain, *Quiet: The Power of Introverts in a World That Can't Stop Talking* (Random House, 2012).

3. Ibid., 2.

4. Peter M. Senge, *The Fifth Discipline: The Art and Practice of the Learning Organization* (Doubleday, Revised 2006).

5. B. Johansen, *Leaders Make the Future: Ten New Leadership Skills for an Uncertain World* (Berrett-Koehler Publishers, 2011).

6. Daniel Hughes (ed.), *Moltke on the Art of War: Selected Writings* (Presidio Press, 1995).

7. Ibid., 4.

8. 'Indo-Japanese Collaborations on LCVs in Trouble,' *India Today*, 15 April 1992.

9. 'How Oberoi Realty Bucked the Trend,' *Business Standard*, 27 October 2011.

10. JP Morgan Annual Report, 2012.

11. 'Clear and Present Danger,' *Economic Times*, 16 August 2013.

12. 'Schumpeter: In Praise of Laziness,' *The Economist*, 17 August 2013.

13. 'Early Detection Helped Genpact Tackle Slowdown,' *Economic Times*, 25 April 2013.

14. 'Speed in a VUCA World: How Leaders of the Future will Execute Strategy,' 2012, www.forum.com.

15. Olivier Leclerc and Mihnea Moldoveanu, 'Five Routes to More Innovative Problem Solving,' McKinsey Q, April 2013.

16. Caroline Y. Johnson, 'Group IQ,' *Boston Globe*, 19 December 2010.

17. Robert Verganti, 'Designing Breakthrough Products,' *Harvard Business Review*, October 2011.

18. Larry Bossidy and Ram Charan (with Charles Burck), *Execution – The Discipline of Getting Things Done* (Random House, 2002), 102.

19. Margaret Heffernan, *Wilful Blindness* (Walker & Company/Simon and Schuster, 2011).

20. Ibid., 19.

21. Ibid.

22. Leonard Fuld, 'Be Prepared,' *Harvard Business Review*, November 2003.

23. Prem Mahadevan, 'The Perils of Prediction; Indian Intelligence and the Kargil Crisis,' Centre for Land Warfare Studies & KW Publishers Pvt Ltd., 2011.

24. Tom Engelhardt, 'From 9/11 to ISIS: The Massive Failure of U.S. Intelligence,' *Salon Magazine*, 1 October 2014.

25. Chris Wood, 'The Man Who Predicted the Subprime Crisis,' *The Telegraph*, 22 September 2007.

26. 'Dr. Doom Twitter,' *New York Times*, 15 August 2008.

27. Nelson D. Schwartz and Vikas Bajaj, 'How Missed Signs Contributed to a Mortgage Meltdown,' *New York Times*, 19 August 2007.

28. 'Another Failed Outlook: NOAA/NCEP Totally Botch 2013–2014 Winter Outlooks for USA and Europe – Exact Opposite Occurs!' 8 February 2014, http://notrickszone.com/2014/02/08/another-failed-outlook-noaancep-totally-botch-2013-2014-winter-outlooks-for-usa-and-europe-exact-opposite-occurs.

29. 'How Did the Farmers' Almanac "Nail" This Winter's Forecast? That's a Secret,' 6 March 2014, www.newswork.org.

30. 'The Farmers' Almanac Outrageous Forecast: A Frigid, Snowy Winter and Stormy Super Bowl,' *The Washington Post*, 26 August 2013.

31. George S. Day and Paul J.H. Shoemaker, *Peripheral Vision; Detecting the Weak Signals That Can Make or Break Your Company* (Harvard Business School Press, 2006).

32. 'How Missed Signs Contributed to a Mortgage Meltdown,' *New York Times*, 19 August 2007.

33. Saras Sarasvathy, 'Are You Feeling Uncertain? Great! How Developing a Taste for Uncertainty Can Create Great Opportunities,' *Economic Times*, 30 August 2013.

34. Nate Silver, *The Signal and the Noise* (Penguin Books, 2012), 135.

35. Alvin Toffler, 'Still Shocking After All These Years,' *New Scientist*, 19 March 1994.

36. Ibid., 35.

37. Philip E. Tetlock, *Expert Political Judgment: How Good Is It? How Can We Know* (Princeton University Press, 2006).

38. Louis Menand, 'Everybody's an Expert,' *The New Yorker*, 5 December 2005.

39. Patrick Hruby, 'Experts' Predictions of the Future Have a History of Being Wrong,' *Washington Post*, 12 December 2012.

40. Ibid., 39.

41. Philip E. Tetlock, *Expert Political* (Princeton University Press, 2005), 59.

42. Ibid., 39.

43. 'Identifying the Arrogant Boss,' *Science Daily*, 25 July 2012.

44. 'Does Your Firm Need Political Risk Cover,' *Economic Times*, 26 December 2012.

45. Ortwin Renn (ed.), *Risk Governance; Coping with Uncertainty in a Complex World* (Earthscan, 2008).

46. Ibid., 45.

47. Christopher Dann et al., 'The Lesson of Lost Value,' *Strategy+Business*, December 2012.

48. Ibid., 47.

49. Frank Plaschke et al., 'The Art of Risk Management,' *Boston Consultancy Group*, April 2013.

50. Ibid., 47.

51. Ibid., 49.

52. Clayton M. Christensen et al., 'The Big Idea: The New M&A Playbook,' *Harvard Business Review*, March 2011.

53. 'HP Board Ousts Apotheker, Whitman in as CEO,' *IDG News*, 23 September 2011.

54. 'Is HP Competing for 'Worst Board Ever Honours'?' *Reuters*, 22 September 2011.

55. 'Voting to Hire a Chief without Meeting Him,' *New York Times*, 21 September 2011.

56. 'Clear and Present Danger,' *Corporate Dossier Supplement*, 17 August 2013.

57. Donald Keough, *The Ten Commandments for Business Failure* (Penguin Books, 2008).

LEARNING IN THE VUCA COMPANY

An infant falls nearly a thousand times before learning how to walk. Adults give up after one or two attempts. Why is this so? How is this growing up? Despite obtaining a sound education, followed by complex experiences in the corporate world, we are nowhere near a child in learning abilities. Instead of gaining, we have lost something as we grow up.

Learning has been part of our lives since the days of hunter-gatherers and has continued through the Greek 'corporations' and medieval guilds. The coming of the industrial age put a stop to self-learning and discovery due to its emphasis on imparting rote skills, perfecting the same tasks every day – a facet aptly reflected in our assembly-line education system. Further, cultural degeneration of organizations has robbed individuals of skills. The world has moved ahead, but the learning environment and methodology have remained rooted in the industrial mindset.

Though the importance of learning is widely acknowledged, many managers remain cynical. They look at learning as something of 'questionable value' that diverts the attention of employees from 'real work.' Learning is also viewed by many managers as something that releases human potential, not something that improves the bottom-line. Another point to be noted is that managers like stability and predictability. This is somewhat inconsistent with learning, which encourages constant questioning and repeated re-evaluations of established practice. So learning has yet to gain a strong central position in many corporations.[1]

Today, no organization can survive, much less prosper, only on the basis of intelligence, competency and skills of a handful of people. Learning disabilities can cripple an organization whether in the profit or the non-profit setting. Both need to be learning organizations for them to live up to the challenges of a world changing rapidly, socially, economically and politically.

What are the learning disconnects in organizations today? There is a wide gap between what organizations do and what employees want. Organizations want to teach people how to do things. Employees would like advice on how to learn. They would like to find, sift and evaluate information on their own. Organizations want thoroughly researched and carefully developed courses for their employees. The latter want fast, current information bites with little or no development time needed.

Companies want to provide polished speakers and stunning presentation materials; employees find credible experts in specialized areas and on-the-job coaches more useful. The former want to find and disseminate 'one best way' to do something; what is actually needed is an environment in which employees develop divergent ways of thinking about problems. Employees find it a chore to wade through reading material and courses. They dislike the idea of too much externally provided training instead of individually motivated learning.[2]

A recent article in *Harvard Business Review*[3] commented that

> [i]ndeed, eminent experts who are the source of dominant assumptions may be less likely than up-and-comers to challenge those assumptions. Your experts needn't be the most famous people in their fields. Sometimes a talented team of young and forward-looking researchers can be more effective.

The purpose of learning is to constantly challenge the status quo and change mindsets. As Einstein noted, 'No problem can be solved from the same consciousness that created it; we must learn to see the world anew.' Learning is complete only when the learner has internalized or embedded the concepts and can apply it to a situation. Present training methods create an atmosphere of 'entitlement' and passivity where training resources are largely wasted. Employees in a VUCA world need more interpretative abilities. They have to draw on a variety of skills to adapt to unpredictable changes. To do that, they need more support from leadership rather than attend more 'edutainments' as most corporate training programs have turned into today.

ADAPTABILITY IS THE KEY

In such an uncertain and fast-changing, globally interdependent business environment, we need a manager and leader who can quickly let go of the past and adapt to changing circumstances. No individual, including a highly charismatic CEO, can train or command someone else to alter attitudes, beliefs, skills, capabilities, perceptions or level of commitment. Instead, the practice of organizational learning, which involves developing and taking part in tangible activities, will change the way people conduct their work.

Peter Senge in his book *The Fifth Discipline* introduces the new paradigm of learning. In place of training, we start with reviewing our attitudes, long-held beliefs and mindsets. The book outlines seven learning disabilities that afflicts individuals and organizations.

1. 'I am my position' – with this disability, individual units in the organization focus too closely on their own positions

and responsibilities, thus missing out on bigger pictures and inter-unity.

2. 'The enemy is out there' – the disability enables us to find an external agent to blame ('no one can catch a ball in that field,' 'the customers betrayed us').

3. 'The illusion of taking charge' – we should face up to difficult issues, stop waiting for someone else to do something and solve problems before they grow into crises.

4. 'The fixation on events' – leads to 'event' explanations that are true for now but distract us from seeing the longer-term patterns of change behind the events and understanding the causes of the patterns to events.

5. 'The parable of the boiled frog' – is in relation to the maladaptation of organizations to recognize gradually building threats to survival; just as the frog placed in a pot of water brought to boiling temperature will not attempt to jump out of the pot but adjusts to the temperature and slowly dies, such as Kodak. Kodak, a 131-year-old company, had been dying slowly for past 25 years, but the management was blissfully unaware of this fact. In India too, companies such as NOCIL had a slow demise for the same reason.

6. 'The delusion of learning from experience' – is when our actions have consequences in the distant future or part of the larger operating system, which makes it impossible to learn from direct experience.

7. 'The myth of the management team' – school trains us never to admit that we do not know the answer, and most corporations reinforce that lesson by rewarding the people who excel in advocating their views, not inquiring into

complex issues resulting in 'skilled incompetence' ('people who are incredibly proficient at keeping themselves from learning').[4]

Perhaps the single greatest liability of management teams is that they confront complex, dynamic realities with a language designed for simple, static problems. Senge further quotes Management consultant Charles Kiefer: 'Reality is composed of multiple-simultaneous, interdependent cause-effect-cause relationships. From this reality, normal verbal language extracts simple, linear cause-effort chains. This accounts for a great deal of why managers are so drawn to low leverage interventions.' For example, if the problem is long product development times, we hire more engineers to reduce times; if the problem is low profits, we cut costs; if the problem is falling market share, we cut price to boost share.[5]

Today, the only universal language of business is financial accounting. But accounting deals with detail complexity not dynamic complexity. It offers 'snapshots' of the financial conditions of a business, but it does not describe how those conditions were created.[6]

The 12 cases discussed in this book showed that the failures were due to one or more of these learning disabilities.

Concepts like TQM, Kaizen, business process re-engineering and large-scale information management tools such as ERP and CRM, which rely heavily on change management, have either failed to take root or their performance has been sub-optimal due to learning disabilities. The retail and banking industry in India has not been able to take advantage of data analytics to benefit from consumer behavior, primarily due to the presence of learning disabilities.

Once behavioral changes take place any type of new initiative can be introduced. This mindset change is brought about by a learning process and consists of typically three steps – acquiring, interpreting and applying knowledge. According to Harvard Business School's Professor David Garvin, to move toward a learning organization, we have to implement three principal types of learning.[7] These are:

1. Learning from the Past – Experience

Experience is the best teacher. Certain knowledge can be gained only by doing things, not by studying or talking about them. We learn from experience in two ways: repetition and exposure. Repetition helps us to perform the same tasks more efficiently over time. Exposure, on the other hand, ensures the addition of new skills by working in unfamiliar environments or by shouldering new responsibilities.

Surprisingly few companies take the time to reflect on their experiences. At a company where I worked, we had an outstanding new product launch. All elements of marketing function worked seamlessly to create the success, which was not repeated again. Why? Some core people left, others moved to new functions and responsibilities, many artifacts were lost and with memory lapses and within a short period there was no knowledge of this launch retained in the company. In the same company, there was another launch of a hi-tech product where the only competitor was a multinational company with 100 percent of the market share. Through innovative marketing practices, we were able to create a significant market for our product. The story was recorded and included in induction training programs.

As an organization ages, it draws lessons from what has worked in the past and applies them to the future. It will draw the most lessons from past successes, leaving it particularly ill-equipped to deal with the challenges that don't mirror past conditions. Success can be a killer for innovation. It's from failure that we learn the most valuable lesson.[8]

It is always cheaper to learn from others than to learn from your own experiences. Many times, the cost of personal and organizational failures can be too high. In most cases, failure may not be catastrophic but failure to learn would certainly be.

Hitler Did Not Learn from Napoleon and Made Identical Mistakes

Hitler who decided to invade Russia in 1941 made no attempt to learn from Napoleon's disastrous failure of Russian invasion in 1812. Both had brought Western Europe to their knees in a short time and were flush with the invincibility halo. They decided to invade Russia in summer hoping to wrap up the victory within three months. Therefore, neither had equipped their armies with winter clothing or supplies for a long campaign. They *assumed* that Russia would ask for terms of surrender within this period.

Hitler, as with Napoleon, disregarded prudent advice from his senior commanders calling them cowards. Hitler who started life as a corporal always believed that he had superior insights into military matters than his generals.

Napoleon had an army of half million, the largest assembled till that time. Hitler committed 3.5 million into Russian campaign. Russian strategy in both cases was not to give fight but allow the armies to enter deep into the vast Russian country. Both kept on going deeper into Russia hoping to find the enemy beyond the next hill or town. The retreating Russians, in both cases, had burnt or destroyed everything in their path, their scorched earth tactics. The armies found everything destroyed, villages, towns, bridges and so on. With winter approaching and a long supply line, there was neither food, nor clothing or shelter. Both armies were decimated by Marshal Frost and General Ice, respectively. Less than 5,000 soldiers returned with Napoleon and Germans lost 1.5 million. This brought to an end Hitler's ambitions of European domination, just like Napoleon over 100 years earlier. Why did Hitler refuse to learn from Napoleon's disastrous Russian expedition? He suffered from all four characteristics of failures described earlier in this book.

In a packaging company in India, with two plants, where hot work was carried out, six outbreaks of fire, in identical circumstances, took place within a short period of two years. There was no effort to widely publicize the cause of failure within the two plants, and, in fact, due to adversarial relations between the two plant heads, inter-plant study trips were not permitted. This resulted in these six fires taking place at the two plants, on different lines, and each event was studied in isolation. The reporting at each successive level was filtered and sanitized, creating conditions for the next fire. Learning from past experience is successful where the aim is to improve process not point fingers. Hiding or ignoring of small failures is a recipe for major failures in future.

The US Army runs the Centre for Lessons Learnt, which is responsible for review, analysis, dissemination and archiving of action-taken reports (ATRs). ATR is prepared by the fighting units after every engagement, and its purpose is to identify four learnings from the engagement through observation, followed by insight. The objective is to sustain, enhance and increase the Army's preparedness.

The ATRs are used to create an information sharing culture within the army in which every soldier is a collector of positive (sustain) and negative (improve or change) information followed by five days of 'lessons learnt' training program for middle level officers.

There is a validation process to ensure lessons learnt have changed behavior.[9] Many corporations such as Shell have put into place similar systems.

2. Learning from the Present – Intelligence

Companies need accurate, up-to-date information about the external environment. Intelligence is concerned with the selection, collection, interpretation and distribution of information that has strategic importance. Information can be gathered in three ways:

Search – relies on public sources/documents and involves careful analysis and research. While doing search, companies must collect information from diverse sources, cross-check their findings to ensure reliability, devote enough effort to analysis and interpretation and link intelligence gathering with decision making.

Inquiry – relies on interviews/surveys and involves framing and asking insightful questions. When the required data does not exist, inquiry is needed. There are two basic approaches to inquiry – descriptive and exploratory. Descriptive approaches involve precise, focused questions. Exploratory approaches use open-ended questions to understand the perceptions and needs of users. They involve unstructured interviews, suspension of judgment, keeping an open mind and listening empathically.

Observation – relies on direct contact with users and involves attentive looking and listening. In some cases, even the most thoughtful questions will be ineffective. When knowledge is tacit, known only at a subconscious or non-verbal level, individuals will have trouble communicating clearly. Under the circumstances, direct observation becomes necessary.[10]

To build organizations that can collect information, interpret, analyze and present actionable insights, certain current assumption have to be suspended and space created for development of organization-wide IQ system.

STAR EMPLOYEE MINDSET

As already explained earlier in this book, most organizations, , believe that star performers should be identified, developed and nurtured for leadership roles. It is believed that it is this elite, largely coming from iconic business schools, that would take the organization to future growth and prosperity. It is another matter that many spectacular failures have also occurred under the watch of such stars such as Enron.

Unfortunately, in a VUCA world, this assumption, like many others, does not hold water.

Separating the spectacularly bright from the merely average may not be quite as important as everyone believes. As mentioned in the previous chapter, according to an MIT study group, intelligence is not strongly tied to either the average intelligence of the members or the team's smartest member. And this collective intelligence was more than just an arbitrary score. When the group grappled with a complex task, the researchers found it was an excellent predictor of how well the team performed.

What they are finding is that groups, as entities, have characteristics that are more than just a summing up or averaging of those of its members. Where star performers exist, teams cannot take roots.

> Intuitively, we still attribute too much to individuals and not enough to groups. Part of that may just be that it's simpler; it's simpler to say the success of a company depended on the CEO for good or bad, but in reality the success of a company depends on a whole lot more.[11]

To build Group IQ, the first step is DIALOGUE.

DIALOGUE: Art of Thinking Together

In a VUCA organization, it is important for people to learn to talk openly, and there can be severe consequences when we don't. Dialogue has been introduced in the previous chapter.

'A dialogue is a conversation where there is a free flow of meaning in a group and diverse views and perspectives are encouraged ... Reflection and inquiry skills provide a foundation for dialogue.'[12]

Why dialogue is critical in a VUCA organization:

- inability of formal systems to capture and retain knowledge;
- to move fast we have to slow down – reflect, learn, adapt and move on;

- new concepts essential for survival and growth in VUCA environment are not taught in business schools; and

- employees learn as much from peers as from experts.

There are three basic conditions that are necessary for dialogue:

1. All participants must 'suspend' their assumptions, literally hold them 'as if suspended before us'

2. All participants must regard one another as colleagues, and there must be a 'facilitator' who 'holds the context' of dialogue

3. DIALOGUE allows leaders to exercise power through people rather than on people

Due of the growth of technological complexity in all functions, organizational structures and designs are moving toward knowledge-based, distributed information forms. Consequently, organizations of all sizes will show a greater tendency to break down into subunits of various sorts, based on technology, products, markets, geographies, occupational communities and so on and create subcultures. Organizational effectiveness is therefore increasingly dependent on valid communication across subcultural boundaries.

Dialogue has considerable promise as a problem-formulation and solving philosophy and technology. Dialogue is necessary as a vehicle for understanding cultures and subcultures within the organization and that organizational learning will ultimately depend upon such cultural understanding. Dialogue thus becomes a central element of any model of organizational transformation.[13]

You can make DIALOGUE a vibrant organizational power force through the following interventions:

Strengthen the Invisible Workplace (Social Network)

True leaders – whether they are at the top of an organization or within it – should know that you cannot go into execution mode and retain peripheral vision. You cannot focus both on the woods and on the trees. So you need a network to watch out when you have your head down. There is a tremendous value to being able to shut down and focus – but you put yourself at risk if you don't have people out there scouting the horizon, covering your back.

'More observers leads to a wiser organization.'

'An organization swimming in many interpretations [of all the information available] can then discuss, combine, and build on them. The outcome of such a process has to be a much more diverse and richer sense of what is going on and what needs to be done.'[14]

Having a network of people, who will bring you the unvarnished truth and with whom you can have unfettered exploration are a partial antidote to wilful blindness. Devil's advocates, dissidents, troublemakers, non-conformists, who are normally shooed away in most organizations, are essential to any leader's ability to see into the future.

Knowledge Communities: Building Blocks for DIALOGUE

A body takes in all types of food throughout the day; in the stomach, this food is digested, and after digestion, useful elements are sent throughout the body while the remaining, which is not found nutritious, is excreted.

Knowledge communities or Communities of Practice perform the same function in an organization. They are groups of people who share a concern, a set of problems, or a passion about a topic and who deepen their understanding and knowledge of this area by interacting on an ongoing basis.

They operate as 'social learning systems' where practitioners connect to solve problems, share ideas, set standards, build tools and develop relationships with peers and stakeholders. Organizations and researchers use a variety of terms to describe similar phenomena, such as 'knowledge communities,' 'competency networks,' 'thematic groups' and 'learning networks.' A community of practice is a particular type of network that features peer-to-peer collaborative activities to build member skills and steward the knowledge assets of organizations and society.[15]

In a VUCA environment, organizations, whether profit-making companies or non-profit hospitals and NGOs and governments, need to build knowledge groups due to several reasons:

1. Information in all domains is exploding at an ever increasing rate and forums are needed to distill this information and separate the music from the noise.

2. Discuss and alert leadership to early trends that have yet to reach front pages.

3. The members can collectively throw ideas that individually none of them might have ever thought of. As the Noble Prize winning chemist Linus Pauling said, the key to having a winning idea is to have a lot of ideas.

It should be understood that Knowledge Communities are self-governing, non-hierarchical groups, which though operating under the organization's umbrella are not directed by it. It is not a committee or team that is created by leadership to address a particular concern or action though from time to time management can dip its beak in the knowledge reservoir thus created.

Knowledge Communities become social learning structures existing within the organization, and enlightened leadership can leverage and position it as a strategic tool that can be used in a variety of ways.

Today companies such as Hindustan Unilever have many Knowledge Communities successfully operating in areas such as rural marketing, packaging and so on while till last count Tata Steel had nearly 500 such communities.

3. Learning from the Future - Experimentation

Amplifying Weak Signals

The future does not come suddenly. It only seems so because we have been unable to see the early signs or cues.

Keep a lookout for who in your industry is skilled at picking up weak signals and acting on them ahead of everyone else? Assess your need and capability for peripheral vision. What are your mavericks and outliers trying to tell you? Most organizations have maverick employees with insights about the periphery, but they are rarely tapped, primarily because such employees by nature are rebels who don't respect authority or seniority. I have personally seen many such employees regularly get transferred from one division to another or encouraged to leave. They are handled as if picking hot coal. Beyond employees, there is a class of complainers and defectors who may also possess the ability to pick up early signals. People who work at customer interfaces such as medical representatives, showroom sales persons or those who work at the junction of two disciplines such as technology and marketing also develop such abilities. The problem is that their knowledge is fragmented but through Dialogue and knowledge communities, this knowledge can be consolidated and insights gathered.

George Day, author of Peripheral Vision have presented a framework through a seven-step roadmap for organizations to develop and use peripheral vision. The first five steps focus on improving the process of peripheral vision. The last two steps focus on building broader organizational capabilities and leadership to support locating and amplifying early signals.[16]

Step 1: Scoping: where to look

Step 2: Scanning: how to look

Step 3: Interpreting: what the data mean

Step 4: Probing: what to explore more closely

Step 5: Acting: what to do with these insights

Step 6: Organizing: how to develop vigilance

Step 7: Leading: an agenda for action

The old idea of failure will need to be recast as a part of learning. In a constantly changing future, there will be no failures, only learning experiences. 'Experiment fearlessly,' Tom Peters advised. Strategic plans, which extend present operations forward in sustained growth, 'work brilliantly under conditions where you don't need them.' Use a strategic plan 'called doing things,' he recommended. He also mocked strategic planning, which in some cases tends to become a perpetual process of planning.[17]

Scenario Planning and Wargaming

The three processes Foresight-Insight-Action, in series, are essential to developing forecasts. Foresight is heavily dependent on sensing and intuition. Insight makes sense of foresight. Action is the desired result. You must hit all three steps, in that order.

Yesterday's executives were Men of Action. See a problem and shoot it. Tomorrow's leaders face something much different – dilemmas, not common problems – and they must go slow to go fast, think more and deliberate more.[18]

Professor Rita McGarth in her book *Discovery-Driven Growth*[19] writes that the time-tested, comfortable strategic planning approaches to strategic management don't work well in dynamic, rapidly changing and therefore highly uncertain environments. Consequently, while many companies invest in growth initiatives, the results are uneven. The case studies discussed in this book as well as the swelling number of companies approaching CDR shows that in spite of competent leadership with previous successful stints, there is something wrong with the strategic planning process.

In our dynamically changing world, the environment where we execute is not the same one we originally planned for. However, the underlying objectives of the Strategy Planning process still remain as important today as ever. It is still critical to establish and communicate the strategic direction for the firm. And it is even more critical to align all the elements of the living corporate body to perform in ways that ensure the organization achieves its desired results.

Since the key objectives of setting strategic direction and organization alignment toward those goals remain critical, the process by which these objectives are achieved needs to change.[20]

In the traditional approach to strategic planning, the CEO and executive team participate in a offsite planning session, where they evaluate strengths, weaknesses, opportunities and threats (the classic SWOT analysis), set the future direction for the organization and map out specific action plans to achieve the desired results. They then go back and communicate these well-thought-out plans to the rest of the organization with 'marching orders' as to what the various functional departments will each carry out. So long as the environment remains pretty much as they understood it, this approach was likely to produce the desired results.

But herein lies the failing; the environment now changes at a rate faster than the planning horizon. Said simply, the marketplace dynamics will have changed significantly before the organization has a chance to realize its planned results.[21]

The business model construct offers a fresh way to consider strategy in uncertain, fast-moving and unpredictable environments. In contrast to more conventional perspectives, business model analysis facilitates a more fine-grained comparison of performance across firms, creating a better foundation for the explanation of performance differences between firms. Experimentation and learning – a 'discovery driven' approach – are crucial to identifying and executing against new business models. Strategies are as much about insight, rapid experimentation and evolutionary learning as they are about the traditional skills of planning and rock-ribbed execution. Modeling, therefore, is a useful approach to figuring out a strategy, as it suggests experimentation, prototyping and a job that is never quite finished. Business models often cannot be fully anticipated in advance. Rather, they must be learned over time, which places emphasis on the centrality of experimentation in the discovery of new business models. Third, although we typically give short shrift to considering the erosion of competitive advantages, decline is crucially important to detect and respond to.[22]

Most business models are conceived within the boundaries of a particular set of constraints. As new technologies and other shifts relax or impose constraints, the possibility for new models (and threats to old ones) increases. New models typically emerge when some constraint is lifted; old models often come under pressure when a constraint emerges. Where the assumption in traditional equilibrium oriented views of the strategy process assume relatively little change in the constraints managers operate under, a more dynamic, business model oriented lens suggests that many of the constraints that will be competitively important aren't known at the outset, and will take some time to discover. The dilemma is that while it is usually quite possible to detect such trends and changes, it is difficult to know in advance how to take advantage of them via business model innovation. Such uncertainty places a huge premium on experimentation.[23]

Breakout growth is not only about launching bold, new initiatives. Many good growth programs begin first with incremental growth, which creates investment in learning where big new opportunities lie. That's the point at which many companies go for breakout growth. Many breakout opportunities don't look that way at first – they are the result of combining things until you finally do have a winner. There are, of course, many companies out there making what they hope will be breakout moves. What they often find out, painfully, is that they are using the wrong tools to do it and are therefore taking on risk far beyond the potential payoff. Worse, they are learning less than they could otherwise.[24]

In this scenario, the proper balance of thinking strategically while acting tactically is vital. You could call it the art of being both a thinker (in developing strategy) and a doer (by acting tactically). In business days gone by, companies and teams were defined by the separation of these two skill sets: the thinkers sat in leadership positions, while the doers took on support and line functions. One doing something in the realm of the other was thought odd, if not counterproductive. Consider the traditional ascent to management: you work hard as a doer and eventually move to thinking, and then if you were caught doing, you get chastised for not delegating enough to allow for more thinking time. But the Great Recession called us to do more with less, letting go of the doer/thinker dichotomy and replacing it with something else entirely: teams that embody both. This hybrid skill set is present in the most adaptive professionals. However, teams should be trained in the synergy between strategic thinking and tactical action.[25]

Experiment-Adapt-Improvise

Peter Palchinsky was a young engineer from a coal mining region of what was to become the Soviet Union. He was appointed to advice on several of the grand schemes in Stalin's Five Year Plan. He counseled against the Lenin Dam, which would displace thousands of people and be ineffective in the dry season, advocating the need for smaller projects that were tailored to local conditions and geology.

On the basis of this damaging report, he was declared a counter-revolutionary and executed. 'The more complex and elusive our problems are, the more effective trial and error becomes, relative to the alternatives. However, this approach runs counter to our instinct, and to the way in which our traditional organizations work.' What Palchinsky realized was that most real-world problems are more complex than we think. They have a human dimension, a local dimension, and are likely to change as circumstances change.[26]

The takeaway message for any organization is that Palchinsky recognized that a single grand solution was not the way forward. Problems are complex with a local dimension, and we need to make more use of what Grameen Bank founder Muhammad Yunus would later call a 'worm's eye view.'

His method could be summarized as three 'Palchinsky' principles:

1. Seek Out New ideas: *Variation*

   Try new things

2. Do it on a scale that is survivable: *Survivability*

3. Seek feedback: *Selection*

   Learn from your mistakes as you go along[27]

ALFA FERRICS LTD. —A DYSFUNCTIONAL LEARNING ORGANIZATION

This small company of about 120 employees was set up in the 1980s with Japanese collaboration to manufacture certain ferrous based magnetic products for the auto and sound industries. Till late 1990s, the company was profitable in a protected economy. The opening of the Indian market brought Chinese competition, which made the products of Alfa Ferrics (name changed) uncompetitive, and the company posted its first loss in 2003. Out of a total of nine manufacturers in India at that time, seven closed down their shutters.

The Group Chairman constituted a small team to study the operations and suggest ways to bring the company back to profitability.

The team found the company wrapped in the cocoon of 1980s when Japanese collaborators left the company, unable to make the changes necessary to take the company from the protective environment to cut-throat international competition. The managers took Japanese manuals, production knowledge and techniques of the 1980s as holy grails not to be tinkered with.

AML's A-grade quality was only 60 percent compared to 93 percent in India's only other remaining plant and 98 percent in China which is required for OEM sales. Even a group company had stopped buying. Therefore, the company was forced to sell its products in the secondary market with poor realizations. It had not made any effort to upgrade production from semi-automated to fully automated production line as the Chinese had done. In addition, there was little coordination between marketing and production. Marketing wanted smaller batch sizes while production insisted on large batch sizes. The excess production stayed on the shelves for a long time, steadily losing its quality.

The initial plant capacity of 3,000 tonnes was not expanded to take advantage of the booming auto and entertainment industries as well as to reduce production costs. The Chinese competitors were running 10,000-tonne plants, three times as big. Other observations were that there was:

• little attempt to control costs holistically;

• little dialogue between different layers of management;

- insular management;
- fear to conduct experiments;
- little ability to introduce and grasp new knowledge;
- hidden knowledge throughout the organization; and
- superficial piecemeal attempts to stem downward spiral.

The overall impression was of an organization that had lost its capacity to adapt, innovate and change largely due to the fixed mindset of management, which was content to run the company as in the 1980s. Two examples given here illustrate these limitations.

The team suggested changes in the operations to reduce costs:

A rotary furnace was used to bake the product, which was in the form of wet cakes. It was run on LPG, as designed by Japanese collaborators since in Japan, fuel oil was not used due to environmental considerations. LPG in India cost four times as furnace oil, and consequently our team suggested that the furnace be run on furnace oil.

The management immediately objected saying that the sulfur from furnace oil would contaminate the product cake diminishing its magnetic properties. This was only an *assumption*, and there was no scientific evidence backing this theory. The real reason was a lack of confidence in bringing about a change.

The team decided to write to the former Japanese partners as well as conduct experiments to test this hypothesis. Sulfur premixed with the wet cake batches in ratio from 1 to 5 percent were passed through the furnace. The batches were tested and no degradation in properties was found. Meanwhile, the plant also received a reply from Japan to this effect. The team changed the fuel process at very little cost using equipment and piping lying with various group companies. This reduced the cost significantly as fuel was the biggest item in the cost basket.

Second, the team attempted to reduce packaging costs. The usual method was to sit with the packaging manufacturer and negotiate. The team found that there was little knowledge or appreciation for the technology of packaging in the company. The team conducted a one-day workshop for production, marketing and supply chain managers with an expert. He gave insights into the physics and costs of packaging. Armed with this knowledge, the team sat with the packaging contractors and redesigned several packagings. Further, the team sent material by road to various warehouses throughout the country and tested their condition. With this knowhow, the team selected the packaging, reducing its cost by 30 percent in addition to what was negotiated.

Moreover, the team found the workers very knowledgeable about their role in the production processes and implemented several of their suggestions. No one had thought of asking them earlier.

This intervention brought the company, which was on verge of closure, back to profitability through adaptation, experiments and sharing of knowledge and most important, a change in mindset that the enemy resides within us and not outside, and we can take Chinese competition head on.

The team wished that the other seven plants that closed down had viewed their problems with new mindsets and seen the results.

PAUSE, STEP BACK TO LEAD FORWARD

Since liberalization of the Indian economy in the 1990s, there has been a relentless march by many companies in India toward scorching growth as if the opportunities are limited and unless one grabs whatever one can, the opportunities will vanish. There is little attempt to take pause to review strategy, talent bandwidth and depth, processes and systems. This is one of the causes of failures of a majority of cases discussed in this book and also the rising number of bank NPAs resulting in CDRs. Our management schools also churn out future leaders whose eyes are firmly focused on the road in front of them and finally our top management's concerns on producing top results quarter after quarter makes them concentrate on action at the cost of reason. Leaders who want to take a long-term view and those who desire growth at a slower pace are seen in poor light.

Every driver knows that it is very risky to drive without a rear-view mirror. Not looking through the rear-view mirror occasionally and keeping one's eyes focused only on the road in front is a sure recipe for accident.

We briefly touched on one of Peter Senge's characteristics of the 'Learning Organization' that is slowing down for reflection. Slow is fast and as a corollary, fast is slow. Reflection allows us to take stock of the situation and with better hindsight, you can accelerate. Alternatively, as many of our cases have shown, action without reflection is a sure recipe for failure sometime in future, either dramatically like Lehman Brothers or slowly like Kodak.

Learning through Past, Present and Future gives us an opportunity to take the necessary pauses before embarking on the next course of action. Thinking offers an antidote to our addiction to speed and transaction, replacing it with a conscious, intentional process of stepping back to reflect and deliberate, and then lead forward with greater clarity and impact. Rather than merely doing more, we must learn to pause and to do things differently in order to grow, achieve and innovate. In the book *Pause*, Kevin Cashman[28] advocates pragmatic practice of deep, reflective inquiry for focused problem-solving and for engendering creative insights. All of these practices lead to purposeful change and contribution – an essential part of a leader's everyday life.

'In our fast-paced, achieve-more-now culture, the loss of pause potential is epidemic,' writes Cashman. 'If leaders today do not step back, to stop momentum, to gain perspective, to transcend the immediacies of life, and to accelerate their leadership, we will continue to crash economically, personally and collectively.'

Cashman's work centers around one simple truth: that fast thinking is the domain of management transaction, while slow thinking is the leadership domain of strategic, innovative transformation. He believes every leader is on a journey from being a transaction-focused manager to an authentic leader that inspires real change. At the core of this transformation is the ability to pause. But for most, slowing down to drive performance is counter to instinct, especially when they have been rewarded for speed and action. But stepping forward to act, particularly in complex situations, without first stepping back for information, clarity and connection to what is most important can be disastrous.

We live and lead in an increasingly volatile, uncertain, complex and ambiguous world. But paradoxically, Kevin Cashman contends that leaders today must not merely act more quickly but pause more deeply. Two examples of *Pause* stand out in the Indian environment.

Genpact during 2000–2002 froze expansion and stopped all recruitments. During this period, the company reviewed strategy, practices, processes and systems. With this insight, they embarked on the next stage of expansion.

In 2007, Wipro Consumer Products acquired Unza, a Malaysian consumer goods company. For two years, Wipro did not carry out any top level changes such as key management, change of name, many processes such as HR to bring them in line with the policies of the acquirer company. Wipro learnt the virtues of patience as most of the core group that came with the acquisition did not leave as normally happens in an acquisition. The result was a win-win situation where Wipro brought some things to the table such as negotiating cheaper loans, passing on cost benefits of being part of a big group and Unza brought learning of new product categories and so on. Today, Unza sales targets, growth projections are in line with Wipro's expectations. This happened in a world where 70 percent M&A fail or are suboptimal.[29]

The future is found when you adapt as you go. Stop fighting the wind, take a pause and adjust the sail.

NATURE IS ALWAYS ADAPTING: WHY CAN'T HUMANS?

Nacie Carson in her book *The Finch Effect*[30] says that adaptation is a scary prospect because of how clearly it smacks of change. It never fails to amaze me how averse to change humans are, in spite of the fact that it is a most basic biological facet of our existence. Every minute we live, our bodies are changing: cells are splitting or dying; organs are aging; our perspective is shifting.

And yet we fight change, and loath it, and resent its coming. We fear it – or more specifically fear its unknown quality. It is uncomfortable, difficult and signals the end of something – be it an era in our life or a particular way of doing things. It is out of our control.

But adaptation is not change.

Or, more clearly, adaptation and change are not synonymous. While adaptation implies change, it is not the kind of change that happens to you – it is the kind of change that you make happen, for adaptation implies a conscious response to shifts in your environment. There is something comforting in that fact: adaptation is change that we control.

Adaptation is programmed into the root of our biology, and we are not alone in this programming: everything on our planet is called to adapt eventually or face extinction. But we are alone in the fact that – unlike the plants and animals – we have the power to direct our own adaptation.

Take the finches of the Galapagos Islands. They were 'discovered' by Charles Darwin in the 1830s when he was circling the globe as part of a scientific voyage. When stopping at the islands, Darwin noted that there was evidence that some of the birds he saw rapidly adapted to changes in their environment (a beak shape change here, a different food source there) and, as a result, were thriving. His encounter with these little creatures helped inspire his famous theory of evolution, and today they are known as 'Darwin's Finches.'

The finches are a simple and elegant example of how life is programmed to survive through adaptation. But they are also a great example of what sets humans apart in the adaptive sense: the finches have no conscious control over how they respond to environmental changes – they can no more change the shape of their beaks than they can form a soccer team and win the World Cup.

But as humans, we have the power to direct our response. We can consciously choose how to change the shape of our beaks...or at least consciously choose how we respond to the changes in our environment. And that environmental change we face now, today, is an economic one.

It has not been possible to provide an example of a Learning Organization in India though many, such as Genpact and Wipro, are striving to become one. This is not to say that outside India there are many. Two organizations stand out.

PIXAR: A True Learning Organization

This US-based animation movie studio had the advantage of transforming itself into a Learning Organization as it is a new organization and thus found it easier to embed an organization with desired culture than to transform one with ancient lineage. Behind Pixar's string of hit movies such as *Toy Story* is a peer-driven process of solving problems. Pixar's culture is founded on the following practices:

- Cultural humility – willingness to be challenged: new ideas can come from anywhere, even the junior most person who joined yesterday
- Management routinely encourage non-conforming views
- Success hides problems: management afraid of complacency
- Commitment to accepting failure as essential to success
- Learning from failure part of culture: a whole wall devoted to failed ventures

- Everyone including newest trainee can suggest changes to Director – little barriers to providing feedback: this is very important in a profession like filmmaking where the Director is the star.

- Teamwork is paramount – make your partner look good: getting talented people to work together effectively is tough; this is based on trust and respect, earned over a period of time

- Non-hierarchical environment

Pixar has taken experimentation to a new high. Every movie has several scenes that are shot differently, such as different endings. These are discussed internally and also shown to a test target audience after which a particular part is selected. Some Bollywood directors too have started such experimentations recently. Pixar CEO says, 'You look for people who have seen failure and figured out how to make something from it. The core skill of innovators is error recovery not failure avoidance. We're looking for resiliency and adaptability.'[31]

TOYOTA: Ambition Getting Ahead of Tradition

Even a learning organization such as Toyota Motors can fail on a massive scale. During 2009–2011, it recalled 8.5 million vehicles, largely in the United States, due to manufacturing defects. It was a big blow to a company that prided itself on the reliability of its vehicles.

There were earlier indications of problems such as in 2005 there were more recalls than vehicles sold but problems were allowed to continue. A greater share of Toyota's problems have been laid on its fast expansion to raise global market share from

11 to 15 percent, especially in North America, setting up five factories in quick succession, stretching its supply chain, as well as product development.

Due to immense pressure to launch new models, there was less time for testing. In addition, the company took on unfamiliar suppliers who didn't have a deep understanding of Toyota culture, especially TPS, The Toyota Production System. Nor did Toyota have enough of the senior engineers, known as sensei, to keep an eye on how new suppliers were shaping up. The company also relied on platform manufacturing to realize economies of scale. This also meant that any defect would be magnified throughout the platform.[32] In short, blinded by its topline ambitions, the company overlooked the principles that brought success in the first place. These were:

Kaizan – continuous improvement;

Hansei – responsibility, self-reflection and organizational learning;

Hoshin kanri – process of cascading objectives from the top of the company down to the work group level.[33]

In an interview with *Harvard Business Review*[34] after the quality problems erupted, then Toyota CEO Katsuaki Watanabe addressed this issue, noting that the firm's explosive growth may have strained its production system.

> I realize that our system may be overstretched. We must make that issue visible. Hidden problems are the ones that become serious threats eventually. If problems are revealed for everybody to see, I will feel reassured. Because once problems have been visualized, even if our people didn't notice them earlier, they will rack their brains to find solutions to them.

However, to the credit of Toyota, there was no finger pointing and witch hunting, and the company did not fire a single employee during the period its plants were closed. It relied on the identification of the root cause through the five 'Whys.'

The company turned crisis into opportunity. They looked to see how they had departed from their principles. It used the opportunity to create a culture of transparency. Further, the company globalized its culture – more regional autonomy and decreased response time.

A learning organization, ten years in the making, allowed Toyota to bounce back in a short time.

For better or worse, the world in which we now find ourselves is plagued with ambiguity and uncertainty. Globalization, economic interconnectedness and international financial linkages are the reality of our social, political and economic existence. You might travel the world seeking the best teacher, ultimately to find that it is YOU.

Continuous learning is essential for lifetime growth. You can have a lot of experience but may not be smarter than before. Experience itself is not a guarantee of lifetime growth. But if you regularly transform your experiences into new lessons, each day can be a source of growth. Smart people are those who can transform even the smallest incidents into a source of learning.

Emperor Babur, after the loss of his kingdom, was driven to lead a life of a nomad in deep mountains with his few supporters. One day, he heard a commotion outside his tent and enquired as to what had happened. A soldier responded saying that a wolf had been coming for past three days to look for a meal. The first day, it went into the horses' enclosure and was kicked out. The next day, the wolf entered the sheep's enclosure, and when the sheep started baying, it ran away. The third day, it entered the chicken coup and got away with one chicken. Babur reflected that the wolf was smarter than he was. It is not obsessed with one objective and, if unsuccessful, moved to another while he remain obsessed with Samarkand. He then decided to look elsewhere to fulfil his ambition and started thinking about India.

The Failure Learning Model developed by the author and his colleagues at Saltlabs Consultants as part of their *The VUCA Company* workshop is a practical method of ensuring that when failure occurs, you recover fast and more robust than before.

As J.K. Rowling, author of the Harry Potter series, spoke of her failures at Harvard Business School Graduation Ceremony in 2008,

> ... and so rock bottom became the solid foundation on which I rebuilt my life. You might never fail on the scale I did, but some failure in life is inevitable. It is impossible to live without failing at something, unless you live so cautiously that you might as well not have lived at all – in which case, you fail by default. Failure gave me an inner security that I had never attained by passing examinations. Failure taught me things about myself that I could have learned no other way. I discovered that I had a strong will, and more discipline than I had suspected; I also found out that I had friends whose value was truly above the price of rubies.
>
> The knowledge that you have emerged wiser and stronger from setbacks means that you are, ever after, secure in your ability to survive. You will never truly know yourself, or the strength of your relationships, until both have been tested by adversity. Such knowledge is a true gift, for all that it is painfully won, and it has been worth more than any qualification I ever earned.

SALt©
Model of Failure

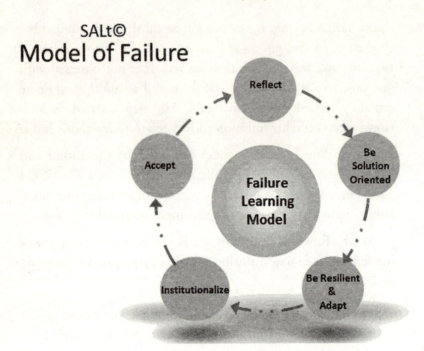

So given a Time Turner, I would tell my 21-year-old self that personal happiness lies in knowing that life is not a check-list of acquisition or achievement. Your qualifications, your CV, are not your life, though you will meet many people of my age and older who confuse the two. Life is difficult, and complicated, and beyond anyone's total control, and the humility to know that will enable you to survive its vicissitudes.[35]

FINALLY, A SLAVE'S WARNING

In ancient Rome, generals who had won a great victory received on their return a triumphal procession through the city's streets. In the procession were slaves and captives, carts loaded with plunder, ranks of marching soldiers and jaunty cavalry.

The conqueror rode in a triumphal gilded chariot led by white horses, and the dazed prisoners walked in front of him. Beautiful women showered flowers on him, and he was crowned with a laurel wreath and wore a purple tunic embroidered with palms under a purple toga embroidered with stars. Always in this triumph a slave stood in the chariot behind the victorious general. Over the general's head he held a garland of laurel, signifying victory. Into the general's ear the slave repeatedly whispered a warning: '*Sic Transit Gloria*' (All glory is fleeting. All glory is fleeting).[36]

NOTES

1. David Garvin, *Learning in Action* (HBS Press, 2005).

2. Suhayl Abidi, 'Close Down Your Training Shops,' *Business Standard*, 9 July 2004.

3. Roberto Vegranti, 'Designing Breakthrough Products,' *Harvard Business Review*, October 2011.

4. Peter Senge, *The Fifth Discipline* (Crown Publishing, 2006), 17–20.

5. 'Notes on the Fifth Discipline,' Stern School of Management, New York University (unpublished).

6. Ibid., 4 and 244.

7. Ibid., 1.

8. Tom Peters, 'Tom Peters on Innovation: Experiment "Fearlessly,"' *Information Week*, 12 September 2006.

9. Marilyn J. Darling and Charles S. Parry, 'After-Action Reviews: Linking Reflection and Planning in a Learning Practice,' *Reflections* 3 (2), 2001.

10. Ibid., 1.

11. Carolyn Y. Johnson, 'Group IQ,' *Boston Globe*, 19 December 2010.

12. Robert Hargrove, *Masterful Coaching* (Jossey-Bass & Pfeiffer, 1995).

13. Edgar H. Schein, 'On Dialogue, Culture and Organizational Learning,' *Organizational Dynamics* 22, Summer 1993.

14. Margaret Wheatley, *Leadership and the New Science* (Berrett-Koehler Publishers, 1994), 65.

15. E. Wenger, R. McDermott and W.M. Snyder, *Cultivating Communities of Practice* (Harvard Business School Press, 2003).

16. George S. Day and Paul J.H. Schoemaker, *Peripheral Vision; Detecting the Weak Signals That Will Make or Break Your Company* (Harvard Business School Press, 2006).

17. Ibid., 8.

18. Robert Johansen, *Getting There Early* (Berrett-Koehler Publishers, 2007), 9.

19. Rita Gunther McGarth, *A Discovery-Driven Growth* (Harvard Business School Press, 2009).

20. Norman Wolfe, 'Strategic Planning Is Dead; Long Live Strategy Execution,' *Fast Company*, April 2010.

21. Ibid., 19.

22. Ibid.

23. Ibid.

24. Ibid.

25. Nacie Carson, 'As Chocolate Is to Peanut Butter, Strategy Is to Tactics,' *Fast Company*, 9 October 2012.

26. Tim Harford, *Adapt – Why Success Always Starts with Failure* (Little Brown, 2011).

27. Ibid., 26.

28. Kevin Cashman, *The Pause Principle* (Harper Collins India, 2012).

29. 'How Wipro Learnt the Virtues of Patience,' *Forbes*, 19 March 2012.

30. Nacie Carson, *The Finch Effect* (Jossey-Bass, 2012).

31. Ed Catmull, 'How Pixar Fosters Collective Creativity,' *Harvard Business Review*, September 2008.

32. Robert E. Cole, 'What Really Happened at Toyota,' *Sloan Management Review*, 22 June 2011.

33. Jeffrey Liker, *The Toyota Way* (McGraw-Hill, 2004).

34. Thomas A. Stewart and Anand P. Raman, 'Lessons From Toyota's Long Drive,' *Harvard Business Review*, July 2007.

35. J.K. Rowlings, 'The Fringe Benefits of Failure, and the Importance of Imagination,' *Harvard Gazette*, 5 June 2008.

36. http://www.usnewslink.com/fleetingglory.htm.

JAICO PUBLISHING HOUSE
Elevate Your Life. Transform Your World.

ESTABLISHED IN 1946, Jaico Publishing House is home to world-transforming authors such as Sri Sri Paramahansa Yogananda, Osho, The Dalai Lama, Sri Sri Ravi Shankar, Robin Sharma, Deepak Chopra, Jack Canfield, Eknath Easwaran, Devdutt Pattanaik, Khushwant Singh, John Maxwell, Brian Tracy and Stephen Hawking.

Our late founder Mr. Jaman Shah first established Jaico as a book distribution company. Sensing that independence was around the corner, he aptly named his company Jaico ('Jai' means victory in Hindi). In order to service the significant demand for affordable books in a developing nation, Mr. Shah initiated Jaico's own publications. Jaico was India's first publisher of paperback books in the English language.

While self-help, religion and philosophy, mind/body/spirit, and business titles form the cornerstone of our non-fiction list, we publish an exciting range of travel, current affairs, biography, and popular science books as well. Our renewed focus on popular fiction is evident in our new titles by a host of fresh young talent from India and abroad. Jaico's recently established Translations Division translates selected English content into nine regional languages.

Jaico's Higher Education Division (HED) is recognized for its student-friendly textbooks in Business Management and Engineering which are in use countrywide.

In addition to being a publisher and distributor of its own titles, Jaico is a major national distributor of books of leading international and Indian publishers. With its headquarters in Mumbai, Jaico has branches and sales offices in Ahmedabad, Bangalore, Bhopal, Bhubaneswar, Chennai, Delhi, Hyderabad, Kolkata and Lucknow.

SINCE 1946